## PRAISE FOR
## PRACTICING SAFE ZEN

"*Practicing Safe Zen* imparts a lesson we all will have to learn if we want to truly mature in our spiritual practice. It asks us to face the emotionally difficult reality of our own idealizations and subsequent disillusionment, of our hopes and fantasies surrounding Zen, Zen teachers, and enlightenment. Nelson takes us through the history of one Zen community torn apart by scandal and teacher misconduct. Yet she also tells the story of how that community has tried to put itself back together, with shared communal responsibility taking the place of hierarchy, authority, and submission. Hers is a Zen that has the potential to outlive—and outgrow—our fantasies of perfectly enlightened, Yoda-like Masters." —**Barry Magid**, founding teacher of the Ordinary Mind Zendo and the author of *Ordinary Mind*, *Ending the Pursuit of Happiness*, and *Nothing Is Hidden: The Psychology of Zen Koans*

"In *Practicing Safe Zen*, Julie Nelson is exploring the beauty of Zen practice and teachings as well as the dangers of the practice and the harm that can be caused by teachers when there is power imbalance and unethical actions. Julie Nelson, herself a Zen teacher, would like to cultivate safe Zen as a teacher in a communal setting. This is a reflective and challenging read, questioning authority, tradition, and lineages. Is Zen beyond conditions or must one take into account the conditions in which Zen is practiced? This is a thoroughly engaging exploration based on deep knowledge of the tradition as well as contemporary research." —**Martine Batchelor**, author of *Women in Korean Zen*, *Principles of Zen*, *The Spirit of the Buddha*, *Walking on Lotus Flowers*, and other books

"Julie Nelson has begun exposing the pitfalls of Zen as a Western Community spiritual practice. Through her own personal experiences and her professional expertise, she illuminates the core problem that may steer Zen practitioners into dangerous territory. In order to do the necessary work of Buddhism—lessening the ego's toxic grip—Zen students need to become vulnerable and allow the Zen teacher to guide them. Yet, in this vulnerable relationship, Zen students may be exploited by their teacher or a community that has succumbed to cult dynamics. In this important work, Julie Nelson points out the underlying problems, how Zen Centers go astray, how practitioners suffer, and how to have a healthier practice place." —**Grace Schireson**, Zen Abbess, president of Shogaku Zen Institute, and author of *Naked in the Zendo* and *Zen Women*

"*Practicing Safe Zen* fills me with gratitude, because here at last, in clear and compelling language, is precisely the book we need for addressing teachers' abuses of power, sex, and money, and for building resilient sanghas that exemplify both compassion and accountability. Julie Seido Nelson's vitally important book should be read by every Zen teacher, board member, and student." —**Rev. Steve Kanji Ruhl**, MDiv, Zen Buddhist minister, author of *Appalachian Zen* and *The Whole Earth Is Medicine*

"A must-read manual, born of the author's long personal experience with misconduct, for how to protect yourself and your sangha from abuse of power, beginning with how to approach and engage safely and wisely with the teachings. Nelson identifies the problem of sexual misconduct in Buddhist communities as rooted in more than one factor, including human psychology, institutional structure and the balance of power. This book belongs on the front shelf of every Zen Center." —**Willa Blythe Baker**, author of *The Wakeful Body*

"*Practicing Safe Zen* dives deep into what every sangha member and especially every person of authority in a sangha must keep in mind. Watch out! Be aware of the perils of cultishness, the pitfalls of spiritual bypassing, the poison of thinking you have arrived, the hazard of minimization, and much more! This is an important read for anyone immersed in Zen community and practice." —**Genjo Marinello**, abbot of Chobo-ji and author of *Reflections on Awakening and Maturity*

"Curious about Zen? Serious about Zen? Either way, read Julie Nelson's edifying and empowering book. It's a vital companion for anyone interested in a Zen path." —**Scott Edelstein**, author of *Sex and the Spiritual Teacher* and *The User's Guide to Spiritual Teachers*

# PRACTICING SAFE ZEN

## NAVIGATING THE PITFALLS ON THE ROAD TO LIBERATION

JULIE SEIDO NELSON

BOOK PUBLISHING COMPANY
RHINEBECK, NEW YORK

Paperback ISBN 9781958972786
eBook ISBN 9781958972793

Library of Congress Cataloging-in-Publication Data

Names: Seido Nelson, Julie, author.
Title: Practicing safe Zen : navigating the pitfalls on the road to liberation / Julie Seido Nelson.
Description: Rhinebeck, New York : Monkfish Book Publishing Company, [2025] | Includes bibliographical references and index.
Identifiers: LCCN 2025002488 (print) | LCCN 2025002489 (ebook) | ISBN 9781958972786 (paperback) | ISBN 9781958972793 (ebook)
Subjects: LCSH: Zen Buddhism. | Zen Buddhism--Safety measures.
Classification: LCC BQ9266 .S433 2025 (print) | LCC BQ9266 (ebook) | DDC 294.3/927--dc23/eng/20250225
LC record available at https://lccn.loc.gov/2025002488
LC ebook record available at https://lccn.loc.gov/2025002489

Book and cover design by Colin Rolfe

Monkfish Book Publishing Company
22 East Market Street, Suite 304
Rhinebeck, New York 12572
(845) 876-4861
monkfishpublishing.com

*To Rebecca Behizadeh and Jill Gaulding,*
*with endless thanks for your discernment, integrity, and leadership*

# CONTENTS

# INTRODUCTION

Perhaps you have only heard Zen mentioned or read a bit about Zen or Buddhist or other Eastern philosophies. You've heard that they promise awakening, liberation, and freedom from suffering. But they also seem bizarre and confusing. Maybe you've seen one of the occasional news stories about a spiritual teacher being sued for sexual abuse. You're skeptical. You wonder why any intelligent person would get involved in (what seems to you to be) just a lot of pseudo-Asian religious claptrap.

Or perhaps you've been leaning towards trying Zen or another Eastern spiritual practice. From what you've learned from reading, listening to podcasts, or watching videos, it sounds great. But so far you have only meditated at home. You are thinking about trying to find a sangha (community) or teacher, but don't know where to start. Will you be welcome? Will there be differences between what you've heard about and how it works "on the ground"? How does awakening work? Are there things you should watch out for?

Long-time practitioners also seek answers. But having more experience, we tend to be mystified about other things. Are my opening (awakening) experiences authentic? How can I know when I am acting from self-centeredness, as contrasted to enacting universal Buddha nature? We hear about a spiritual teacher who abused power and are deeply bewildered about how someone so "enlightened" could have gone so badly off course.

Perhaps you are a spiritual teacher who thinks you already know all that you need to know. To the extent that any of us (including me) take a know-it-all attitude, we are a danger to our students.

Welcome to this book. It's for you.

## WHAT WE DO (AND DON'T) TALK ABOUT

Hundreds if not more books, articles, and websites have been published about the benefits, power, practice, philosophy, and history of Zen practice. This is somewhat amusing, since it is a core principle of Zen that the most important things can't be communicated in words! Silence is an integral part of the practice. The basic instructions are:

Sit down.

Shut up.

Pay attention.

Yet these are really hard for most of us to follow, so some instruction is a good thing. Combining a practice of silence with guidance by words and example can be transformative. The liberation Zen promises is a *real thing*.

Yet precisely because Zen is a powerful practice for liberation, there are also dangers involved. A whole lot fewer publications deal with these.

Let me suggest that you will save yourself (and probably others) a lot of time, trouble, and anguish if you learn about these neglected or silenced topics! This book is my attempt to give you the truth and the whole truth, at least as I understand it after years of practice and hard knocks. It includes not only how to (and why to) practice Zen, but also how not to. It covers what I really wish I'd learned as a student. This book may not be #1 on your Zen reading list, but I recommend that it be #2. And it includes what I believe was sorely missing in my initial training to become a spiritual teacher.

Some of these dangers come from meditation itself. Others arise from misunderstandings. Many arise when our old habit energies, including our desires to get approval and avoid unpleasantness, hijack Zen teachings towards self-serving purposes. No practitioner, from the beginner to the most experienced and esteemed senior teacher, can entirely avoid these dangers. That's not because we are bad people. It's because we are human beings.

## PRACTICING SAFE ZEN

Odd things happen to you when you venture away from the familiar. Sitting as upright as possible, and still, is a physical practice. Strange sensations may arise, as well as pain, and possibly physical damage. So there are physical risks.

Not able to converse or look at our cell phones or bury ourselves in activity, our mental and emotional worlds shift as well. This is meant to be, and often is, liberating. But it's also possible for the practice to invite in emotional damage if we are overloaded with incessant negative thoughts or overwhelming feelings.

Even if you find the physical and emotional dangers in individual practice manageable, there are further dangers. Every group has leaders and histories, and even the most innocuous meditation workshop, mindfulness group, or yoga retreat can have unsavory ones. Many of the cautions in this book could apply to any such group.

But Zen and related spiritual practices go beyond mere meditation or mindfulness. These practices are deliberately destabilizing, at a very deep level. We are led to question all our beliefs, including our fundamental belief about *who we are*. When this process goes well, we discover who we really are. We discover "just this." We start to experience living at a level of presence and embodiment that we couldn't even have imagined before. We fully enter our own lives. This process is life-long, as old knots of habits and karma slowly loosen.

*And* the central teaching of "no-self" presents profound risks. When the process doesn't go well, we may stay simply destabilized. Or we may build back a new identity around false ideas and distorted beliefs. There are so many ways "no self" can be misunderstood! Does "no-self" mean you never get angry? Does "no-self" mean you dedicate yourself to serving your teacher and community? Is achieving the realization of "no-self" a once-and-forever state of Enlightenment? Is that what makes someone a Zen master? If we believe such things, I believe we misunderstand Zen. We are at high risk for suffering harm. Even worse, we may *do* harm.

A safe place to practice, where we can share our wisdom and open our hearts to transformation, is vital to Zen practice. Skilled and healthy spiritual guidance can be very helpful for keeping our practice on track. In the best-case scenario, a healthy *sangha* (community) and a trustworthy teacher will provide the companionship, guardrails, and guidance that is needed. If those are for some reason not available to you right now, this book, I hope, will give you some helpful advice about what to do with some of your personal experiences. If you are looking for a sangha or teacher, I hope it will help you in your search for a reasonably sound one, whether online or in person.

Tragically, however, teachers and sanghas are, in my personal experience with Zen, too often neither trustworthy nor healthy. They can be dangerous. I've seen a tendency to neglect the possibility of emotional damage. Even worse, I have witnessed three major crises perpetrated by abuse of power by authorized, and often widely respected, Zen teachers. What I will call Betrayal #1 in the chapters which follow involved emotional and financial abuses. Betrayal #2 involved emotional and sexual misconduct, followed by additional emotional damage. Betrayal #3 broke commitments yet again. All threatened to chip away at my spirit, and the spirits of other targets and witnesses. If you know anything about the history of Buddhist sanghas or of guru-led communities (or glance at chapter 5), you know that my experience is far from unique. Too often, instead of helping students, teachers have helped themselves to students. Sexual misconduct, corrupt financial practices, bullying, and other abuses of power by teachers happen far, far too frequently.

And the offenders usually get away with it. This is often because it's simply assumed that authorized, lineage-transmitted teachers know best. Or those around the offender may come to believe that staying close to the teacher or protecting the institutions of Zen from scandal is more important than protecting vulnerable students. They refuse to listen to complaints of harm. Or they pretend to listen, but then dismiss. They often turn on the student victim(s), claiming that they are liars, or unbalanced, or that they are just troublemakers who like to create conflict and drama. The direct victims usually end up leaving the community—and perhaps leaving Zen and spiritual practice altogether. Those who witnessed the harm may also leave. Meanwhile, the abusive authorized teachers keep their power. Their personal charisma and teaching about wisdom and compassion continue to attract new students.

In the middle of Betrayal #2, I became a lineage-authorized teacher myself. As you might imagine, I have had considerable reason to investigate deeply what it means to be a teacher. What does it mean if we take seriously the heart of our Zen or other spiritual practice, which is the realization of non-duality? What does it mean to be a student? What does it mean for my home community, Greater Boston Zen Center? What does it mean for Zen on a larger scale?

My hope is that this book will help practitioners, both new and old, approach our work with open eyes as well as open hearts.

## A NOTE ON NAMING AND ACCOUNTABILITY

When mentioning teachers, I have deliberately refrained from mentioning formal teaching titles. This in not out of disrespect, but because these titles often change over time and the variety across different Buddhist groups can be confusing. When I write about "teachers," I generally mean those who are authorized to meet individually with students, since this is a practice that particularly creates vulnerability.

I will be naming some of the teachers I believe—based on personal observation or public and what I believe to be reliable documentation—have committed or minimized abuses. This is a delicate matter, so I name in the text only those teachers who are already in some sense a public figure. They have led organizations that are larger than a single sitting group and/or written books. They have brushed off previous discussions (or attempts to have private discussions) about the harmfulness of their actions. They could be of danger to people who come to them for help—although I would never presume to tell a student with whom they should or shouldn't study. Finally, the teachers whose names I mention are well-equipped to tell their own version of events should they choose to.

Is it unkind to mention the names of some of the people who have harmed others, or taken the harms committed too lightly? Does it break the precept (Buddhist ethical teaching) of "not finding fault with others"? It's often said that nearly every philosophy or religion encourages three values: truth, beauty, and kindness. I believe we get in trouble if we prioritize any one over the others.

I know that, as a lifelong scholar, I tend to enter through the door of seeking truth. Sometimes the truth is not particularly warm or lovely. Yet it is because I yearn for people to experience the brilliant and deep beauty of practice, rather than harm or cruel betrayal, that I write this book. Kindness that is one-size-fits-all, and too "nice" to speak truth to power, is terribly unkind to those who have been harmed by power's misuse. A purely poetic and aesthetic approach to practice is similarly ill-equipped.

So I am writing in accord with another precept of our precepts, that which encourages us to "speak truthfully." Calling for *accountability* is not the same as *blaming*. Blaming is defined as "finding fault with," and is associated with condemnation. It is essentially personalized and backwards looking. Accountability, on the other hand, means accepting responsibility for one's actions—whether one has acted directly as a perpetrator or, perhaps simply through ignorance or inertia, indirectly as an enabler. It results in apologies, restitution, and prevention. The need for accountability arises not because some individuals are bad apples, but simply because to err is human. Accountability is forward-looking and less personal. It involves not only the individual who directly caused harm but also those who are able to influence systems and structures that have failed to support ethical behavior. I am trying (as beautifully and kindly as I can manage!) to call for accountability while avoiding laying blame. I am aware that I carry within myself the seeds of every fault, failing, or weakness I point out in another. I hope that every reader will also remember that every incident I recount took place at a particular time. It's possible that individuals or organizations may have changed between the time that I am writing the time when you are reading.

I also believe that *respect* is not the same as *deference*. Deference is "yielding to the judgment of a superior." There will be readers who will be outraged that I, an upstart with far fewer years of study and teaching under my belt than some teachers I mention, should venture to say anything about them that is not flattering. That sort of attitude, I believe, is a big factor in the atrophying of once-vibrant traditions. In contrast, one definition of respect is having "due regard for…the wishes of others." The teachers I mention have all vowed, many times over, to "refrain from evil," "end delusion" and "enter every Dharma gate." I'm appealing to them from these shared values, and to that part of themselves that made these vows sincerely. We should *all* welcome assistance in waking up to harm that we have caused or tolerated. Or at least (being human) we should be able to tolerate it being pointed out instead of trying to kill the messenger.

My goal is to make Zen safer. In order to do that, we need to face up to our history in the area of abuse. Otherwise, we will keep repeating it.

## OVERVIEW

Part One of this book is addressed to individual practitioners. Many of these warnings would also apply to any sort of meditation practice. My hope is that being forewarned may help newcomers to develop a healthier practice. My even more sincere hope is that *experienced* practitioners will recognize that we all, as individuals, are never guaranteed to be past these dangers, either! At the heart of Zen is a non-dualistic and dynamic understanding of self and other, form and emptiness. At the times we can truly act from this understanding, we are acting as an enlightened person, with wisdom and compassion. But doing so is hard. It is *very* hard. We all carry seeds of greed and hatred. All our usual ingrained habits of thought and action are based on delusions of separation and stasis. To investigate and loosen these, I will also introduce some images—one ancient and one newer—that may help us use our thinking minds (in addition to our opening experiences) to get past "one or two."

Part Two looks at structural issues that create or perpetuate harm. Why do so many teachers and sanghas get derailed, and end up doing harm? How can teachers and other sangha leaders avoid this? Most of this section would also apply to Tibetan Buddhist sanghas and lamas, churches and congregations, yoga communities and gurus, or most any form of community spiritual practice. I write about Zen because that is what I know best. Most of this second part is also useful information for new or newish practitioners, though chapter 8 is especially directed to those with more experience.

When I started writing this book, Betrayals #1 and #2 were in the past, and I thought I was in a sangha that was progressing well in dealing with these questions. But that was before Betrayal #3. So I, and my home sangha, are still learning. I hope you, dear reader, will join me in exploring these issues, and trying to find that next step on this Way.

# PART ONE

## FOR YOU AS AN INDIVIDUAL

1

# WHAT'S HAPPENING TO ME?

THE EMPHASIS in Zen practice is on sitting meditation. We sit upright, silent, and still. At my home sangha, we do this for twenty-five minutes at a time, interspersed with periods of walking meditation. What's this about? What might happen?

## THE LIBERATION AT THE HEART OF ZEN PRACTICE

While people meditate for various reasons—for example, to lower their blood pressure, or manage anxiety—our Zen teachings point to something more profound. While we might start with concentration practices such as counting or following the breath, eventually we want to practice *doing nothing.* Just sitting. This is because our noisy, constant doing and fixing and thinking and planning and judging and even concentrating get in the way of the universe getting through to us. As long as we keep those barriers up, we feel separate from everything "outside." When we can finally relax all that, letting thoughts just rise and go away without chasing them or trying to banish them, the sense of me versus the outside drops away. We realize that our dualistic view is just a delusion: We have been created by, and have been flowing with, the greater whole or oneness all along. We are a wave on the ocean, and we now realize we've been water all along. We finally come home. We realize that our existential suffering and many of our problems in life are actually not inflicted on us, but instead created by our habitual dualistic views.

While it is no substitute for the sort of visceral, bone-deep *realization* of non-dualism that Zen points to, I find that some images of non-dualism help me picture what's going on. They also help me notice when I've slipped back into relying on dualistic thought.

We usually understand our world by putting things into clearly demarcated bins or categories: *This* is me, *that* is you. *This* is Buddha, *that* is sentient being. We understand things to be objects or entities that exist on their own. A chair is a chair, and different from a table. And what is more, it will stay being a chair. We might picture such distinctions in the simple way shown below.

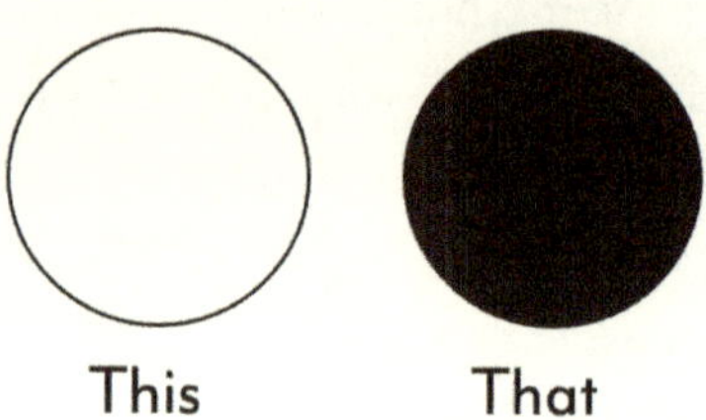


In terms of our daily lives in the relative world, this way of thinking is usually highly convenient. We distinguish a chair from a table. This prevents us from having to continually test whether our table is comfortable to sit on!

But, to paraphrase a very old Buddhist story about King Milinda and a chariot, what if we took apart the chair. Are the legs the chair? The rungs? The seat alone, when the legs are elsewhere? It's only when those pieces of wood *are related to each other* in a particular way that we call them a chair. An ancient text reads:

> When this is, that is.
> From the arising of this comes the arising of that.
> When this isn't, that isn't.
> From the cessation of this comes the cessation of that.[1]

There is something fishy about the idea that anything exists on its own.

So a Buddhist understanding of the universe is different. We and everything else in the universe exist only as, and in, interdependence.

We are not the separate objects or entities we think we are. And nothing is permanent. We suffer when we deny these facts. We try to deny interdependence by distancing ourselves from unpleasant things. We try to deny impermanence by holding onto things we like. These are what the Buddha taught as the Three Marks of Existence: *Anatta* (no self), *Annica* (impermanence), and *Dukkha* (suffering).

As Buddhism moved from South Asia to China, *Chan* Buddhism, which is the Chinese root of Japanese Zen (and Korean *Seon* and Vietnamese *Thien*) was developed. This combined imported Buddhist practices with elements of Chinese Taoist and Confucian philosophies and indigenous religions. Chinese understandings of *yang* and *yin* can be helpful for understanding how what we usually think of as opposites are actually complements.

Yang energies are associated with lightness, activity, heat, and positivity. Yin forces are associated with darkness, receptivity, cold, and negativity. Neither is considered superior to the other. They are more like two sides of the same coin: without one side, we could never distinguish the other. We may think of heat as the opposite of cold. But if we never knew heat, how would we know if something were cold?

To illustrate how these two forces, while different, are actually interconnected, mutually interdependent, and two sides of a dynamic whole, the Chinese invented the diagram shown below.

The white shape that resembles a teardrop or tadpole represents yang. The black one is yin. Yet both are contained within a single circle, and inside each teardrop is a dot (or tadpole eye) of the other color. This illustrates that there are no separate "white thing" and "black thing," only interdependence. What is more, the diagram is meant to be seen as representing swirling movement. I like to see it as two tadpoles swimming in circles in a very tiny fishbowl. This movement evokes the Buddhist teaching of impermanence: Nothing stays in place. Instead of "either/or," we are in a universe of "both/and."

Does the yin/yang symbol indicate oneness and unity since there is one circle? Or two-ness and separation since there are two colors? In Zen we would answer "no" to both questions. Or maybe "yes" to both. The symbol points to a reality that is beyond "one versus two."

Note that this dynamic combination is not simply "finding a place in the middle" of a simple polarity, on some simple continuum. There are no in-betweens, no grays, no "meh." Such an understanding might be pictured as follows.

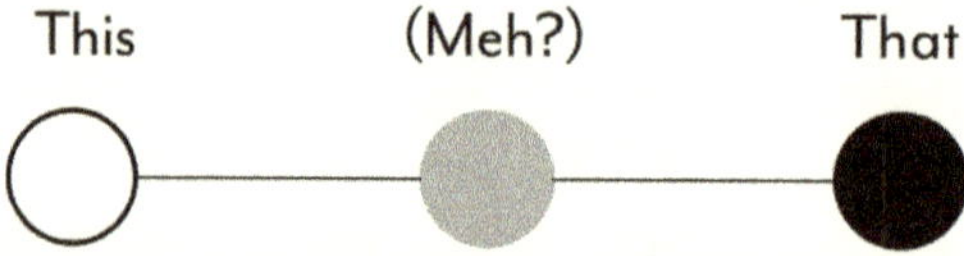


In the yin/yang diagram, the black stays fully black, and the white stays fully white.

Many years ago, I created a diagram I call a compass, to contrast how our usual either/or thinking gets in the way of a relational understanding, using words. In the compass, shown below, the west direction indicates yang, and the east is yin. North is the yin/yang, non-dualistic understanding of interdependence and dynamism (that is, impermanent and always changing, both/and). South is our usual dualistic "this/that" understanding of things as separate and static (that is, fixed or unchanging, either/or).

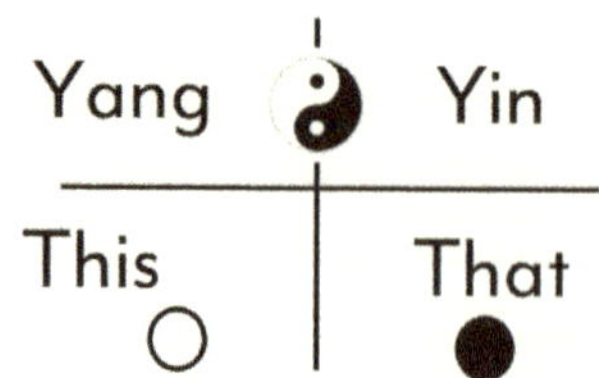

I'll be using this by putting a word in each of the four quadrants. The top (north) pair of words will illustrate the both/and relationship, where yin and yang forces are in dynamic, swirling interdependence. The lower left (southwest) indicates what we get when "this" is imagined to exist alone, without "that." The lower right indicates a similar imagined existence of an opposite "that" alone. So the bottom half represents separation, a focus on distinct unchanging "things," and a dualistic relationship of either/or.

While the compass is intended only as a tool for understanding, I think that, if understood, it can help us see some of the fundamentals of Zen practice. The *Sandokai*, a foundational text of Soto Zen by eighth-century Chinese teacher Shitou Xiqian, evokes these swirling, do-not-be-attached-to- "things," not-one-not-two, relationships:

> The subtle source is clear and bright;
> the branching streams flow in the dark.
> To be attached to things is primordial illusion;
> to encounter the absolute is not yet enlightenment.
> Each sphere, every sense and field,
> intermingle even as they shine alone;
> interacting even as they merge,
> yet keeping their places in expression of their own…
> Light is also darkness, but do not think of it as darkness.
> Darkness is light; but do not see it as light.
> Light and darkness are not one, not two,
> like the foot before and the foot behind in walking.
> Each thing has its own being which is not different from
> its place and function.
> The relative fits the absolute as a box and its lid.

I will use the yin/yang diagram and the compass in later chapters to explain the hazards involved in misunderstandings of "no self" (chapter 2) and teacher-student relationships (chapter 4). Yet these images of yin/yang and the compass are also not static in meaning. Use them if they are helpful.

And then, even if they are, throw them away, too.

Zen is going to mess with your head. As the ancient Zen text, "Affirming Faith in Mind" by Sengcan says, "What is, is not. What is not, is." If your initial reaction to it, and other statements that seem nonsensical and contradictory, is confusion, you are quite normal. And this is a feature, not a flaw. At some point in our practice, we start to be able to make sense of teachings that go beyond our usual belief in dualisms. But in the meantime, a lot of very wise teachings will appear to be nonsense.

Yet, unfortunately, our profound Zen teachings and practice may be misapplied or misunderstood. While the path is well worth walking, we will likely encounter some bumps and quicksand along the way.

## CONTRAINDICATIONS

In medical-speak, a treatment or technique is "contraindicated" when the treatment itself can cause harm. Intense or prolonged Zen practice—or any kind of intense meditation or mindfulness practice—may be contraindicated in some specific situations. While I am not qualified to give psychological advice, let me share what I've learned from the research.

Untreated victims of trauma, as well as those actively suffering from some kinds of very serious mental health issues, may be poor candidates for extended meditation practice. It is very common for memories and emotions to bubble up during meditation practice, seemingly of their own accord. But for someone suffering from chronic PTSD or severe anxiety or depression, these can come on in waves that are absolutely overwhelming. Go ahead and give a moderate amount of meditation a try! If your condition is not too severe, you may find meditation helpful. But if you find that difficult thoughts and feelings are becoming even more powerful—as though meditation simply gives them space to expand and take over—silent sitting practice may not be healthy for you, at least at this time.

Others may experience a strong sense of psychological dissociation or depersonalization. They come to feel distant from their environment, their emotions, their behavior, and themselves. They may feel numb or blank.[2]

While very rare, some individuals have even experienced psychotic episodes while sitting quietly and introspectively for substantial periods of time. Such a person loses touch with reality and may experience, over days (or years), hallucinations and confusion. The research on meditation and epilepsy is inconclusive. While there are accounts of meditation bringing on seizures, there are also arguments for using meditation as a form of therapy (along with medication).[3]

Meditation has many real and transformative benefits, but it is not a cure-all. We talk about spiritual "waking up" in Zen, but the first thing one needs to wake up to may be one's own need for psychotherapy, more social support, and/or medication. In the meantime, you may need to shorten the periods of time you sit in meditation or avoid long retreats. Or you may need to temporarily give up silent sitting entirely, perhaps doing only chanting and studying for a while. Or you may need to focus entirely on your treatment plan, putting Zen entirely on hold. Only when disturbing thoughts and feelings can be safely held in stillness of meditation will prolonged meditation be useful.

Often the best thing a wise Zen teacher or other sangha leader could do, for those suffering adverse effects, is to refer you to where you can best get appropriate help. Zen teachers are usually not qualified doctors, psychotherapists, or psychiatrists. (Even when they are a therapist, ethical issues about dual roles should prevent them being *your* therapist.[4]) Not all teachers are well-informed about these issues. A teacher may deny or minimize the harm that can arise in meditation. Or your teacher may fail to recognize when your condition is beyond the limits of their expertise. If you are a student in such a situation you may, unfortunately, need to buck the teacher and other sangha leaders and seek appropriate help on your own.

Teachers and sangha leaders can and should get better at recognizing contraindications. Professor Willoughby Britton, a psychologist at Brown University, and her team have put together resources to help meditation teachers "do no harm."[5] They encourage screening students for such contraindicating conditions, monitoring the effects of meditation, and learning how to do "mental health first aid" should a crisis occur. The "safety toolbox" developed by Britton's team, as well as other resources, are also distributed available at the Meditating in Safety website in the United Kingdom.

In our sangha, we welcome anyone to try out our weekly sitting groups. But we've added a screening question about sources of support for mental health issues to the application for our longer retreats. We could still benefit from educating ourselves more about these issues.

## PHYSICAL MALADIES

The standard stock picture of meditation is of a young, healthy woman in a leotard sitting in full lotus position and looking totally at peace. Hah! Meditation is physically challenging.

This is especially true if one is not young or is living with a physical disability. Some especially rigid Zen centers may demand that participants sit in full lotus position, with each foot on top of the opposite thigh. Even if we *can* get into that posture, it could be permanently damaging, especially to our knees. For most of us, who didn't start training in this posture at a young age, sitting in full lotus is impossible.

Serious physical harm can be avoided by allowing a variety of positions. People may still sit on standard cushions on the floor, but in a half-lotus, cross-legged, or kneeling position. The use of extra cushions, kneeling benches, and chairs can offer even more supportive alternatives. While still recovering from a concussion, I did parts of one retreat lying down with my head on a round cushion and my knees bent, feet on the floor. I've also seen this position used by people with severe back problems. In some statues Buddhas rest on their sides. I've heard of "seated meditation" being effectively practiced while lying in a hospital bed. The important thing is to find a posture in which the spine can be as erect as possible, and which can be held with minimal or no fidgeting for a substantial period of time.

Some degree of discomfort, though, is inevitable, especially on long retreats. Learning to sit still, even when you've got an annoying itch or an aching knee, is a crucially important practice. Our brain tells us that we have to

> SCRATCH!
> MOVE!
> DO IT RIGHT NOW!

Not paying so much attention to the demands of our brain is the beginning of insight. We start to understand how much our brain lies to us. We start to learn to be okay with reality as it is, even when painful, instead of always trying to fix it right away. As we continue to practice, we come to find that our entire perceived self and world are delusory. (This doesn't mean we aren't individuals, or we don't fight injustice. But realizing that we have habitually filtered everything through a screen of "what's in it for me?" progressively frees us from attachment to our perceptions and beliefs.) It all starts with not scratching an itch.

So how do you know when you are doing yourself damage versus when you should just bear with the pain for the sake of practice? The rule of thumb I learned is that if the pain goes away when you get up and walk, it's probably not doing you any permanent damage. Just continue your practice. If the pain doesn't go away, you should, when you go to sit again, try a different position, or different cushions, or move to a chair.

Even if you aren't in pain, overemphasizing and straining at meditation can lead to physical illness. Hakuin Ekaku, an eighteenth-century Japanese Zen teacher, described a "Zen sickness" involving feelings of heat and cold, ear-ringing, sweats, weakness, and fatigue. Hakuin described a contemplation practice designed to bring one's energy lower in the body as a remedy.[6] Practitioners of Tibetan Buddhism talk about "lung" or "rlung" (pronounced "loong") stress-related problems that can arise from over-concentration. These may include pains, digestive issues, and insomnia.[7] Relaxation and changes in diet are among their suggested remedies.

## SLEEPY OR TENSE

Beginning students commonly complain that sitting meditation practice "Isn't working for me." As soon as you sit down, you may get sleepy and start to drift off. You feel dull. Or you may find that you "can't let things go"—whatever you were thinking about, worried about, planning or remembering before you sit down is still fully occupying your mind after you sit. You feel tension and struggle. Your mind doesn't pay the least attention to your commands to count your breaths, follow your breath, or just sit. Whichever it is, dull mind or busy mind, you end up frustrated.

You may be told that the proper way to sit in Zen meditation is to be both alert and relaxed. In our usual ways of thinking, that seems impossible. We understand alertness as a concentrated focus, and relaxing as letting it all go. How could we possibly do both at the same time?

To examine the issue of alertness *and* relaxation in these images, note that alertness is yang and relaxation is yin. A compass looks like this:

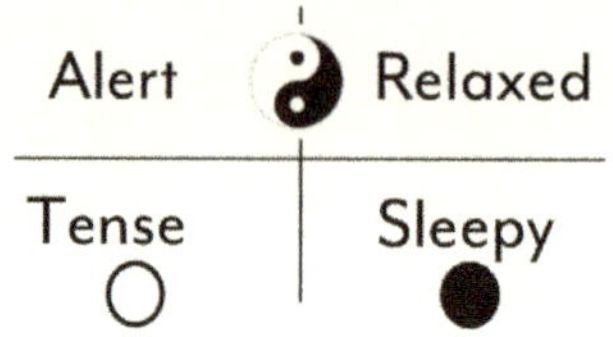


The top pair illustrates the both/and relationship, where our yin and yang forces are in dynamic interdependence. This sort of alertness is not tense, worried, defensive, narrowly focused, or busy, because it is completely open. We are alert to whatever the universe wants to give us. But that receptivity involves yin. The lower left (tense) indicates what happens if we fall into a rut of exclusively yang activity (usually focused on something in particular). The lower right (sleepy) is what happens if, conversely, our dark yin energies eclipse our yang alertness.

Physically, this means that we are neither rigid nor collapsing. In sitting posture, we let our lower body become thoroughly grounded (yin) and sink into the earth, while our upper body, simply through the rise and fall of our breath, reaches for the sky (yang). In seated meditation it is possible to be 100% alert—feeling more alive than we ever have!—*and* 100% relaxed, with nothing at all to be tense or worried about. *Fully* feeling the yin and yang energies in our posture naturally straightens one's spine in a dynamic way. Many dancers and other athletes know about this physical manifestation. It may look to us like the person who leaps unbelievably high has a special relationship with the air. Actually, they have a special relationship with the ground: the upward movement starts *downwards*.

If we don't learn to feel in our bones this sense of alertness *and* relaxation and accept that both are part of a constantly turning wheel, we will always be trying to fight sleepiness by raising tension and vice versa. This is, metaphorically, just fussing with various shades of gray. The way to come to understand this alertness *and* relaxation in your bones is to engage in dedicated, continued practice. Advanced practitioners of "just sitting" will sense this more than beginners.

*And*, because the relationship of yin and yang is always swirling and changing, we give up (when we remember to!) fighting with ourselves when it *isn't* what is happening. When we sit and only "busy mind" comes up, we become the Bodhisattva of Busy Mind until that leaves us. When only sleepiness comes up, we become the Bodhisattva of Sleepiness until that leaves us. Zen is our whole lives. Busy mind is "suchness." Sleepiness is "suchness." Nothing left out. Nothing permanent.

As Korean Zen teacher Seung Sahn put it,

> Clear mind is like the full moon in the sky. Sometimes clouds come and cover it, but the moon is always behind them. Clouds go away, then the moon shines brightly. So don't worry about clear mind: it is always there. When thinking comes, behind it is clear mind. When thinking goes, there is only clear mind. Thinking comes and goes, comes and goes. You must not be attached to the coming or the going.[8]

So keep practicing.

## BLISS

How could bliss become a *pitfall*? It feels good! Many start Zen practice thinking that overwhelming feelings of peace and contentment are not a trap but the goal.

I remember early in my meditation practice an experience that I named for myself as "sweet breath." Sitting and watching my breath, at times the breath itself would feel inexpressibly lovely. Just in. Just out. So beautiful. Then later, at a retreat, I experienced a bliss state even more strongly. We were several days into a week-long retreat and I was pretty much aching all over. Suddenly, without any sense of leaving my body (which would be psychological dissociation), these all just faded into the background and the foreground became a vast expanse of peace and ease. It lasted maybe a half hour. By the time of that retreat I'd practiced long enough to know that I didn't need to try to either end it or extend it. As the bliss state gently passed away and the aches returned, I simply watched the process.

The problem is not in these feelings themselves but in getting attached to them. Once we've experienced bliss, we may think "Wow, now I've really 'got' Zen!" And we think that the point of our meditation, the next time we sit, is "to get back to that state I experienced last Wednesday." We think we're failing somehow if we don't. We may imagine that Zen teachers go about in such a state all the time.

We begin with concentration practices and learn with time and practice to develop some degree of calmness and clarity of mind. Yet Zen is not about achieving a particular mind state. Zen is about being okay to be with reality as it is, right here and right now. Maybe achy, or maybe feeling anxiety churning in our gut. Or maybe peaceful. "This is it" applies to all these states.

Keizan Jokin, a Japanese Zen teacher born in the thirteenth century, advised, "Do not attach yourself to a sublime feeling of the way."[9] The Surangama Sutra, which is even older, notes that "a feeling of infinite serenity" may arise in one's mind.[10] Yet, it is listed in the context of a long list of "demonic" traps for unwary practitioners! It is "not unwholesome" in itself, the sutra notes, if one recognizes its transient nature. But if we believe that it is some kind of special achievement or should be permanent, then we have become confused. Trying to get back to that bliss state, in other words, means we are reminiscing about "last Wednesday" rather than fully living today.

This also harkens back to a basic Zen teaching. Some other religions (and even strains of Buddhism) consider heaven and hell to be separate realms, one of which you will enter after death. In a compass diagram, hell (all yang and heat) *versus* heaven (all yin and coolness) would be shown as the either/or dualism in the bottom cells. In Zen, we see them as both right here, right now. We become liberated not by escaping our problems and "hell realms" but by radically accepting that these are part and parcel of our life. As Charlotte Joko Beck put it, "What makes it unbearable is your mistaken belief that it can be cured." Our lives are made up of samsara *and* nirvana, in dynamic relationship. If we try to stay in coolness and bliss, we will miss half of our real lives.

Would you really *want* to be off in a bliss state when someone you love dearly dies? Sometimes people confuse Zen equanimity with emotional distance and flat-lining. Far from it. Instead, by not attaching to the stuff we like and trying to push away the stuff we don't like, we can ride all the ups and downs, living fully through it all.

## VISIONS AND OTHER WEIRD STUFF

Keizan Jokin further noted that,

> Sometimes your body may feel hot or cold, rough or smooth, stiff or loose, heavy or light, or astonishingly wide-awake.... Your mind may feel as though it is sinking or floating, dull or sharp, or as though you can see outside the room, inside your body, or the body of buddhas or bodhisattvas.

The Surangama Sutra also mentions a number of different kinds of visions, altered perceptions, unusual sensations, and heightened or numbed feelings. It also talks about odd abilities such as being able to see in the dark or inside one's body, or to hear things happening a great distance away. "Aha," you might think if you experience these. "Finally, something is happening!" In some varieties of meditation practice such hallucinations and special abilities might be welcomed. They may even be the goal of the practice.

Not so, typically, in Zen. Keizan followed his list with, "Such sensations are caused by a disharmony of mind and breath." The Surangama Sutra calls them "demonic." In Japanese lines of Zen, we call them *makyo*.[11] The usual advice from a Zen teacher is "Don't worry, they will go away." One is advised, as I was, to neither try to develop them or suppress them, but just not get too involved with them.

Why? Most of the time the driver behind makyo is our own bored brains or needy psyches. Our brains, crazy to begin with, and then really annoyed when their demands aren't getting top priority, will get up to all sorts of tricks to try to amuse themselves. And, in our usual state of greed, hatred, and delusion we may grab at a weird experience as some sort of personal "accomplishment" or supernatural elevation. Yet Zen is not centrally about getting "far out" experiences or polishing the achievements of our little selves. Far from it. It is about really living our lives, *these* lives, right here. And it's about going beyond our self-centeredness.

I also dissent a bit from the advice I was given. In *The Shamanic Bones of Zen*, Zenju Earthlyn Manuel argues that things like visions and energy healing are an integral part of Zen.[12] There is no avoiding the fact that magical occurrences figure prominently in ancient Zen and Buddhist texts! Some were certainly later additions and exaggerations, but perhaps not all of them. Manuel argues that these are ignored in contemporary Zen mainly because we have adopted an overly rationalistic mindset.

The way I see it is that weird experiences are just like anger or sexual attraction in that they are all just energies arising. Simply indulging in them unreflectively can be harmful. Yet, as human beings, we also can't fully repress them without doing harm to ourselves. We need to feel them arising *and* inquire as to whether they contain useful information or the spark for appropriate action.

For example, if I see that my spike of anger is only indicating that my ego has been bruised, I can see that the wise move is to just let it go. If it is anger at injustice, however, it has the potential to be an energizing force for wise and compassionate engagement. While I have never experienced visions during Zen practice, I do have a rich dream life. Ninety-nine percent of the time my dreams seem to be just the noise my brain makes as it consolidates the sensations of the day. I can ignore those. But, boy, that one percent! Some of those have brought the hidden to light and changed my life! Other Zen practitioners have also experienced "weird" but meaningful things. For example, Zen scholar Steven Heine has written quite seriously about a couple of "apparitions" that were important to him.[13]

So yes, these things happen. Without thinking of them as any sort of accomplishment, inquire if they have something to tell you. If they just seem to be noise and happen once in a while and are not too upsetting, keep practicing. Center back in your body and breath. Eventually your busy, thinking, imagining mind will likely learn to take more of a back seat. If they seem to carry important information, bring that wisdom into your life. But if weird things are persistent and very disturbing, consider whether meditation may be contraindicated for you.

We, and I hope most sanghas, warn people at the end of retreat about re-adjusting to the outside world. Perceptions of time have probably become distorted. One needs to remember that a red traffic light is not just brilliant—it also means stop. It's wise to put off making major life decisions for several days. A retreat can be a marvelously supportive environment for deep practice. But it's different from daily life. And only as we do the work of integrating our practice into the realities of our lives are we living the path.

## STRONG EMOTIONS

It is common for sitting practice—and especially prolonged sitting practice—to bring up strong emotions. You may suddenly feel great love and joy. Or great anger, sadness, or fear. If you find feelings such as anxiety or depression become overwhelming, meditation may be contraindicated for you. But some degree of emotional arisings is normal. They have various causes.

On the positive side, sitting practice may allow old, unprocessed, knotted-up emotions to release. As is well known to most massage therapists, counselors, and yoga teachers (and at least some academics),[14] emotions may be stored in various parts of the body. The practice of sitting silently and still, with your spine as erect as possible, may create a somatic state in which the previously ignored can finally be attended to. I recall one time in particular where I could physically feel an emotion "bubbling up" inside me—like a burp!—and releasing itself in about ten seconds of quiet crying. Our Zen practice, on such occasions, is simply to be with the feeling. There is no need to analyze it, or try to find the story behind it, or note it down. If you want to bring it up later with a therapist, that's fine. But in Zen practice we simply continue sitting. The sitting itself forms a safe "container" into which strong feelings can arise and then fall away.

At other times emotions may arise simply because your small mind feels bored to death. It generates some internal drama to entertain itself. You may, for example, find yourself absolutely *enraged* by the fidgeting of the person next to you! Or you may get terribly anxious about what you're going to say the next time you meet with a teacher. Our practice is to neither repress nor indulge such feelings. Just feel them, and, as you can, let them pass as you continue to sit and breathe.

Sometimes you may experience what psychologists call *transference.* They define it as redirecting the feelings you have about one person onto someone else. (This will be discussed at more length in chapter 5). I'm not sure, myself, that the original feelings have to be about a *person.* I recall at one early retreat feeling attracted to a man who I'd never talked to, for no other reason than that he made the coffee in the morning. I *do* love coffee!

If you know that distracting emotions including transference may happen, and are prepared for them, they may not be a problem. A little shot of reality—such as talking to the fidgeter or coffee-maker once silent practice ends—is often enough to dispel the feelings or at least shrink them down to size.

## OVERCONFIDENCE

The ancient texts have more to say. Keizan includes in his list of strange conditions, "Sometimes, you may feel as though you have wisdom and can understand the sutras or commentaries thoroughly." The Surangama Sutra repeats this same refrain after many of its first descriptions of demonic influences:

> What the practitioner has gained is temporary. It does not indicate that they have become a sage. There is nothing unwholesome about their state unless they think that they are now a sage. If they do think they are a sage, they will be open to a host of deviant influences.

I am (alas) very familiar with the feeling, "Now I've really seen through into reality! Now I've really got it, once and for all!" For years, I left most retreats with something of this feeling. And then, as it wore off, I inevitably realized—by looking at my actions—that I am still far from wise.

This is normal, and to be expected. Here is an old Zen story involving Mara, a personification of forces that tempt people to go astray:

> One day Mara, the Evil One, was traveling through the villages of India with his attendants. He saw someone doing walking meditation whose face was lit up in wonder. The person had just discovered something on the ground in front of them. Mara's attendant asked what

> that was and Mara replied, "A piece of truth." "Doesn't this bother you when someone finds a piece of truth, O Evil One?" his attendant asked. "No," Mara replied. "Right after this, they usually make a belief out of it."

This phenomenon is a big reason why finding a trustworthy Zen community is so important to practice. The natural urge of any person who has had a substantial, authentic, sudden opening experience (sometimes referred to as "sudden awakening," *kensho* or *satori*) is to want to show it off. We want a merit badge that everyone can see! We feel superior and special. We might even believe that now we are ready to teach others. We may speculate that from here on, our life will be rosy. We make the serious error of becoming attached to, and making an identity out of, what is in fact only a passing glimpse.

This is actually kind of hilarious, because in the moment of awakening, there is no self to which a merit badge could possibly be pinned! But our little selves return with a vengeance the nanosecond after that opening has passed.

One of the main jobs of those with more experience with practice, then, is to help newer folks recognize and get past this quicksand. If you excitedly describe your enlightenment experience to a teacher, you'll probably get an underwhelming response. The tone will probably be, *That's nice. Now what about your daily life/koan/precepts study?* A little deflation, at this point, is a good thing.

Others of us may not have a "big bang" type experience, but perhaps just lots of little openings where something lets go. We don't feel the universe turning inside out, but we have many moments of seeing some particular object, belief, or emotion in a new way. I like to think of these as times of "en-*lighten-up*-ment," since one sign of authenticity is that they help us take ourselves a bit less seriously. After a few of these, though, we might likewise come to think, "OK, *now* I've got the hang of it!"

I've heard it said that awakening is "sometimes fast, always slow." As human beings, we carry heavy loads of personal and social karma. We have unhelpful habit energies that only unwind, it seems, one at a time. We have psychic knots, related to our own histories and emotional constitution. Awakening is *always* just a new beginning. Then comes integration of that awakening into our lives. Repeat. Repeat again. Repeat over and over. We are on the Path for our whole lives. Unfortunately, this sometimes seems to be forgotten, even and especially by those further along on the path. That's why there are many more chapters in this book.

### DESPAIR AND SPECULATION

The flipside of getting carried away by joy and feelings of accomplishment is becoming misled by feelings of extreme despondency and despair. The Surangama Sutra includes a number of these in its list of fifty "demonic" states.

One such state is believing that one has made no progress in the practice at all. Feelings of dryness or bleakness in the practice may make us despair. We've been practicing and practicing and haven't had an opening experience at all! We may blame the universe and feel cheated. More likely we blame ourselves, and wonder if we are, deep down, defective. Don't give up. Even though I don't know you, I can say with perfect confidence: You are *not* defective.

I don't believe that authentic opening experiences are under an individual's control, nor the control of any teacher. As far as I can tell, practice does not *make* them happen. We have zero control over the timing. Consider poor Ananda, Shakyamuni Buddha's long-time attendant, who, the story goes, remembered every word of the Buddha's teachings. Yet while he witnessed one person after another—and even the serial killer Angulimala!—being enlightened after encountering the Buddha, he himself was not enlightened until *after* the Buddha died. And he wasn't the only one to practice for years before anything happened. Take heart from these stories!

My understanding is that the timing of openings is (at least from a human point of view) random. I think of them as a something like a momentary glitch in our mental habit of "selfing." That process for some reason misses a beat, and…the bottom falls out of the bucket. The universe is not at all being withholding about it. In fact, it is constantly jumping up and down in front of us trying to get noticed! When we practice, we start to turn down the volume of our noisy selfing and tune in to our "receivers." Our selfing membrane thins and we quiet down to the point where we can actually hear, see, and feel. The timing of a breakthrough (into no hearer separate from the sound heard, or no see-er separate from the object seen), however, can't be foretold.

Judging from my own experience and many conversations, I'd say that *everybody* who practices has at some point experienced the feeling, "everybody else here in the zendo 'gets it,' except me." These feelings are normal and to be expected. As an introvert, I especially identify with how the Surangama Sutra describes the desire to "flee into the mountain forests because one cannot bear the company of other people." The sutra also warns us about becoming attached to any theory, or to speculations about the future. The problem with any joy, despair, or fear, or any thought or theory, is not simply that they arise. The emotions and thoughts just arise, and *their arising* is the truth of that moment. They turn into dangerous beliefs when we attach to them and think them incontrovertibly true. Real scientists know better than to talk about "truth" in any fixed and eternal sense because any theory, explanation, or prediction is always dependent on what we know at this time. Zen figured this out centuries ago. We simply cannot know the future, no matter how much we plan or speculate.

Given the environmental, social, and political challenges we are facing in the 21st century, it's very tempting to fall into fear and despair. I find it somewhat comforting to learn that some people in 8th century China apparently felt the same way. The Surangama Sutra warns against concluding, from observation of the "raging fire of the world," that the world is coming to an end. Zen advises us to not get lost in speculation. Zen encourages responding to situations as best we can while not being attached to the outcome.

It's interesting to note that the traditional orientations towards time in the Asian cultures in which Zen developed is quite different from that common in the industrial West. There is a lot of veneration of elders and ancestors in traditional Zen. A number of older Zen texts bewail the fact that the golden age of practice is in the distant past. Now, these texts often say, we have only a weakened, corrupted version, and things will probably get worse from here. In the West, elders are more often considered to be useless and past their prime. During the twentieth century, at least, and still in many quarters now, the future is believed to be where it's at. We may expect that the progress we've made—in science and technology, in women's rights, in reparations to exploited groups, in mindfulness, and so on—will just continue to make life better.

Notice that both despair and utopian dreams are mere speculation. We tend to absorb our culture's myths. In reality, we do not know what is coming next.

## FINAL THOUGHTS

Zen is about waking up. Although it generally helps relatively healthy people deal with their troublesome thoughts and feelings, it is not a cure for serious mental illness. It involves tolerating physical discomfort, but we should not persist to the point of damaging ourselves. The goal is not to experience any particular mind state or display any peculiar powers. We don't become instantly wise. We can see rosy and disastrous scenarios being invented by minds and recognize them as only speculations.

2

# CHOOSING A SANGHA

MAYBE YOU'VE practiced on your own for a while and have read a book (or many books) about Zen. Books usually encourage finding a supportive sangha (Zen community) and working with a teacher. It's too easy to delude ourselves when we try to practice alone! So now you start to look around. What should you look for when you check out a sangha? What should you watch out for? Or perhaps you are a leader in your spiritual community: What should people be finding, or *not* finding, when they try out yours?

## TRADITIONAL (AND POSSIBLY VERY HELPFUL) SANGHA PRACTICES

What should you expect to see and do when you decide to try out a Zen community?

Sangha practice involves meditating silently for long periods in a room with others doing the same. You will generally find people bowing along with the group. We do slow walking meditation in a line and chant in unison with others. We often figure out what we are supposed to be doing simply by observing what others are doing.

Zen communities often try to be welcoming places and build a sense of community. While the silent practice remains at the core, sanghas may warmly welcome you or hold social events. Perhaps the members engage in practices of mutual aid. You may be encouraged to devote more time to sangha activities by attending classes or discussion groups, volunteering to help with sangha administration, or participating in volunteer activities of social service. The sangha will ask for donations to help pay its rent or mortgage and other expenses.

Many Zen communities encourage or require all participants to wear certain colors of clothing (often black or at least drab) or even special robes or Asian-style work outfits. You will probably notice subtle (or obvious) signs in clothing, position in the zendo, and forms of address that distinguish newer students from senior students and all students from authorized teachers. Those who have done some training are often given new (Dharma) names. At a retreat, you may be woken up at 4:30 a.m. It may seem to you that some of Zen's elaborate rituals (such as formal meal practice or the precise use of bells) are *designed* to make you screw up.

You will hear talks about "no-self," and may be encouraged to "let a talk wash over you." You will probably hear a lot of obscure terminology, perhaps in Japanese, Korean, Vietnamese, or Pali. You may be invited to meet privately with a teacher for spiritual guidance. It will seem like some folks have special knowledge that you don't have.

I have experienced all these things in my years of Zen practice. In addition, in the tradition in which I practice we study both the writings of Eihei Dogen (as in Soto Zen) and koans (as in Rinzai Zen). Both of these make clear just how far removed from typical understandings of language and logic Zen can be! We are encouraged to trust that we are being guided in the right direction, even when things don't seem to immediately make sense.

If all goes well, this will all be in service of helping you along the Way. You will be asked to donate only amounts of time or money that are reasonable given your situation. You will constantly be assured that you *yourself* are Buddha nature, even if you don't realize it yet. The relative uniformity of movements and dress will not be harshly enforced; it will start to make sense to you as a way of creating an atmosphere of quiet and harmony. Your questions, your mistakes, and even your skepticism and criticism will be welcomed as part of the process. Teachers will be respectful of your physical and emotional boundaries and not set themselves up as someone superior to you in all ways. You will be able to practice while remaining true to your basic moral values.

## THE PERIL OF CULTISHNESS

While "cult" has become an unfashionable term, designations such as "high control," "high-demand," "charismatic," or "authoritarian" are now often used to mean the same thing. Psychologist Margaret Thaler Singer, in her 1995 book, *Cults in our Midst*, defined a high-control group as "[One] that forms around a person who claims to have a special mission or knowledge, which they will share with those who turn over most of their decision making to that self-appointed leader."[15] Cultishness may be most pronounced in those spiritual practices which teach that the guru is an incarnation of the divine who must be worshiped and obeyed. While that is not the case in Zen, Zen sanghas can also tend towards cultishness.

### THE CULTISH LEADER

Charisma. The main thing I know about it is that I don't have it. But there do seem to be people who have the power to able to awaken certain energies in people simply by their presence. Individuals may find themselves feeling deeply warmed and loved at a mere glance from such person. The charismatic individual can "light up a room" and make others feel revitalized and uplifted. They may inspire religious fervor, sudden insights, or political zeal. Some may, from what I hear and read of others' experience, stimulate real spiritual awakenings.[16] These feelings and experiences are commonly perceived as *emanating from* the leader.[17] The experiences stimulated may be so overpowering that—at least for some of those involved, and for some period of time—critical thinking goes out the window. Previous reservations are immediately cast aside and awe and devotion to the charismatic leader take their place.

I haven't personally experienced such overpowering by a spiritual teacher. This is perhaps because my initial openings didn't involve teachers, or perhaps because I haven't found my teachers to be particularly charismatic. But descriptions of such events resonate with an experience I had in a romantic situation some years ago. It seems to be human nature to want to put absolute, cosmic-level interpretations on our strongest emotional experiences. Thoughts of "soulmate" and "destiny" and "this is *meant to be*" arose strongly in me in that situation. Humans also tend to (mis-)perceive such energies as externally-generated.[18] Had I been more naïve, I could easily have believed that the relationship was *creating* the new sexual and emotional ranges I discovered instead of simply awakening them. I may have believed that these were therefore unique to that specific relationship. As for some of the decisions I made while under the influence: All I can say is that they seemed like good ideas at the time.

Charisma and strongly felt "spiritual connections," I think, are neither good nor evil in themselves. They just are. They may be put to good purposes or harmful ones—or often some of each. Charismatic leaders have inspired life- and nation-changing spiritual renewal and democratic solidarity. But they have also inspired mass suicides and campaigns of bloody violence.

What about the charismatic teacher who inspires a genuine spiritual awakening? What happens next depends greatly on the spiritual and emotional maturity of the teacher.

The teacher may understand that while they are a channel for the absolute, they are also still a limited and flawed human being. In this case they will hold the devotion and trust given them by their students very lightly and carefully, knowing that it is rightly directed at the absolute and not at them personally. Their goal in the teacher-student relationship will be to help the student mature. The energy and connection to the absolute that the student initially perceived as emanating from the teacher *has never been anything other than the student's own.* Spiritual growth leads towards the student realizing this and becoming better able to follow the way in their own day-to-day life.

Or the charismatic teacher may believe that they really *are* special, deserving of devotion, and infallible. They may come to believe this over time even if they didn't at the start—and might never admit they believe it now. If they are infallible, then it stands to reason that they know best about everything. They become authoritarian and controlling. Instead of encouraging students' spiritual growth they (subtly or overtly) encourage students to think of themselves as fundamentally and forever inferior and reliant on them. Depending on a student's level of emotional and spiritual development, a student may gravitate toward this belief even if their leader *isn't* particularly charismatic. The group ends up being a cult.

### CULTISH PRACTICES

It's a bit eerie and disconcerting to realize how many of our typical Zen practices are also techniques used by charismatic or authoritarian leaders as part of a gradual and insidious campaign of "thought reform." These include maintaining silence, moving and chanting in unison, and peer pressure (even in such subtle forms as following the group in removing one's shoes)! Margaret Thaler Singer also includes in her book on cults activities such as displays of warmth and affection; sleep deprivation; systems of rewards; notions of special knowledge; encouragement to suspend one's rational thought; spiritual hierarchy; and complex and ever-changing rules. The use of somewhat obscure language or phrases with changed meanings, she writes, is an additional "thought reform" technique.

Zen teacher Grace Schireson, in her scholarly article, "The Promise and Peril of Buddhist Meditation," mentions another sign of cultishness: "Leader/community dictates personal choices in clothing, occupations or relationships."[19] This outward uniformity has been shown, in psychological studies, to lead to other sorts of conformity in thinking and behavior.

Going in alone to see a teacher also can carry hazards. A high-control teacher may take advantage of the situation, engaging in inappropriate touching or making inappropriate requests.

### WHAT DISTINGUISHES A CULT

Singer tells us that it is often hard to tell a healthy group from a cultish one. This is because the techniques of thought reform are insidious and leave people unaware they are being controlled. People around the fringes of the group may often perceive nothing amiss at all. But Singer's work can help point to some of high-control groups' distinctive aspects, which are not characteristics of healthy groups. To flesh out those aspects a bit more, consider:

- Veneration of the leaders. The leaders are served by the members (rather than vice versa) and create systems of control to assure this. The members trust and rely on the leaders to an excessive degree.
- The group "love-bombs" new recruits with excessive displays of warmth and attention.
- The leaders and their senior followers suppress questions, member communications with each other, information from "the outside," and dissent. People who disagree with the leaders are shunned or evicted. The leaders may pressure members into making donations of money, time, and effort in excess of what is reasonable. These donations are often used for purposes that are more self-serving than those publicly expressed.
- Very importantly, leaders and their elite helpers make extensive use of Orwellian doublespeak, that is, using words euphemistically or even to mean their opposite.

If you see any of these things going on, keep your eyes open. If you see a lot of this going on, run!

### WHO CULTS ATTRACT

I was even more struck when reading Singer's book by who it is she says cultish groups attract. You are probably already aware that people who are lonely, depressed, isolated, or in crisis may be particularly susceptible. While we may resist the idea, that description probably fits most of us in Zen, at least to some extent. If we weren't desperately looking for something, why would we give up beautiful days and entertaining pursuits to spend hours sitting silently on a cushion?

While we might think that intelligence and education should make one cultish-proof, Singer also pointed out that many cults have successfully targeted colleges and universities in their recruitment strategies. Not uncommonly, the leaders will be educated, apparently rational, successful, and even professional people. My home sangha happens to have long been situated between Harvard and MIT and attracts many of just this sort. (Uh oh.)

Most striking to me was Singer's insight that cults also tend to attract good, altruistic people. They attract people who want to be on the side of the right and true. Cults attract people who want to do good things, people who want to save the world. Many were attracted to Jim Jones' People Temple in the 1970s, for example, by its message of anti-racism and its utopian ideals. (Hundreds of them later, on his orders, drank poisoned Kool-Aid.) Put another way, cults may attract people who want to "save all beings," as we chant in the Four Bodhisattva Vows.

The sanghas I've been in have been full of good, altruistic people.

## NO-SELF: A CENTRAL (AND SOMETIMES MISUNDERSTOOD) TEACHING

The teaching of "no-self" (anatta) is an especially tricky one to understand. Does it mean I'm really not me? That this body doesn't really exist? Misunderstood, it can open us up to cultish influence.

### WHAT ZEN REALLY TEACHES

Our Zen teaching is that we don't have separate, permanent selves. I have no fixed self—that is, no essential self that preexists before activity and relationships. There is no stable boundary dividing me from the rest of the universe. A delusive belief in an enduring self that is independent of others in fact poisons our lives. The folk belief is that it is my job to take care of me. I need to make my life better or more pleasurable or more righteous than it is right now. I perceive my personal drama (rehearsed and reviewed endlessly inside my head) as the main event—as *this*. Everything around me I perceive as something more like scenery—as *that*. And not only do I perceive and categorize things in terms of my own interests, but I also pursue them or avoid them according to my purposes. But I will never get all the things that I want. I will never avoid all the things I don't want. This is the cause of a perpetual feeling of unease or dissatisfaction.

In some ways, this is glaringly obvious. What I think of as "my opinion" this week, perhaps I perhaps picked up from you in our conversation last week. What I called "a banana" this morning was separate from "me." But after I eat it, I'm made up of banana and acting with banana energy. Some of the banana that became me will end up as sewage. And this entire me will, at some point, also return to the dust from which it was formed. (We don't like to think about that last point.)

The world we live in, when viewed from the perspective of distinctions, is the world of form—of diversity, of many, of the relative. The very same reality, viewed from the perspective of no distinctions, is the world of emptiness—of oneness, of the absolute. Yet this oneness, this emptiness of distinctions, is not a characterless void. It is fertile. Among the many things that arise from activity and relationship is undeniably this so-called thing I call myself. The yang and yin of form and emptiness can be illustrated as:

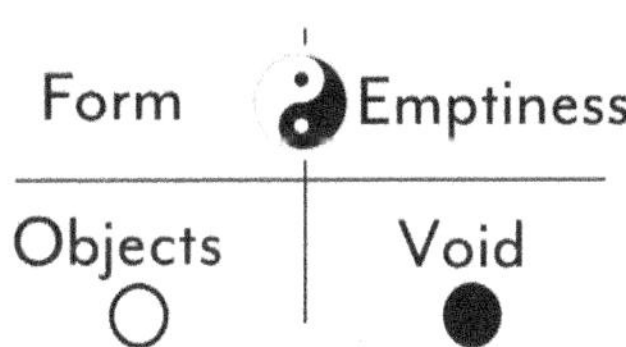


We arise in all our variety and distinctiveness—just not as enduring *objects*. The alternative to being an enduring me is not non-existence, or some kind of dark pit. It's just that instead of me being a separate object, everything in reality flows. You know what music is, right? Can you put your finger on it? If not, does that mean it doesn't exist? Like music, we are flow and change.[20]

From the perspective of emptiness, we are both nothing and everything. That is, we are no*thing*—not an object or entity that persists. Yet because we are utterly inseparable from the rest of the universe and from all time, we are also the entire universe at all times. We are boundaryless. From the perspective of form, however, the demands of living in the relative world require a different approach. We must recognize that there is differentiation and that boundaries are important. When chopping carrots with a sharp knife, it's best to acknowledge the difference between carrots and our fingers!

A good metaphor for how we can be both differentiated and not-differentiated at the same time is that we are each a wave on the ocean: We are never anything other than ocean water (emptiness), yet, for a while we appear as a wave (form) distinguishable from other waves. In emptiness there are no distinctions. But that doesn't mean that emptiness is a vacuum. In the world of form, we are physically and psychologically differentiated. We just aren't actually separate.

If you haven't realized it already, a trustworthy, well-grounded teacher may help you see that you are much more than you usually think, and much less. You are not an enduring self, and you are the entire cosmos. When you do realize this, you and the teacher can share the feelings of gratitude, joy, and awe that come with this discovery. That is likely not something you share with many others in real life, and so it can feel very special and intimate. Then the job of the trustworthy, well-grounded teacher is to try to help you do the lifelong work of integrating that realization into your daily life. The most trustworthy teachers will openly acknowledge the fact that they are also still working on the same thing and are not without clay feet. They will encourage you to, more and more, develop your own sense of when you are on the Way and when you are not.

### HOW THIS TEACHING GETS TWISTED

So, back to our question of cultishness. True Zen practice requires that we keep healthy interpersonal boundaries. While it may seem at first like a contradiction, we need a reasonably healthy ego to do Zen! I don't want an overblown ego: If I put up too-high walls around myself, I will try to reject being influenced by other people, and so reject my place as part of the wholeness of life. Clearly, constricting and impermeable boundaries around myself will not help me enact "no-self."

But if we have weak, overly-permeable boundaries—and especially if we confuse such weak boundaries with becoming no-self!—we open ourselves up to exploitation by other humans. In the world of form, we need to be able to discern for ourselves what is right rather than live as an extension of someone else. We need to have gotten to a reasonable level of psychological maturity and integration. Only then can we safely begin to see through the fictions (of permanence and separation) the ego likes to create.

I first thought about this decades ago, inspired by the work of Christian Process theologian Catherine Keller.[21] She looked at the representations of masculinity and femininity in Western myth and culture. Keller coined the term "separative self" to represent the masculine-associated high-boundary mythical being who (while exploiting other beings) believes they can exist with no dependence on other people. The converse, the feminine-associated mythical no-boundary entirely supportive and dependent (and exploitable) being, she named the "soluble self," as in how salt dis*solves* in water.[22] Since the Chinese associated yang with masculinity and yin with femininity, we can express these insights in the compass like this:

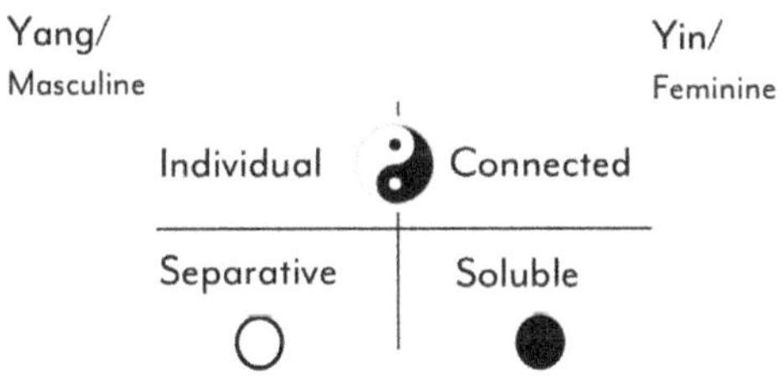


The person who thinks of themself as individual and separate lives in a myth of isolation. The person who believes they can simply merge into someone or something else attempts to give up their individuality in favor of engulfment. In reality, we are both individuated *and* created by nothing other than vast interdependence of causes and conditions.

The danger of cults, then, lies in rejecting the idea of myself as a separate, enduring thing, but doing so in the wrong sphere. We might, in pursuing no-self, try to jettison our individuality (our good sense, our own judgment) completely. We might aim to dissolve ourselves into a set of true-sounding beliefs and an apparently wise leader. If we do this, we've taken teachings meant to point to emptiness and inappropriately applied them to our relations in the world of form.

This is in contrast to the sort of appropriate intimacy that can develop between a well-grounded teacher and a student described earlier. The intimacy between a student and a teacher should certainly not be characterized by unquestioning loyalty and slavish devotion to some human being who we have idealized. And it should not develop into the kinds of intimacy that exists between lovers, family members, or best friends. (More on this in chapter 4.) Since you interact with those folks more in real life, they actually know you better, in many ways, than your teacher knows you. You may feel a special resonance with your teacher, but your relationship must stay within the bounds of spiritual friendship and guidance to be safe. You are still the one in charge of your life.

## AN EXPERIENCE WITH CULTISHNESS

First, a bit of background. I started meditating at age forty-one, in 1997. This was when both my marriage and my career had fallen apart within the same few months. At first, I practiced alone, simply finding that silent sitting as needed helped me manage my panic. After that I attended an Insight Meditation (Vipassana) center for a couple years. I began my Zen practice sitting with a small, independent group in Newton, Massachusetts in 2003. I was attracted to Japanese Zen because the Newton group's teacher, James Ford, seemed so approachable and warm. And, frankly, because the Zen group was closer to my home.

Over time, though, the group grew and became affiliated with other groups and other teachers in the New England area. Eventually it turned into Boundless Way Zen, a self-styled "school" of Zen founded by James Ford along with his student Melissa Blacker and her husband, Korean Zen teacher David Rynick. As more students moved up through the teaching ranks, its council of transmitted teachers grew to include a number of other teachers who led sitting groups in a variety of geographic locations. After a while, James Ford retired and moved away. I stayed on, choosing a new teacher, Josh Bartok (also a student of James), and took on progressively more leadership roles within the organization.

During this growth period, Melissa and David solicited from the wider membership logistical and financial help for purchasing and renovating a property for use as, at least in good measure, a Boundless Way retreat center. My son and I helped build bunk beds and I and many others donated money. The resulting temple in Worcester, Massachusetts became a place where members of all Boundless Way sitting groups, and their teachers, could gather.

In 2018, I was vice president of one of the two relevant boards. (I won't bore you with the details about why there were two boards.) That's when I discovered the cultish aspects had taken hold over part of the organization.

The two teachers who were behind the creation of the temple were advanced Zen practitioners, very experienced, and warm and welcoming human beings. But one of them, in the middle of a week-long retreat when he was supposed to have been guiding my spiritual practice, lobbied me instead. He told me that he and his wife were clearly superior in spiritual authority to the other five teachers on the council. Therefore, he said, they should be able to decide who to invite to teach with them on retreats at the temple—and, by implication, who to exclude. He wanted my support for this, as a board member.

I was appalled. I was shocked by his assertion of superiority. I found his interruption of my practice in the depths of the retreat to be entirely inappropriate. I feared that I would be disenfranchised from studying with my own teacher at the retreat center I had helped develop.

These two teachers had gotten deeply involved in the business matters of the organization, having by now succeeded in hand-picking many of the people who served in non-teaching leadership positions. Many board members saw their job as serving the teachers rather than as serving and caring for the sangha. They trusted these two teachers completely—not only on matters of Zen practice, but on matters of finance, real estate, and institutional history.

I tried to counteract some of the misinformation that sangha members were receiving, but flows of information were managed carefully in a top-down manner. The president of the board I was on, who was a close associate of the two teachers, once wrote to me about a communication I made, "I must insist that you…always discuss any action you propose with me first to ensure that I approve."

I saw plenty of doublespeak. "Listening carefully," for example, was used to describe rushing to make a change with only minimal, tightly-managed discussion. "I've been harmed by that person" was, I heard, said by one of these teachers when someone did not supply sufficient agreement and deference. The disagreements within the teachers' group were described as "interpersonal conflict" when what was going on was an abuse of authority. The whole power play was described by the two teachers as necessary "in order to better spread the Dharma."

People who raised questions were pressured to conform or shown the door. The president of the other board, who merely wanted a slower and more deliberate process, was forced out in what seemed to me an especially cruel manner. What was supposed to be a board business meeting with him in charge was instead orchestrated to be a ritual with the teachers clearly in charge. The board president was coerced into making an emotional public apology (for what, remained unclear), and then voted out. I heard from others that I had been bad-mouthed, too.

I learned later that dysfunctional power plays had been going on for some time both in the wider sangha and within the teaching council. One of the teaching council's disputes was concerned with a student's devastation, and subsequent complaint, after being verbally abused by one of the two teachers. The five other teachers on the council all ended up deciding they had had enough and would rather separate than continue to battle with those two teachers. By early 2019, they had all exited Boundless Way, taking "their" sitting groups and students (including me) with them. We regrouped as the Greater Boston Zen Center.

So ultimately, those two teachers won. The efforts and funds that had gone into providing a place for retreats by the larger group ended up turned towards more local purposes. These included providing those two with a comfortable, rent-free home and substantial stipends—benefits not enjoyed by any of the other teachers.

When I had tried to draw attention to the power plays and misinformation, the good people at the temple with whom I engaged often simply couldn't believe that these teachers could be motivated by anything other than the highest purposes. What I saw as valid critique they saw as unprovoked aggression. What I saw as a need for accurate information, they dismissed as unnecessary quibbling. Many times, I felt confused, as though I was trapped in a fun house with distorting mirrors. I could no longer tell what, or whom, to trust. Consensual reality had broken down.

I believe I was seeing the results of some pretty effective thought reform. I call this "Betrayal #1."

## SOME CRITERIA FOR CHOOSING A SANGHA

So, how can you tell if a Zen group is healthy, versus leaning towards cultishness? Almost all groups will, as noted above, share some practices that, on the surface, may appear cultish. For example, you will be generally expected to do some amount of "going with the flow" until you learn the ropes. Most Zen groups will seem welcoming. And, unfortunately, most teachers who are authoritarian are very good at hiding this fact. It may be difficult, when you first start practicing, to discern what is going on.

This is a case where an ounce of prevention is worth a pound of cure. For reasons to be discussed later, it is generally far easier to detect cultishness *before* you are in the group than after you have become involved. Once you've opened your heart, you become more vulnerable. After a controlling authority figure has sunk their talons deep into your soul, it's much harder to get loose.

Some ways of checking out a sangha before you get involved aren't all that useful. Going by the recommendation of current members is not all that reliable since they themselves may be teacher groupies. Checking the qualifications of the teacher in terms of background, lineage, memberships, or education may tell you something—or may tell you nothing at all. Some of the most cultish teachers have stellar credentials. Noticing that the teacher(s) have written books or recorded talks that you like is *definitely* unreliable. "Do as I say, not as I do" happens in Zen, just as it does elsewhere.

I'd suggest, first, investigating yourself, second, gathering information, and third—if you dare! —doing a little experimenting.

### KNOW YOURSELF

Who are you? What are you like? Do you see yourself very easily in the positions I described earlier: lonely, depressed, isolated, or in crisis? Did you have an abusive or neglectful childhood, especially perhaps one with an alcoholic parent, that has left you more attuned to others' needs and feelings than your own? Your wisest first step out of this may not be into a zendo. You may be far too vulnerable to love-bombing, or to teachers who seem to promise to be that perfect parent you missed. Perhaps medication, therapy, or a support group such as Al-Anon would be a better first move. Zen will be safer after you know yourself better and have developed healthy personal boundaries.

Or perhaps you feel pretty good, but you're looking for a flashy, fabulous experience? You've heard about head-over-heels, fireworks-like sudden enlightenment experiences and want to get you some of that good stuff for yourself? We sometimes only half-jokingly say we should post a sign over our zendo door saying, "Enter Here After You've Tried Everything Else." You'd obtain thrills more quickly and predictably by taking drugs or engaging in extreme sports—though I don't recommend them, for safety reasons! You can even find programs that promise fabulous "enlightenment" in a single weekend (for a price, of course). You may be likely to mistake charisma and false promises for spiritual wisdom.

To find Zen practice satisfying and safe, you need to be ready to settle in for the long haul. Maybe you've had some opening experiences or will have some after you begin practicing. But achieving them is not really the point. From the first time you sit, you are doing the Buddha's practice. And a lot of the time it will seem (to your restless small mind) dead boring and pointless. You might wait to come until you really know that all those other things can't address your burning questions.

### GATHER INFORMATION

Before you even go the first time, do internet searches on the teachers' names, and the name of the group, and words such as "cult," "controversy," "abuse," "scandal," and "misconduct." Read what you find with an open and critical mind and weigh the arguments or evidence. Be aware that cultish groups often defend themselves with *ad hominem* attacks on their detractors, or with counter-lawsuits.

Also scan the group's website looking for evidence of total teacher-centrism. This is often signaled by worshipful prose about their many accomplishments. (Respectful summaries of qualifications, on the other hand, are normal.) The lack of a meaningful ethics policy or little mention of non-teachers in leadership positions are also worrisome. Passing these tests doesn't always mean that a sangha is safe but failing them can be a bad sign.

After you're involved, consider asking to see documents related to finances, real estate, or to anything about which you have a concern. Many sanghas say they strive for transparency—until you ask.

If you can, talk with people who have left the sangha, or left positions of lay sangha leadership. Find out why they (really) left or stepped down. The reasons may be innocuous. But the more I've been around sanghas and heard from others, the more stories of disillusionment due to teacher abuses of power I've heard. Yet such people often leave quietly. Or they give some plausible but untrue reason. Or they step down from dealing too closely with teachers but don't want to give up their community of fellow students. I wish I had talked more to the people who left Boundless Way early on. When I finally did, I heard of troublesome behavior going back years.

### TRY DISAGREEING

Running some subtle experiments could be especially revealing. Try suggesting something new, expressing disagreement with a teacher, or making a reasonable critique of something a teacher has done. (If the teachers are out of reach, try directing your comments to one of their close associates.) Do so in a respectful way—so, initially at least, do this privately or in a small group. Your suggestion could be about something as trivial as whether to put salt in the morning oatmeal, or whether shoes should be placed to the left or right of the door.

How do they respond? Are you treated as a reasonable adult who may have something interesting to contribute? While no guarantee of safety, that's a positive sign.

Or do they get immediately dismissive or defensive? Are you quickly shut down with a curt "this is the way we do it"? Do they act like they are the parent, and you are their unruly child? Are you regarded with tight-lipped disapproval? In a really cultish group, even just *hesitating* too long before you enthusiastically agree with a teacher can be enough to bring out this protective ammunition.

Unfortunately, many cultish leaders have fine-tuned empathetic listening skills that they can use to get your confidence. They seem to treat you as a reasonable adult—"really hearing you"—in order to sink their claws even deeper into your spirit. I've succumbed to that sort of subtler manipulation more than once. So if you made a reasonable suggestion and were met with "listening," ask yourself some additional questions: Did your critique actually lead to positive change? Does this person actually agree with you, or are they just good at saying what people want to hear? You might need to check what they are saying to others.

If you really want to draw defensive ammunition from cultish leaders, suggest starting a study group about abuses of spiritual power. Maybe research a couple past scandals in your lineage or school and start talking out loud about them. See if the sangha leaders try to twist your suggestion into something that misses the point. See if the sangha leaders try to blame the problem on a few bad apples. Or you get a too-easy, "Oh yes, that happened, but we've already dealt with it," or a "That's not a problem here" response. Those would be on the mild end of inadequate responses. You may be asked, "Why do you always make trouble?" You may be talked about as a poor student and diagnosed as possibly mentally disturbed. So, do this early on. Once you've already felt this sangha to be your spiritual home, such betrayal will be incredibly painful.

You might have to run such experiments more than a few times. If you persist in posing questions to a truly annoying extent, a healthy teacher will probably talk with you about more appropriate ways to express your views. A healthy leader may suggest you bring your concerns to the board, or the ethics ombuds, or run for a sangha leadership position. They may need to set reasonable boundaries out of self-protection, such as "I'll read your complaints, but I won't always be able to reply." But you will get the feeling that dissent, if not always entirely welcome, is at least tolerated. An unhealthy sangha will move quickly to try to divert you, minimize your concerns, shut you up, marginalize you, or kick you out.

### PAY ATTENTION

Finally, trust your gut. Do you get little twinges now and then, as if something is off? Pay attention to them. As the Japanese Zen teacher Ikkyu counseled, "Attention. Attention. Attention." In Zen, we open our hearts. We need to keep our eyes open as well.

## FINAL THOUGHTS

In the previous chapter, we looked at a number of initial warnings given in the Surangama Sutra. These were directed to who are relatively new to the path—who, in the words of the Sutra, are experiencing "mental darkness." After these, the sutra always refers to the practitioner as a "good person," so someone who has started to reap some of the fruits of the practice. At around the thirtieth of the fifty states, the emphasis changes from states that do damage to oneself to states that do damage to other people. "The good person" who has become convinced (by the demons) of their own superiority loses the ability to see what is going on with themselves. They can turn into a teacher who attracts followers who are willing to turn over their power.

This is not to say that all Zen groups should be considered cultish. But it's important that we be aware of the power of our practices to disrupt our usual senses of identity and discernment. When used in a healthy way, our practices crack our self-centeredness and open us up to the fact that we are the universe. When used in an unhealthy way, these same practices may break down our resistance so that other human beings can use us. The chink in our self-centeredness may merely mutate into blind loyalty to an untrustworthy high-control leader or group of leaders.

How do you find a (reasonably) healthy teacher and sangha, and protect yourself from harmful ones? Here's some advice that's come down through the ages, from Shakyamuni Buddha, via Eihei Dogen, Taizan Maezumi, and finally as expressed by Bernie Glassman:

> [I]f you want to practice, if you want a good teacher, if you're looking for protection and support, nothing can be more essential than remembering that you are the Three Treasures.[23]

You are *already* Buddha, Dharma, and Sangha. You need to realize it for yourself. No person or group is going to give this to you.

# 3

# THE PITFALL OF SPIRITUAL BYPASSING

I HAVE already described some perils that lie along the Zen path when we think about joining a sangha. What about when our individual practice itself becomes a trap? This is a more subtle danger and one that none of us are likely to ever escape fully.

## AVOIDING PERSONAL GROWTH

The term "spiritual bypassing" comes from the work of psychotherapist John Welwood. He wrote,

> Spiritual bypassing is a term I coined to describe a process I saw happening in the Buddhist community I was in, and also in myself. Although most of us were sincerely trying to work on ourselves, I noticed a widespread tendency to use spiritual ideas and practices to sidestep or avoid facing unresolved emotional issues, psychological wounds, and unfinished developmental tasks.[24]

We "spiritually bypass" when we use our Zen practice to avoid the hard work of achieving personal integration and emotional maturity.

Robert Augustus Masters, in his excellent books, *Spiritual Bypassing* and *Bringing Your Shadow Out of the Dark*, vividly describes the causes and effects of this phenomenon. I can't repeat all of this wise analysis and advice here, but let me comment on a few signs of bypassing I've witnessed in myself and others.

## FANTASIES ABOUT SPIRITUAL TRANSFORMATION

Are you a good person? Are you a bad person? Chances are that one of the reasons you came to Zen is because you want to be a better person, a good person. Perhaps less angry. Maybe more compassionate. Probably wiser, so you don't continue doing so many things you later regret. Less insecure. Able to feel better about yourself. More happy and peaceful, certainly. You've heard that the Buddha promised a way to end suffering. Becoming less tortured by our own psychological knotty places—the places in ourselves we can't examine without experiencing shame and pain—sounds like a good deal.

Maybe if we do the sitting, do the bowing, get some insight into "form and emptiness" and so on, we can get to a place of joy and serenity. In the realm of the absolute, Zen teaches, good versus bad doesn't apply, anyway. And we are all Buddha nature. We may think that, since our selves don't really exist, that they don't really matter. "So, those parts of ourselves that feel nasty can just be dropped off," we might assume. "We can spiritually transcend them."

I know I had some of this fantasy when I started meditation. One of things I hate most is feeling regret. Knowing I made a bad decision and missed out on something good, or perhaps even harmed someone, is really uncomfortable. I secretly hoped that Zen practice would turn me into a person who would always know what the right thing was to do. I also sometimes felt that I, in particular, unlike the rest of humanity, was lacking something in my capacity for compassion. Other people often seemed so warm and understanding in situations where my inclination was to keep my distance. I secretly hoped that Zen would give me a personality transplant. I so wanted to be good.

I suspect we all have our own lists of fantasies, rooted in our own deep sense of woundedness. I suspect this simply because I'm assuming that this book is being read by flesh-and-blood human beings. Life can be hard, and we like to imagine that pursuing a spiritual path will make our life easier. If we can't recognize that we have secret fantasies, it may be because we so strongly believe in them. Yet pursuing a path of spiritual development without paying equal attention to our very human emotional and relational development is dangerous. And it may make us a danger to others.

### EMOTIONAL FLAT-LINING

One sign of bypassing is confusing Zen equanimity with emotional flat-lining. Masters talks about this as "exaggerated detachment" and "emotional dissociation."

We may dismiss uncomfortable feelings as soon as they come up—or turn to a meditation practice to avoid them. We may approach Zen only on a purely intellectual plane. We may deny to ourselves that the emotion is arising at all. We may say that we simply have no desires. You may walk around with a serene expression on your face. If you've practiced for a while, you may actually believe that you have advanced to a level above the fray of ordinary disappointment and conflict. We, and many who are familiar with Zen only from popular media images (and advertising!) may believe that we are "very Zen."

Far from it. We've merely rejected all our normal human desires and feelings as bad and tried to drive them underground. This is nowhere near becoming awake and living a full life.

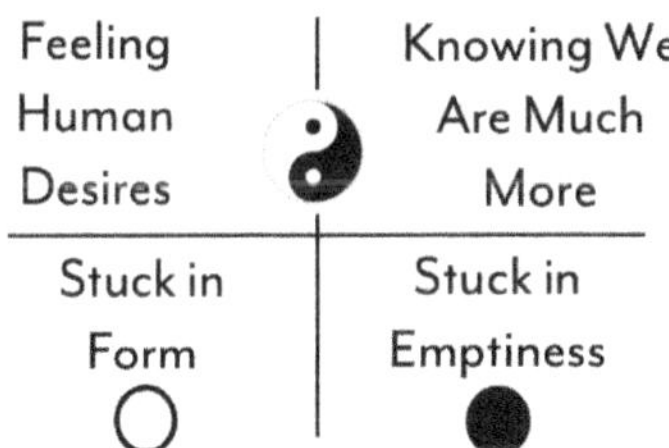


When we live only in our "small selves," as limited karmic beings who think we are separate and permanent, we tend to measure the whole world by whether or not it lives up to our desires and expectations. We see the world of form and distinctions, but nothing more, and are on a constant hamster wheel of trying to satisfy our craving. Zen promises us something better.

*And* it is equally dangerous to try to live *only* in our universal "big self." If we do so, we deny the equally present (though always changing) reality of our bodies, needs, feelings, and thoughts. We are again foundering in attachment—but now it's attachment to the absolute! As expressed by centuries ago by the Korean Zen monk Chinul,

> Some people do not realize that the nature of good and evil is void; they sit rigidly without moving and, like a rock crushing grass, repress both body and mind. To regard this as cultivation of the mind is a great delusion.... If they could see that [thoughts of] killing, stealing, sexual misconduct, and lying all arise from the nature [of mind], then their arising would be the same as their non-arising.... As it is said, "Do not fear the arising of thoughts: only be concerned lest your awareness of them be tardy."[25]

That is, be aware of what you are thinking and feeling. Work at this if you have tended to bury your feelings in the past! And know that you are more than just these. Experienced Zen practitioners often describe sitting practice as creating a little space between oneself and what one is feeling, as if creating a "container" in front of yourself in which you can drop the feeling. Either way, this gives you a chance to take a look at it. You are both fully present to it *and* not overwhelmed or identified with it.

### THE NICENESS TRAP

Spiritual bypassing may also manifest in a way that allows feelings and emotions, but within a decidedly dualistic view of good vs. bad ones. It may show up as a condemnation of anger or judging, usually accompanied by an overblown and blind compassion. We may confuse anger—a natural human energy—with aggression, and label it "bad." We may similarly confuse compassion with constant warmth and niceness. We may assume that everyone is always "doing the best they can" and deserves our empathy and indulgence, no matter how harmful their behavior. We may feel that constantly opening up to others, and always striving to be careful of their feelings is the right thing to do. We may consider any criticism or conflict to be inimical to Zen.

But this is just another version of the false, boundaryless version of no-self. As Robert Augustus Masters puts it,

> [U]nchosen empathy, automatic and innate, can be far from a good thing...Our defining edges, our shape, our integrity as a separate person become mushy.... [F]using with them emotionally...gets in the way of being able to effectively relate to them.[26]

This contrasts to what he calls "chosen" empathy where "cognition and feeling work in healthy tandem." We might fit this in a compass as follows:

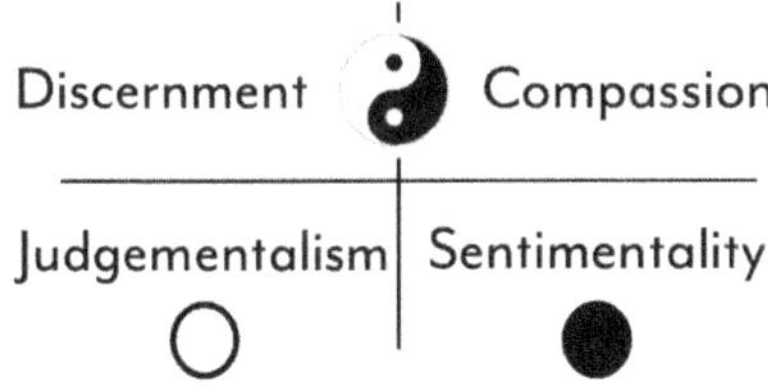


Our mind will always be making judgments because that's what minds do. Sometimes these judgments are decidedly self-serving or condemnatory in an *ad hominem* way and would be best ignored. But sometimes they involve comparisons of what we observe to standards of truth, morality, justice, or care. To judge from those standpoints can be valuable. We can call out a harmful behavior or position (that is, call for accountability for a human error) without making a blanket judgment about a person (that is, condemning an individual for their supposed bad character). If we refuse to judge at all, however, and let everything and everyone in, we over-connect. Our intention to be compassionate dissolves into mere conflict-aversion and sentimentality.

Masters writes:

> When we are driven by blind compassion, we cut everyone far too much slack, making excuses for others' behavior and making nice in situations that require a forceful "no," an unmistakable voicing of displeasure, or a firm setting and maintaining of boundaries. These things can, and often should, be done out of love... Judgment is not necessarily equivalent to condemnation!... Real compassion can be fierce when it needs to be, without loss of heart.[27]

We do others no favor when we fail to hold them accountable. Zen is not reducible to a bumper sticker saying, "Always Be Nicer."

### THE JUDGMENTALISM TRAP

It is possible to go too far in the other direction, too. I've heard of Zen groups at which even beginners are harshly berated if they step with the wrong foot or do an incorrect number of bows. Or, armed with the Buddhist precepts, we might consider ourselves to be the ultimate arbiters of right and wrong and go around constantly calling other people out. Or we may turn our judgmentalism inward. My guess is that most of us have had the thought, "I'm the worst Zen student in the room." Some of us are cruelly judgmental about ourselves most of the time. Where's the liberation in that?

The difference between healthy discernment and unhealthy judgmentalism is, as shown in the figure above, the co-presence of compassion. When we attempt to correct others, is it for their good and the good of the community? Or is it to make ourselves feel superior? When we vow to liberate all beings, can we remember that the being who is, right now, sitting where you are sitting is included?

By natural temperament I lean towards this extreme rather than towards niceness. If you get any insight from personality typing, I test as a Meyers-Briggs INTJ and an Enneagram Type 8. The J stands for judging in contrast to perceiving (P). The T stands for leading with thinking in contrast to leading with feelings (F)—and I lean heavily in the T direction. An Enneagram Type 8—in case you haven't figured it out by the motivation behind this book—is highly concerned with ethics. This can cause problems in relationships with people who are less judging-oriented and more feeling-oriented. Because I lead with logic and reasoning and value straightforwardness, my attempts at discernment and calling for accountability may come across as pushy and insensitive. I need to remind myself to communicate the compassion side more clearly and deliberately.[28]

I also have had to deal with a very loud and persistent inner critic. Masters makes a distinction between our inner critic and our inner conscience: the latter includes compassion for vulnerable parts of ourselves, while the former does not. He suggests looking for the compassion when we have self-judgmental thoughts. If compassion isn't there, then he likens the voice to an annoying mosquito and suggests we don't need to take it seriously.[29]

Zen is not reducible to a bumper sticker that says, "Always Be Right."

### DISEMBODIED ZEN

We may neglect to pay attention to our personal histories and our bodies. So you've experienced severe physical or emotional trauma? "That's just your story. Get over it," some pseudo-Zen teachings (and teachers) might advise.

Our bodies tend not to comply with that instruction: whatever we are failing to deal with will likely show up as tension, illness, an ache in our head or a churning in our gut. The pseudo-Zen solution is to avoid giving any importance to our bodies and what they are trying to tell us. We may treat our physical being as no more than a necessary nuisance for living our spiritual lives.

I knew a Zen practitioner who tended to look askance at putting much care into settling into sitting, or doing body scans, or engaging in other somatic practices that are often thought of as part of or complementary to Zen practice. As time passed, however, this person's spiritual practice appeared to be hijacked by their body and its urges. I'm guessing that this was due to "spiritually" denying bodily urges that they didn't dare acknowledge. This was unfortunate and ended up causing harm.

### SHADOW

The key to continuing on the Way, and not getting tempted into this bypassing, is to become intimate with those parts of ourselves to which we have been blind. Usually these are ones we have labeled "bad" and want to deny we have. We may tend to hold to a belief that they make us somehow less than everybody else. (Probably at some point in our life some authority told us that we *were* bad and less-than-everybody-else.) In fact, these hidden parts, called "shadow" in much of the literature, just mean we're human. Feeling that we are somehow, uniquely, beyond the pale is just another way our ego has of assuring us that we are really separate and special! We need to wake up to the truth that what we perceive as ourselves are, on the one hand, a total fiction, and on the other entirely connected with and dependent on the entire universe. Even our worst parts are "just this." Zen, being unconditional, assures us that even those parts can be worked with.

There is a huge difference between the desire to be a good person and the Zen goal of waking up to all that is, in this moment. The first may be what gets us into the practice to begin with, but the latter is what Zen is really about. The problem is that being good is a project, and we have a natural desire to want to succeed at our projects. We also have a natural tendency—well documented in the psychology literature on "confirmation bias"—to see the things we want to see while tuning out the things that might disturb our beliefs. So to the extent that our deepest desire is to be a good person, that very craving will itself tend to block us from noticing when our shadow has taken over. When our deepest desire is, instead, to be awake, we will want to be awake to our yucky parts too.

There are many ways of learning to engage with our shadow. Spending months or years (and usually a good deal of money) meeting with a good and trustworthy psychotherapist is one. This can bring to light some of the links between our self-defeating behaviors and the way we have been formed by family and social trauma and other pressures. For some, this one-on-one talk therapy will be the best way of starting to gain some intimacy with what has been hidden.

Others may find a somatic approach—where a qualified therapist, counselor or coach helps one get back in touch with one's body—to be the best entrance gate. Others nurture their emotional maturity through "circling" and other structured group practices. A few are lucky enough to get their psychic education more organically through everyday human encounters with wise and emotionally mature people. For those unable to find (or afford) such ongoing personal support, books and workshops may be helpful.

The work is not all about digging up dark stuff, though. We may also, as Masters reminds us, find some gold—some repressed vastness and gifts—as we explore our shadows.[30] I suspect, though, that only doing reading or attending some one-shot-events would be insufficient on their own. This is hard, potentially frightening work and requires an ongoing, supportive, and safe environment populated by at least a couple of fully present human beings. The environment needs to be safe so we can be vulnerable. And it needs to be relational since there is nothing like having to deal with another human being to bring out our shadow side. And it needs to be lifelong.

Practice with a Zen teacher and sangha can go either way—it may encourage spiritual bypassing or help one get past it, depending on their degree of authenticity. Or it can do some of both.

### MY EXPERIENCE

It's very tempting in writing about this to put in examples of spiritual bypassing by *other* people. While one's shadow is largely invisible to oneself, it often is obvious to those who have to deal with us! The preciousness of pseudo-equanimity or the vapidness of overblown empathy, for example, can make you rather annoying to those around you. I've seen a case where it appeared to me that a Zen practitioner's long-buried self-hatred, rooted in guilt about their past adultery, had suddenly exploded. This caused extensive damage, while the person involved remained somehow oblivious. But I'll spare you any more of my amateur psychologizing since I only really know my own psyche, and then only partially.

I did a couple years of psychoanalytically- and spiritually-informed one-on-one psychotherapy after my divorce. This helped me to get in touch with some of my childhood emotional wounds. I have no doubt that my parents loved me. Yet their backgrounds in families damaged by alcoholism, along with pressing life circumstances, meant that I grew up with a certain amount of neglect and exploitation. I covered these with exaggerated self-sufficiency and productivity, and by burying my own needs. To this day, I still have to watch for these habits. I'm still surprised when someone else points them out.

A somatic breathwork workshop also helped me realize one of the roots of my deep dissatisfaction with myself. Growing up as a preacher's kid, I'd internalized that I should "be like Jesus" and bring salvation to the world. That's rather grandiose. At the same time, I also was very conscious that I *hadn't* saved the world yet. So I believed I was an utter failure. I waffled between thoughts of grandiosity *or* total failure. Releasing these beliefs opened me up to finding the yin/yang of the middle way. This means accepting that I have value *and* limitations.

As humans we are both valuable, Buddha-nature beings and limited, flawed karmic selves. I was attempting to spiritually bypass my human limitations by taking on a superhuman "spiritual" quest. I needed to find out that I was actually just (and incredibly lucky to be) human. The best I can do, in terms of being as awake to that experience and responsive to the world, is the best I can do. Whew!

Significantly, my Zen practice helped me release some of my fantasies about Zen practice. One day, after I'd practiced a couple years, I was unlocking the car to go visit a friend. But making that visit meant I was foregoing a weekly dance event I often enjoyed. I let myself fully feel my FOMA (fear of missing out). At that moment, I realized that instead of banishing them, Zen includes and holds even my bad decisions, fears, and regrets. My full human frailty. There is nothing to run away from. In the realm of the unconditioned, Zen assures me that making a mistake does not negate the reality of Buddha nature. I felt great relief. "No hindrance, and therefore no fear," we read in *The Heart Sutra*. Zen practice is truly liberating and transformative—just not in the way we expect.

I used to occasionally experience a deep fear that I was essentially, chronically, and uniquely lacking in the quality of compassion. Once, during a retreat, these feelings arose. In that place of stillness, I finally recognized it as a story based on a firm belief I was carrying. I had (wrongly) equated being compassionate with having a warm personality. I can definitely be compassionate, but I tend to manifest compassion in more practical and firm ways (as, I discovered later, is common with INTJs). I'm probably not the first person you'd turn to when your feelings have been hurt. But if you've suffered an injustice, you might find me vigorously on your side. By looking at what I had been devaluing in myself, I found some positive qualities.

I still have to watch out for the negative, judgmental, hyper-productive shadow aspects of my natural inclinations. I have no illusions that I am done with spiritual bypassing.

## RETREATING FROM LIFE'S PROBLEMS

While coined to refer to avoiding engaging with unpleasant parts of our own psyche, I'm going to take the liberty of generalizing the idea of spiritual bypassing to avoiding other things we find unpleasant. This generally includes our problems of daily life, such as:

- Are the kids rowdy in the evenings? "I'll commit to some evening Zen sits."
- Does my spouse resent me for leaving them to deal, alone? "Clearly that is a sign that my spouse is less enlightened and doesn't recognize the importance of my spiritual path."
- Is my co-manager bullying the people working for us? "I think I'll recommend they go on a Zen retreat."
- Am I getting ever deeper in debt? "I'm learning to live in the moment!"

You get the idea.

It's (too) easy and comfortable to turn to spiritual practice as a cure all. It *is* difficult and uncomfortable to deal with tired children, have a serious conversation with your spouse, confront your co-manager about their behavior, or put together a realistic financial plan. But Zen is about living life, *this* life, fully. If one uses Zen as a reason to escape problems, it's a danger.

What about monastic life? Most of us in the West these days live as householders with jobs, families, and bills. Yet some do choose a traditional, celibate, monastery-based life. I've never tried it, so I can't speak with any authority about it. But I'm pretty sure that Jon Kabat-Zinn's insight, "Wherever you go, there you are" applies there, too. I suspect that if you enter a monastery primarily because you want to move *towards* a deeper spiritual life, you may find fulfillment there. And you may serve all sentient beings. But if instead you mostly want to *escape from* the challenges of family relationships, sexual intimacy, householder responsibilities, and so on, you would just be taking a spiritual bypass.

## FORGETTING ALL BEINGS

One can still find in some forms of Buddhism a goal of personally escaping rebirth into this suffering world. But Mahayana Buddhism (of which Zen is part) developed some centuries after the time of Shakyamuni Buddhism and went in a different direction. The Bodhisattva vows to stay *in* this suffering world until *all* beings are freed. As Joan Sutherland explains,

> [E]nlightenment is about the brilliant illumination that lifts us out of the suffering world and is the focus of classical Buddhist literature; endarkenment is about the radiance of the deeps that lets us find home in the world. Endarkenment is the heart that breaks open to life, rests comfortably on the unfathomable mystery of existence, and is easy with uncertainty, complexity, and

> what courses underground. Enlightenment and endarkenment are both essential to awakening.

Enlightenment is the yang, and endarkenment the yin.

In the Four Bodhisattva Vows, we vow to "save," "free," or "serve" all beings (depending on the translation used). We really are not separate from the universe. If we forget our vow, and try to cut off a "little me," whose individual spiritual achievement is the goal of practice, we've missed the boat. There is no way we can really disconnect from it all.

We are not only connected to family and coworkers but also through our citizenship, our consumption, and through many of our daily actions to everyone and everything in our nation and world. And when we are realistic about it, much of our life depends on other beings' death. Even if we are a vegan living in a grass hut, we still can't help cutting short the lives of bugs and bacteria, not to mention grasses. There is no way we can always be pure and guiltless in how we connect.

So what *can* we do? We can be our limited human selves and do the best we can.

Thich Nhat Hanh is well-known for his advocacy of "Engaged Buddhism."[31] A Zen monk, he spoke out against the hatred and violence destroying his country during the Vietnam War. He later brought his teachings of nonviolent social action to bear on other occasions of violence and injustice. Bernie Tetsugen Glassman started Zen Peacemakers,[32] and founded organizations addressing problems of unemployment, homeless, and other sources of suffering in New York City. There are other notable leaders, as well.

We can't all be them. But we can do, and must do, what we can. Ignoring the suffering of the world is not the Bodhisattva way. Meditation should not just be a middle-class "lifestyle" indulgence.

So, should we be sitting on our cushions when we could be out doing something? To some extent, *yes!* If we don't first carefully examine our own seeds of greed, hatred, and delusion, we will act out of hatred rather than love. I've been around too many groups in which activists self-righteously divide the world into the "good guys" (us) and the "bad guys" (them). Then they go to war and create more conflict. I believe it is true that peace in the world begins with peace in ourselves. Our time on the cushion prepares us to act strongly and firmly, but without adding to violence and pain. Sometimes "Don't just do something, stand there!" *is* the right rule to follow.

I believe sitting may also support those who are suffering in ways that don't particularly make sense to our rational minds. Once, while sitting in meditation at a retreat, I experienced the room of meditators as a sort of wetland. Long disparaged as useless swamps and filled in, wetlands have more recently been discovered to play an important role in ecological systems and especially in water purification. I felt that the zendo was a place of purification for the toxic emotions and beliefs in the world. In this still place, with none of us adding to their strength, those energies might get a chance to settle out. I know that I have had moments of despair when I suddenly didn't feel so alone. Was I being held at that moment by someone sitting? Perhaps someone somewhere was doing the Tibetan practice of *tonglen*, where suffering is breathed in, and compassion breathed out.

Remember that yang activity and lightness is of one dynamic and ever-changing whole with yin stillness and darkness:

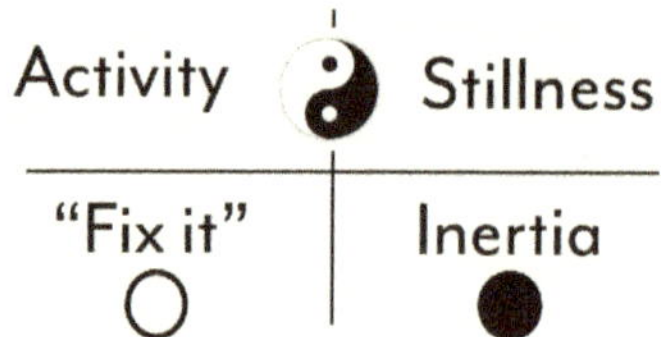


If we merely set out impatiently and unreflectively to "fix it"—or more likely, fix *them*, whoever we think is causing the problem—we may add to the violence in the world. Yet neither do we want to be like "rocks crushing grass."

Most of us shouldn't take sitting as the whole of our practice. Are we situated in a social and political location in which we have some power to speak out? Some power to change things, some power to do our bit? If we decide to sit on our cushion *instead*, we are being irresponsible. Zen isn't about being permanently on retreat.

## FINAL THOUGHTS

Zen is our lives. As humans we have psyches and bodies, relationships and responsibilities. These are alive and constantly changing. If we think we can stick anything in a back room and forget about it, we are on the wrong track.

4

# THE POISONOUS "I HAVE ARRIVED"

It is not unusual to become overconfident even relatively early in one's practice. A first experience of waking up (or *kensho,* as it is referred to in Japanese Zen) may feel so powerful that you think "Now, I've really got it!" You may think that you have now reached the summit of Zen. A little deflation at this stage, as previously noted, is a good thing.

But what about after a few years? Or maybe ten or fifteen or more? Perhaps you have now had a number of dramatic enlightenment experiences. Or maybe, for you, it's been a slowly developing but profound, cellular-level understanding of no-self, impermanence, and suffering. Maybe you've read many books and engaged in much scholarly study. You've taken on positions of responsibility in your Zen community. You may believe you are a much better person than you were when you started.

Or maybe you've even *written* many books or published many scholarly works on Zen. Perhaps you've become an authorized Zen teacher and teach a good-sized community of students. Maybe you've even reached the highest level of teaching status possible in your school of Zen. Perhaps you even have hundreds of students and many Dharma heirs. Certainly, then, you've really arrived, right? Aren't you at the peak of Zen achievement? Aren't you someone everyone should look up to and try to imitate?

Uh, no. Let's go back to basics.

## BEGINNER'S MIND

Shunryu Suzuki's *Zen Mind, Beginner's Mind* has long been a popular first book for starting Zen practice. According to Suzuki,

> The goal of practice is always to keep our beginner's mind…If your mind is empty, it is always ready for anything; it is open to everything. In the beginner's mind there are many possibilities, in the expert's mind there are few.[33]

He continues with the warnings:

> In the beginner's mind there is no thought, "I have attained something." All self-centered thoughts limit our vast mind. When we have no thought of achievement, no thought of self, we are true beginners…. You should not say, "I know what Zen is," or "I have attained enlightenment."

And he stresses that this is "the most difficult thing" about Zen practice.

Tell me about it. This goes totally against all my personal and social karma and conditioning. First, we accomplish crawling, walking, talking. Then there is first grade and second grade. Our graduations are marked with ceremonies and parties. We then might aim to check off the achievements of partnering, parenting, and job or career goals. We get gigs for our band, or gallery shows for our art. We improve our fluency in languages, our cultural competency, or our weight-lifting ability. Or perhaps we have achieved a greater ability to hold alcohol or refined our shoplifting skills. Whatever our goals, we're constantly measuring and aiming for more. Even when mostly what we are successful at is failure, we still have that measuring stick out. How can we *not* bring our habits of marking achievements to Zen?

## THE THOUGHT OF ACHIEVEMENT

In fact, from a certain angle, Zen practice is full of markers of achievement. Older texts often talk about gaining "merit." In my school, we get to wear a *rakusu* (bib-like garment) when we have studied and formally received the precepts. Senior students take on service and leadership positions of increasing status and responsibility. Schools use a variety of titles to distinguish roles and ranks. Teachers, we may presume, are people who *can* say, "I know what Zen is." We may revere them as "Zen masters" and "enlightened beings," believing that they have passed the finish line of the Way. This fits right in with our conditioned views that work for the other parts of our lives.

If that is the angle from which we regard Zen practices, we've lost it. We've made Zen into just another self-improvement project. We've made an opening experience into just another merit badge to use to adorn our small, self-centered self. Zen's transformative power lies not in never *having* thoughts of achievement—since thoughts arise outside of our control—but in not *believing* them. "Don't believe everything you think" is a useful bumper-sticker version of the ancient teachings. Thoughts of "I have accomplished something" happen. The danger is getting stuck in them.

I had a successful career as a Ph.D.-holding university-level academic. I practice Zen in a city (Cambridge, Massachusetts) where you can't throw a rock without hitting an institute of higher education. Our sangha has a large proportion of well-trained, whip-smart high achievers. An excessive focus on knowledge and ambition can be a problem!

Here's a good story about a Zen teacher and an academic:

> Nan-in, a Japanese master during the Meiji era (1868-1912), received a university professor who came to inquire about Zen. Nan-in served tea. He poured his visitor's cup full, and then kept on pouring. The professor watched the overflow until he no longer could restrain himself. "It is overfull. No more will go in!" "Like this cup," Nan-in said, "you are full of your own opinions and speculations. How can I show you Zen unless you first empty your cup?"[34]

We are so geared toward accomplishment that Zen requires that we do some fundamental nervous system or cellular rewiring. The mind of achievement needs to back up and let beginner's mind arise afresh. Over and over and for our whole lives.

While sometimes I try to take the measure of other people, my tendency to measure achievements is most pronounced when turned back on myself. I'm find I'm almost constantly checking to see how *I* measure up: Did I get a pass or a fail on that? Have I inched up, or fallen back? By how much? Am I better or worse than that other person? But this need not be the case. One of the things that helps me get my inner life untangled is my dreaming. One night, in a dream, I came face to face with a toll collector who had clearly been in his booth for far too long without a break. Ceaselessly judging who would pass and who would not, he'd become old, thin, and grizzled. He had long matted hair and several days' growth of a beard. His eyes were rheumy and crazed. His teeth were unbrushed…and, in shape and position, looked just like mine. As I started to wake up, I realized that *I* am the toll collector. I desperately need to take a break from all that judging. I am seriously in need of the soul equivalent of some sleep and a shower.

I then had an image arise in my half-asleep mind of a measuring stick and of the Bodhisattva of Compassion with her thousand arms. I realized that with all her hands, she could easily hold that measuring stick. So now I often visualize handing it over when it's getting in my way.

What is all this self-improvement stuff about anyway? I hooted out loud when I read the title of Joan Tollifson's book, *Death: The End of Self Improvement.*[35] Now *there's* a nice reminder of a Zen perspective!

## NON-ACHIEVEMENT IS NOT NON-DOING

So Zen practice isn't about climbing some fixed ladder. Yet neither is it just sitting like a rock crushing grass. We are in a constantly changing, swirling, world of both emptiness and form. Perhaps some examples can help make this clearer.

Suzuki also famously said, "Each of you is perfect the way you are…

and you can use a little improvement." We are perfect because we are already Buddha, though we better not think that "my" Buddha nature is some personal possession or merit badge. Meanwhile, we can all use a little improvement because we are also limited karmic beings with plenty of habit energy to work through. In the dynamic relationship of yin and yang, both statements are true.

It is also often said in Zen, "Do your best, but don't attach to the outcome." That is, we need to act in this burning world with all the compassion and wisdom we can muster. We make the impossible vow of saving (or serving) all sentient beings, as the expression of this intention! And yet, if we try to measure ourselves by how successful our efforts have been, we are right back in the mind of achievement:

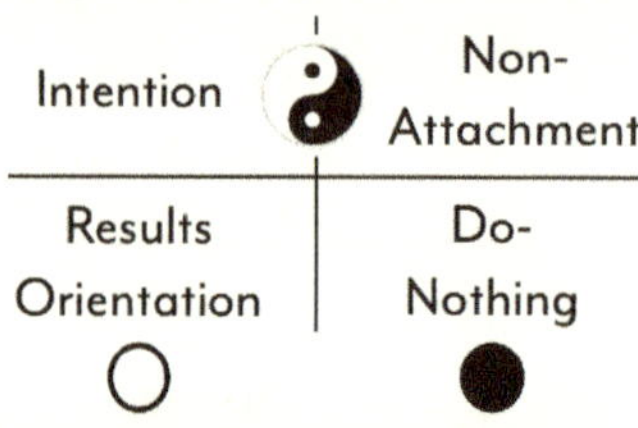


We respond to the situation in front of us as best we can. The rest is not up to us.

## THE BELIEF THAT "I HAVE ACHIEVED"

So what is so poisonous about believing in the thoughts, I know what Zen is, or, I have attained enlightenment? Not only do they take *you* away from the path, but you can also end up misleading others as well.

The Surangama Sutra warns us about the delusion of thinking oneself to be a sage. The first ten "demonic states" it describes affect those who are experiencing "mental darkness." So those are warnings for relative newcomers to the practice, who have not yet had their Dharma eye opened. But there are forty more demonic states to go! At the twentieth, the sutra starts describing the affected individual as "the good person."

This is someone who has been on the path awhile and experienced some illumination.

The warnings about the dangers of overestimating one's spiritual accomplishments just get stronger. For example:

> They may then have a vision of their own superiority, for which they feel an overwhelming gratitude. Immediately a boundless courage and intensity may arise within them so that they come to believe that their resolve is equal to the resolve of all Buddhas. If they understand this state, they will not suppose that they have become a sage, and they will not become confused. Eventually the state will disappear of its own accord. But if they think that they have become a sage, a demonic insanity will enter into the depths of their mind.

Again, note that it is not that feelings of superiority *arise* that is the problem, but the mind of "I have arrived" that believes them.

The tragedy is that if we are suffering from this delusion of being a sage, we are usually so deep in it that we don't notice. We may admit to having human foibles now and then, sure. We may even speak or write eloquently about humility and the need for "beginner's mind." But, deep down, any belief that we have permanently "got it" and no longer have any work to do—even in just one tiny part of our lives!—will influence all our actions. We may be subtly but thoroughly convinced of our own goodness, and our own superiority.[36]

## TEACHERS AND STUDENTS CREATE EACH OTHER

Mariana Caplan's book, *Halfway Up the Mountain*, describes at great length the dangers that come along with "premature claims to Enlightenment." "The reality of the present condition of contemporary spirituality in the West," she writes, "is one of grave distortion, confusion, fraud, and a fundamental lack of education."[37] I'm afraid, given my own rather turbulent history in Zen, that I tend to agree with her (though I maintain hope that there are also exceptions). And I agree with her in attributing this mess to the too-common belief of teachers that they *have*, in fact, "arrived." (The fact that this might be a widely shared understanding of what "Dharma Transmission" means will be discussed in chapter 6.)

This can be especially dangerous to the students in the context of meeting individually with teachers, as offered by most Zen sanghas. The purpose of these meetings is to provide the student with spiritual guidance along the Way. Yet primarily because of teacher exploitation—or even just misunderstanding—of their own role and power—these meetings can present dangers.

## POWER, DUALISM, AND DANGER

If the teacher-student relationship is approached in a dualistic way, it's very easy for us to fall into thinking that teacher and student are distinct and separate entities. And when we think of interpersonal relations dualistically, we can only envision three kinds of relationships. The first is one of separation and hierarchy, leading to domination. The teacher is on top and the student is below. The teacher is thoroughly enlightened. The student is in the darkness of ignorance and delusion. The teacher has knowledge and power, and is assumed (at least by many students, and too often by themself) to have "arrived." The student submits to their instruction, and looks up at them with reverence and devotion:

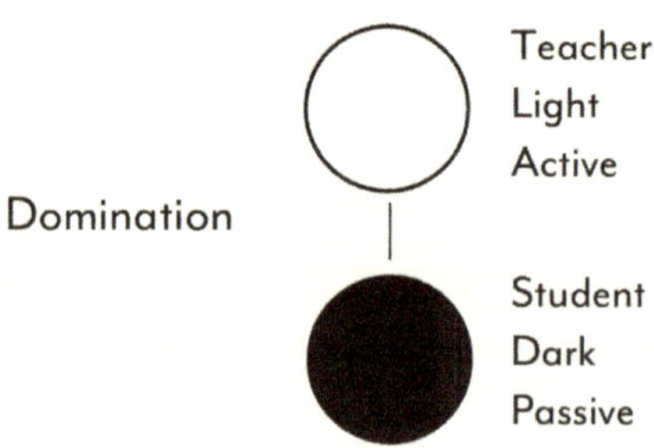

Unfortunately, there are plenty of examples in the literature, as well as traditions carried on in Zen communities, that seem to encourage what some call the "guru model" of teaching.[38] This perspective, however, denies both the human weaknesses of the teacher and the Buddha nature of the student. Rather than *inter*dependence, it prescribes abject *de*pendence of the student on the teacher.

Psychological research has also found that, under many conditions, the fact of having power actually changes how one's brain works in rather anti-social ways. People who get used to having power often tend to become overconfident in the rightness of their views, reckless in their actions, and demonstrate little empathy for, or willingness to listen to, others.[39] This often hurts the people around them and also leads to failures in their organizations. Assuming that "power corrupts" everywhere and always, some have become very leery of *any* structure that allows for differences in power.

The second possible relationship is one of merger. The student who submits may ultimately aspire to merge with their teacher, to essentially lose themselves in their teacher. We might picture this as a single light circle into which the student's dark circle has been absorbed.

Isn't the end goal to banish all darkness and become a teacher oneself? Keizan Jokin, for example, speaking of the relationship between his Dharma ancestors Eihei Dogen and Koun Ejo, wrote "Master and disciple became one. The light of their minds' eyes merged, like water combined with water, or sky merges with sky, without the slightest discrepancy." While I believe Keizan was trying to make the point that Ejo *really* understood what Dogen was teaching, I dislike the language he used. It just reduced two to *one*. Yet there can't be *inter*dependence with just one. Other ancient commentaries on teachers and students often make statements such as Keizan's, but then follow them (in that "contradictory" Zen way!) with an equal assertion of difference and distinction.

Robert Augustus Masters, in his book, *Spiritual Bypassing*, discusses this type of relationship, this "fusion." He writes that fusion (or merger) is unhealthy because it "does not demonstrate true union or intimacy;

instead it demonstrates a kind of interpersonal homogenization.... [It] signals not that our separateness has been transcended but that it has been marginalized; our boundaries have been collapsed rather than expanded."[40]

It may seem that we have really become "no-self"—the student has disappeared! Simultaneously, it may seem that we have gained "sage"-hood. But in actuality we have just handed all our personal power over to another human being.

It might seem that the only way that students and teachers could meet each other with mutual respect would be to meet as equals, in some sort of we're-all-on-the-same-level democratic model. Neither, it is imagined, has more power than the other. This might be mentally pictured as two circles on a horizontal line.

It may seem that this might be a better model for teaching in our contemporary world. The domination and merger models, after all, date from the very rigid social systems of ancient India and China and medieval Japan. I've found this "equality model" tempting. But the reality is that the teacher *does* have more power—students have come to *them* for something, and not vice versa. Marilyn Peterson, in her book on such relationships, identifies false equality as just another trap. The teacher is charged with using their power for the good of the student, but this responsibility can be daunting.[41] It would be easier to either overuse their power (domination) or pretend to not have any (equality).

While set up as a worthy ideal in some realms (e.g., one-person-one-vote), perfectly equal relations are of a mostly mythical nature. Few interpersonal relationships are exactly equal in power given variation not only in experience and knowledge but also money, status, intelligence, articulateness, maturity, and self-confidence. Even seemingly irrelevant things like attractiveness, height, and qualities of one's voice go into determining one's power in social situations.

The egalitarian ideal is also distinctly and irreversibly *two*. There is no interdependence. There is no vulnerability, and because of that, also no intimacy. The peer image neglects to take into account the way that, in a close relationship, the teacher and student will influence and in fact co-create each other. If neither side is open to influence, the relationship exists at arm's length, at best. Masters writes about the problems of "dissociation" or being "overboundaried," where we utterly refuse to be receptive and instead keep the walls around us very high. This may "masquerade[e]...as spiritual detachment and equanimity," when in fact it represents the rejection of intimacy and emotional flat-lining.[42] The desire to be independent at all costs sets up an unhealthy separation. It seems safe because it refuses vulnerability, but that sense of safety comes at a great cost.

### A SAFE AND UNEQUAL RELATIONSHIP

I first thought deeply about the issue of power *and* caring in the context of women's traditional caring roles as mothers and in work such as nursing, early education, and childcare. In these roles, the person providing care has some degree of power over the person being cared for. They have greater knowledge and skills and are usually in a position to deal out rewards and penalties. None of the models we've looked at so far would be healthy for such a relationship. We would consider a caregiver who followed one of them in regard to children to be domineering (domination), smothering (merger), or neglectful of their all-too-real responsibilities (equality: "Go ahead and run into the street if you want—I'm just your buddy").

Is it possible to have relationships that are hierarchical in terms of some type of power, *and* yet caring and mutually respectful? The evidence from women's traditional caring labor suggests so.

Recent psychological research also backs this up. It seems that it is only a subset of people with power who experience anti-social brain changes. It is leaders who see their power as an *opportunity to accomplish things*, and perhaps especially things that benefit themselves, who tend to become overconfident and lacking in empathy. They may disregard the feelings and views of subordinates simply because their exclusive focus is on getting the job done. Or they may see their power in personalized terms, as an opportunity to exploit others for money or sex, or to build up their ego. But people who see their power mainly in terms of *responsibility* exhibit more *pro*-social behaviors. They tend to do better by their subordinates and organizations. They listen to other's ideas and opinions, act with less recklessness and impunity, and seem to remember that while the task is important, so are the people.[43]

This can only really be understood, I believe, if we can get over our habit of thinking dualistically. We need thinking that includes dynamism and interdependence. Let's get back to the yin/yang diagram, taking the light, active parts as representing Zen teaching, and the dark, receptive parts as representing being guided. What can this tell us?

The yin dot within the yang suggests that the Zen teacher, even though they are primarily yang and active in this situation, still also has an element of being a student. They need to be able to be receptive, to listen, to admit when they don't know, and to learn new things. Fourteenth-century Korean Zen teacher T'aego exhorts us to "Be like our original teacher, Shakyamuni, keeping on progressing, energetically."[44] Not even the Buddha could stop practicing! I earlier shared an old Chinese story in which an arrogant scholar was dissed by a Zen teacher by being likened to a completely full teacup—no room there for anything to be added. Not even a Roshi can rest on their laurels and stop learning. No one is fully enlightened.

A teacher needs humility. Why is that often in such short supply? Our culture values light over dark, yang over yin, knowing over not-knowing. Knowing and light are "good." To not-know or acknowledge our own darkness is "bad." To not know threatens us with being on the downside of the hierarchy of domination. To admit to a lack, a darkness, is to realize that one's quest to be good and pure has failed. It can feel shameful. Limited karmic selves don't like that, and they rise up to buttress and defend "me" when challenged or criticized.

The best Zen teachers, I believe, have made friends with their own darkness, their own failings, their own shadow. Being human, a teacher may find that their limited karmic self still initially rises up in outrage when someone questions or challenges them. But emotional and spiritual maturity, one would hope, would allow them to investigate the possibility that their behavior could use a little improvement. Admitting being in the dark, after all, is not shameful…when you understand yin and yang.

The student, while primarily yin and receptive, also has an element of yang and activity, as represented by the light dot within the dark area. They do not lose their self-authority. In the yin-yang understanding, they have—and would do well to develop and exercise—their individual judgment and power of discernment. As Reb Anderson says about Zen practice, while "We can't do it by ourselves," at the same time "nobody else can do it for us."[45]

In the yin/yang understanding, a student learns from the teacher, and sometimes has to trust that the teacher understands something that they do not. But they do not blindly follow the teacher. They receive, but don't simply knuckle under to being on the downside of a relationship of separation and hierarchy. They listen, but don't try to lose themselves in mystery and "crazy wisdom." The wise student doesn't try to get the teacher to tell them what to do with their life. They recognize that teachers are still fallible humans. The black tadpole swimming in the tiny fishbowl has both receptivity and an open eye.

Wise students should even expect to experience some amount of disappointment in relation to a typical teacher's guidance and behavior: Because no teacher has totally arrived, a student with integrity will be somewhat selective about what they choose to take from the teacher and what they choose to leave. Thinking that you have to either *totally* accept or *totally* reject your teacher's messages and behavior is just another case of falling into dualism. Even the worst teachers sometimes say useful things. Even the best teachers will not live up to your ideals. Perhaps your teacher smokes or reads trashy romance novels. Is that really so awful?

There is one important caveat to this, though. If a teaching feels *really* "off," or the teacher's actions seem unethical, or you get cultish vibes, then more than just selectivity is required. Overlooking truly harmful, abusive actions in order to stay with (and support) a teacher is just another form of spiritual bypassing. Staying true to oneself in such cases may require challenging the teacher. Or calling out the misconduct. Or heading for the exit. Perhaps you will still find guidance in their podcasts or books, but you can borrow their books from the library and keep your distance from the person.

Teachers who feel they have arrived will encourage students to trust them completely. They may convince their students that they offer the *only* path to awakening. Students who attribute "arrival" to their teachers may fall into such blind acceptance even without encouragement.

That's not the place to put your trust. As Zen teacher Taizan Maezumi put it, "In order to discover your own direction, it is important to have great faith in yourself. Know that buddha nature and all kinds of virtues and wisdom are you yourself. See yourself as nothing but the very nature of being."[46] Then, he notes, what is left is to mature in the practice and live from this compassionate nature.

Recall that the yin-yang diagram is dynamic, swirling. The tadpoles swim in circles; nothing stays in place. Today I may take the role of the teacher in relation to someone, but when I'm with my own teacher, I'm her student. And things change when the situation moves. When I take my car in for service, I'm the ignorant one and the technician has the power. Sometimes we lead, sometimes we follow. That's the dance of our life.

The backwards-S-shaped "line" between the black and white tadpoles creates a boundary between the two shapes. Black, while it contains the white "eye" and continues "swimming," does not at any time seep into the white, nor vice versa. The roles remain clear. There is no pretense of sameness; there are no shades of gray.

It turns out that maintaining this clear boundary is vitally important for using power with respect and care. I knew, in my career as a university professor, that it was important to not get too chummy with particular students or ask students for favors.[47] But I understood this mostly as a way to avoid accusations of favoritism or of letting students "buy" a higher grade. I also taught a course that included the topic of sexual harassment and recognized the damage done by unwanted sexual attention. Yet I didn't feel powerful when I assigned grades. To me it was just a chore. Only after Betrayal #2 in my sangha (to be described in a later chapter) did I become fully aware of a teacher's moral obligation to turn towards issues of power and keep up a clear boundary for the good of the student.

## TEACHERS AND STUDENTS IN PRACTICE

A conceptual understanding of a dynamic, safe-but-unequal teacher-student relationship is a start. But what might this look like in practice?

### ARE TEACHERS NECESSARY?

Working with a teacher is absolutely necessary for waking up, say some ancient Zen texts and contemporary teachers. Some even assert that you need to commit to *one* particular teacher and then stay loyal to them come hell or high water. Or they highly praise those students who do.

I believe that these are misunderstandings. Perhaps a person might think this way simply because they personally came to awakening through the guidance of a teacher and can't imagine it otherwise. It seems to me, though, that such beliefs can also arise from, and contribute to, domination or merger misunderstandings.

Let's take the issue of loyalty to a teacher, first. Loyalty *to a person* is not a virtue. Blind loyalty to a person causes us to overlook their mistakes and perhaps even their falsehoods and their crimes. This is as true in Zen communities as it is in politics.[48] When you think about it, the saying that "Good friends will help you bury a body" is actually rather gross. Loyalty to our own fundamental values should take precedence.

What about the necessity of a teacher? *The Platform Sutra* contains the teaching of Huineng, the seventh-century Chinese Sixth Ancestor of Zen. Huineng was very clear on this point: "If you can't realize [your original nature] by yourselves, you need to find a good friend to show you how to see your nature. But if you realize this by yourselves, you don't need to look for a good friend somewhere else. And if someone insists that you have to find a good friend somewhere else before you attain liberation, that place doesn't exist. You will attain liberation when you meet the good friend inside your own mind."

In case that isn't clear enough, consider this version of The Three Refuges: I take refuge in the pure dharma-body buddha in my own material body. I take refuge in the myriad-fold transformation-body buddha in my own material body. I take refuge in the future and perfect realization-body buddha in my own material body.[49] Fundamentally, we awaken in and by ourselves, or we don't awaken at all. The crucial Three Treasures are in each of us, without exception, not "out there" somewhere.

Even more ancient than Huineng's teachings is the image of the *pratyekabuddha*, a person who is enlightened without recourse to teachers or other guides. And, of course, there are the examples of people who come to enlightenment and practice alone, as hermits.

What, then, is the importance of the external, historical Buddha (Shakyamuni), the Dharma (as a set of teachings) and the sangha (as people in a community)? And, although they are not even mentioned, what is the importance of Zen teachers? They all can be *very* helpful. They can help us to wake up and to live out the lessons of our awakening and the precepts in the world. They are, furthermore, the way that teachings enter the world and become transmitted from generation to generation. Living our Zen vows in the raging world is more challenging than doing so in a hermitage. And isolated hermits don't help others along.

I would never deny the great value of the ancestors, sutras, and communities! But is it strictly necessary to work with a teacher? No. Teachers and sanghas are helpful to us as carriers of the teachings and as "good friends." And each of us in a sangha has, in turn, a role to play in supporting others. But if—not having faith in our own Buddha nature—we head down the road of loyalty to a particular person or group instead, we are off the path.

So if you *do* work with a teacher, and want to do it in a healthy way, what might that look like? I'll give two examples. In the first I contrast what koan practice might look like under a domination model versus under a yin-yang model. In the second I give my best understanding, at the moment, of how individual meetings with a teacher (*dokusan*) should be regarded.

### EXAMPLE 1: KOAN PRACTICE

The following is a chart that I put together for myself, contrasting how I used to understand koan practice with a teacher, and how I conceive of it now.

| **Hierarchical-Separate** | **Yin-Yang** |
|---|---|
| The teacher (sage) gives the student (disciple) a koan. | The tradition/curriculum, via the teacher, gives the student a koan. |
| The student works on the koan. | The student sits/lives with the koan. The koan works on the student, enters the student. The student's process is one of breaking open in that particular direction, so that the koan may enter. |
| The student presents the koan, hoping to match the way others have presented it in the past. | The student presents the koan as it resonates with them. |
| The teacher, armed with spiritual authority (and possibly notes listing the correct presentations), judges when the student's work is complete. | The teacher is someone who has personally experienced awakening, possibly including through the entry of koans, and who is able (at least most of the time) to meet people face-to-face without a personal agenda. The teacher may be assisted (but not directed) by notes on how the koan has manifested in other students in the past. |

| | |
|---|---|
| If the student's presentation is not correct, the teacher tells them to keep working with the same koan. | The teacher may feel that distance, artificiality, intellectualizing, resistance, timidity, strategic action, or other manifestations of "selfing" are behind the student's presentation of the koan. The teacher may give the student a nudge or suggest that the student sit/live with this koan a while longer. |
| Failure on a koan is bad. | Failing, as well as looking foolish, are not flaws in koan practice. They are features. Deep koan work requires loosening up our habit energies around ideas of success. |
| If the student's presentation is correct, the teacher passes them on the koan. | The koan, once it enters the student, manifests as/through the student. The teacher who is sufficiently in touch with both the student and the koan recognizes a genuine presentation and affirms it. |
| The teacher is always right. | The teacher who (because they are also a limited karmic being) is not, at that moment, sufficiently in touch with both the student and koan may (a) humbly say, "I'm not seeing into this right now." or (b) make a mistake, affirming a presentation that is not genuine, or failing to recognize one that is. |

| | |
|---|---|
| Going on to the next koan is a sign of progress. | Each single koan could be a lifetime practice—the particular opening presented is only a start. But our curriculum gives us many. This helps both teacher and student keep from settling down. Additional koans also often require the student to awaken in a somewhat different way, so that flexibility is developed. Many koans are repeated in the curriculum because (1) we forget—the "passing" of a koan is a thing of that moment, not an accomplishment for all time (2) the koan may enter a new way in another round. If the teacher has affirmed a not-really-genuine presentation, there will be more opportunities to explore that entry point. Having many meetings over time, and humility on the teacher's side, will both help with the not-affirming-a-genuine-response teacher mistake. |
| Students trust the teacher. | Teachers and students trust the process. The student trusts that they, themself, are Buddha nature. |

| Cake metaphor: the student is the oven, the koan is the cake. The teacher is the judge of when the cake is done. | Cake metaphor: the koan is the oven (the source of energy), the student is the cake (what the Dharma energy enters into), and the teacher attempts to be the toothpick, picking up on any crumbs (of "selfing") that still stick. |
|---|---|

#### EXAMPLE 2: INDIVIDUAL MEETINGS

The following is the text of a handout I created, intended for new students.

> Welcome to dokusan, a private meeting with a teacher.
>
> Teachers take on the solemn responsibility of always acting in the *student's* interest. Zen teachers are here to help you wake up—to awaken in, with, and for the world.
>
> Dokusan meetings are usually short—5 to 10 minutes at most—and meant to be focused on your practice. This could mean your formal practice on the cushion or your daily practice as you deal with the messiness of your life. Teachers will hold what you tell them in confidence (except for the special cases described in our sangha's Ethics Policy).
>
> Teachers are not some special species of "enlightened being" who, if you please them with the quality of your practice, will give you something that you seek. Neither is a Zen teacher your parent, therapist, partner, lover, or best friend. (Because of the problems caused by such dual roles, our Ethics Policy forbids them.) Zen teachers are simply human beings who have probably been on the path longer than you, and who try to help

you avoid traps and point you in helpful directions. They are not experts on everything, and they do not give you anything. You already are Buddha nature.

Unfortunately, the long history of Zen sanghas indicates that practitioners can sometimes become confused about the teacher-student relationship. A teacher may become arrogant or start using a student to meet their own financial, emotional, or sexual needs. Warning signs of these include a teacher becoming rigidly intolerant of dissent or requesting that a student keep their secrets or meet with them more privately. (*Students* are allowed to share anything that happens in dokusan, except for koan demonstrations.) Any such behavior should be immediately discussed with others, including sangha leaders.

For their part, a student may idealize the teacher, consciously or unconsciously giving over power that they should keep for themselves or demanding from teachers inappropriate sorts of attention or guidance. The teacher might point this out if it happens, or the student may find a "reality check" with a therapist, good friend, or senior student helpful.

So let's meet. Don't worry if you don't have a specific question or something earthshaking or clever to share. Even just bowing to each other is a true meeting.

As far as Buddha Nature is concerned, there is no difference
between sinner and sage...
One enlightened thought and one is a Buddha,
one foolish thought and one is an ordinary person.
—Huineng

## BEGINNING AGAIN...AND AGAIN

But Zen is not all confusing titles and customs and doom stories. Our literature also includes inspiring stories of those who were able to shed their belief in achievements. Here's one about a know-it-all ancient scholar:

> Deshan was a scholar of the Diamond Sutra and traveled to southern China to stamp out what he considered to be heresies there. Nearing his destination, he sought to buy refreshments from an old woman.
>
> She asked what he was carrying, and he replied, "Notes and Commentaries on the Diamond Sutra."
>
> The old woman said, "I hear the Diamond Sutra says, 'Past mind cannot be grasped, present mind cannot be grasped, future mind cannot be grasped.' Which mind do you want to refresh?"
>
> Deshan was dumbfounded and unable to answer.
>
> Deshan went on to study with a Zen teacher. He burned all his notes and commentaries, saying, "Even though I have exhausted the abstruse doctrines, it is like placing a hair in vast space."[50]

Deshan was able to accept defeat at the hands of a woman—which would have been especially surprising in that patriarchal culture. He was able to give it all up and start over. (There's also a really sweet story about when Deshan is an old man and very senior teacher, and humbly accepts correction from the temple cook.[51]) It's a great loss, though, that wise women Zen teachers never get recognition as such, or even names, in these old stories.[52]

Even more to the point is a story about Zhaozhou, an esteemed teacher in his old age. Here it is, as recounted by Dogen: "When Zhaozhou...aroused the aspiration for enlightenment and was about to begin a journey, he said to himself, 'I will ask about dharma of anyone who surpasses me, even a seven-year-old'.... When asking a seven-year-old about dharma, an old man like Zhaozhou bows. It is an extraordinary aspiration, the mind art of an old buddha."[53]

Dogen goes on to suggest that the seven-year-old could also be a girl—who he calls "a dragon princess." May we all stay this willing to learn!

## FINAL THOUGHTS

Contemporary Zen teacher Shohaku Okumura reminds us,

> When we understand that our goal is eternal, infinite, and absolute, no matter how hard we practice, no matter how deep our understanding, compared to the infinite, we are zero. We cannot afford to be arrogant.... No matter how small or great our accomplishments, they are all the same compared to the infinite.... We should be down to earth. This is our practice.[54]

# PART TWO

## WHY ZEN FORMS AND INSTITUTIONS MATTER

# 5

# TEACHERS ARE POWERFUL

UNLIKE OTHER spiritual practices that emphasize beliefs, doctrines, or scriptures, a long tradition in Zen emphasizes working individually with a teacher. In most Zen sanghas students are encouraged to meet alone with a teacher for spiritual guidance. When Buddhism arrived in China from South Asia it had to adapt to the Chinese cultural emphasis on family loyalty. It did this by creating the concept of a Zen "family tree" or lineage. From its East Asian beginnings, Zen has emphasized "mind to mind" transmission from teacher to student.

## WHAT A GOOD TEACHER CAN DO

We will leave the question of what, in particular, can only be "transmitted" by teachers for chapter 6. Meanwhile, as a practical matter, the idea that only some people have received "transmission" distinguishes teachers from students and empowers them. Teachers are generally seen as spiritual authorities; students are seen as learners.

This is quite a delicate situation, since Zen also teaches that students are also *already and always* Buddha nature, and that no one can realize this except *for themselves*! How can these two sides of the tradition be made compatible?

Endowing someone with a position of power and authority cuts two ways. One way is helpful: The powerful person uses their power for the benefit of the less powerful. In Zen, a good teacher will recognize the power, understand how it affects their relationship with students, and use it very carefully and with humility. They will understand that they are not the *source* of the Dharma for their students, but simply spiritual friends (*kalyana mitra*) who may be able to help guide others along the Way.

Having (probably) been on the path longer than their students, they can give talks that draw on their own experiences. These can add immediacy and relevance to the sense of Zen a student may get from readings. They've also experienced some of the traps and quicksand for themselves. Their own struggles to avoid or escape common pitfalls will help them guide others through such encounters. A skilled teacher will "catch us out" when we get waylaid by our delusions and our stale beliefs. I have certainly been "caught out" many times! While no one can *make* us wake up from our self-centered dream, good teachers can help us move in that direction. At the very least, it's good to have some largely trustworthy people around who will point out to us when we are dreaming.

## TEACHER-CAUSED HARM

Or the person with authority can cause harm. I can say with full confidence that all Zen teachers, no matter how advanced, are never perfectly enlightened beings. We are still human and fallible, and still working out our many karmic and psychological stuck spots. As such we may still harm, or at least confuse, our students. I've coined the term "psychopompogenic harm" to mean "harm caused by someone who offers spiritual guidance."[55]

Sometimes when teachers harm it is thoroughly unintentional and probably unavoidable. Even the best teachers are human and will make occasional mistakes. Hopefully, the harms we cause will be relatively small, and the teacher will engage in atonement and repair. Stay around long enough and you will also hear about teachers who developed dementia in their old age or suffered from mental illnesses of some sort. Even if sustained meditation practice was not contraindicated for a person when they started into Zen, it may become so later on, and teachers are not immune. (Did I hear somewhere that "things change"?) Long-time practitioners may need to take a sabbatical from Zen teaching, or even from sitting meditation itself. They may even need to leave teaching or practice permanently. Situations of teacher incapacity may cause a great deal of confusion and harm. When such situations arise, much discernment and compassion is needed from the sangha.

Our societies are also rife with racist, sexist, homophobic, transphobic, neuro-normative, ableist, ageist (and so on) beliefs and conduct. Even if subtly expressed, unconscious assertions of privilege (or of unhealed wounding and self-hatred) may result in teachers making some students (or peers) feel unwelcome or unseen. We all are works-in-progress when it comes to overcoming cultural biases. Even well-intentioned Zen teachers and sanghas will cause harm because these biases take concerted effort and time—and to get to *all* of them, a full lifetime or more—to unlearn. That doesn't mean we shouldn't try.[56] But it does mean that change may be slower than we like.

What about the case where a student *has* felt welcomed, heard, and understood? Feelings of gratitude, trust, and belonging naturally arise. These feelings may help a student grow in the Dharma. Or, too often, they may be exploited and the student left betrayed.

## SCANDALS AND SECRETS

The longer I practice, the more fellow practitioners I find who are on their second, third, or fourth spiritual community—or have given up entirely. They encountered teachers who acted like bullies. Or know-it-alls. Or who spread around things told to them in confidence. Or demanded complete, unquestioning loyalty. Who misspent funds, lied to authorities and to the sangha, or, yes, violated sexual boundaries. Or they simply did little things that made a student feel "icky" one too many times. Spiritual leaders abusing their power is something of an epidemic in Zen, in other Buddhist sanghas, and in groups offering spiritual practices in general.

Eido Shimano, Joshu Sasaki, and Taizan Maezumi were some of the first Zen teachers to come to the United States from Japan in the 1960s. In 1983, Taizan Maezumi's sexual misconduct came to light.[57] In 2010, the Zen Studies Society in New York, led by Eido Shimano, was roiled by evidence of his decades of serial sexual misconduct.[58] News about Joshu Sasaki's long-running habit of sexual abuse broke into wide public view in 2012.[59] Cultural differences between Japan and the U.S. as well as the "free love" subculture of the 1960s are often said to have contributed to these patterns. The way spiritual authority was conceived of and handled in these groups, however, seems to me to have likely played the major role.

And the problem has not been limited to the past or to teachers from Japan. Robert Aitken, another esteemed early Zen teacher, joined in signing an open letter concerning his own Dharma heir, John Tarrant, who now leads the Pacific Zen Institute. The letter urged Tarrant to address the pain of the many students of his who had reported experiencing "serious, persistent abuses of power and boundary violations."[60] Apparently the rift between Aitken and Tarrant was long-standing.[61] Two teachers who studied with a student of Tarrant's have recently been disciplined by the Soto Zen Buddhist Association (SZBA) for ethical violations. One was the person who created harm in my own sangha, primarily by engaging in sexual misconduct.[62] The other, (Michael) Dosho Port, attempted financial abuse. The board of the Nebraska Zen Center, which he filled with people loyal to him, attempted to sell the Omaha temple to buy him and his wife a home—in northern Minnesota.[63]

It's also not just a problem in that line of teachers. In 1970, Richard Baker wrote the introduction to Sunryu Suzuki's *Zen Mind, Beginner's Mind.* In the early 1980s, mounting evidence of Baker's sexual and financial misconduct forced his resignation as Abbot of the San Francisco Zen Center.[64] "Big Mind" leader Dennis Genpo Merzel and his lineage group, The White Plum Asanga (WPA), parted ways in 2011 over concern about Genpo's many abuses of authority.[65] In 2019, Ezra Bayda, another WPA teacher, was fired by the Zen Center of San Diego because of "multiple instances of sexual misconduct."[66] In 2024, the WPA parted ways with teacher Michael Shikan Brunner of One River Zen due to his "unprofessional conduct…involving violations of sexual boundaries."[67]

Nor are the offenders exclusively men, or exclusively in the Japanese Buddhist tradition. Even though the vast majority of sexual abusers are men, some women do bully or cross other financial or emotional boundaries. And Seung Sahn, leader of the Korean-tradition Kwan Um Zen (Seon) school, had sexual relationships with more than one female student.[68]

These issues are not just a problem for Zen Buddhism, or just in the U.S. In 1999, Mariana Caplan included quotes from (among others) Reginald Ray, founder of a Tibetan Buddhist group, in her book on humility in spiritual practice.[69] In 2020, thirteen former senior students and employees of Ray's Dharma Ocean sangha wrote an open letter describing his "longstanding patterns of emotional and spiritual abuse."[70] Abuses by Chogyam Trungpa and others at Shambhala International have been extensively documented.[71] Theravada leaders in Thailand recently came under fire for theft and sexual misconduct.[72] Communities in the Insight Meditation (Vipassana) tradition have not escaped scandal.[73] Other groups that engage in South Asian-inspired spiritual practices, including Sivananda Yoga Vedanta, have had notable problems with abuses as well.[74]

So far I've only mentioned the fairly public scandals. My impression, however, is that Zen *secrets* are even more numerous. I've found that those "in the know" (mostly teachers and a few longtime students) can list many others who are known to have overstepped boundaries. But those cases have never been publicly documented. They remain unknown to those not on the grapevine.[75] And even adding those cases would not make a complete accounting. Many victims remain silent out of (the often very realistic) fear of not being believed and/or suffering retribution.

In the last few years, I have talked with several people who were so personally devastated by abuse that they left Zen practice altogether. Yet their stories tend to involve teachers overstepping emotional, financial, or sexual boundaries in ways that were relatively subtle. The teachers, hidden behind their star reputations or puppet boards, easily deflect criticism: The big lie is passed off as a white lie; the inappropriate touch is said to be mere friendliness; the ridiculous expense is portrayed as somehow necessary; marriage to the student is said to preclude the possibility that she was controlled and abused. It's hard for truth to get believed over counter-claims by authorities, especially if the authorities are skilled manipulators. These cases may never go public and be associated with a teacher's name. If you're not angry after reading this, you're not paying attention.

Teacher abuse of power is not just a "bad apple" problem, caused only by a few "bad" teachers. Those who make headlines for egregious and serial abuses may be predators who have relatively rare emotional deficits (and no desire to overcome them), but if so they are still just the tip of the iceberg. *Any* teacher can end up abusing power—including me. All of the teachers I will mention later in this chapter have some quite wonderful qualities. Some students continue to fruitfully learn from them. Thinking that teachers can be sorted neatly into those who are "bad" and those who are above criticism is just another type of rigid this-versus-that thinking.

## SPIRITUAL POWER AND RELATIONSHIP

The key factors in the relationship between a Zen teacher and a student are power and trust. In many realms, we relate to each other as adult peers, with equal personal responsibilities. However, in others, one adult has something the other needs. This makes the relationship asymmetric. The one who has some specialized knowledge has some degree of power over the person seeking that knowledge. If I am in a relationship with someone and I don't know as much as they do, I am to some degree at their mercy. I trust a lawyer with my legal affairs, ask a psychotherapist to hold my secrets, or put my medical care in the hands of a healthcare professional.

Legal, counseling, and medical professional groups have well-known ethical codes mandating that the service provider must always act for the well-being *of their client.* While people often think the word "fiduciary" just has to do with money, it actually refers to a person with a legal or ethical obligation to act in the interests of others.

So why does a person seek a spiritual teacher? Buddhism promises relief from suffering, and we generally work with a teacher because we hope that they will help us get that. Because the teacher has received Dharma transmission, we tend to take this as a sign that they "have" something (i.e., enlightenment, Buddha nature, *satori*) that they might share with us if we follow their guidance. Students can and do project all sorts of imagined abilities onto more experienced practitioners. We want to believe that *someone* has gotten their life under control and that they can show us how to do this, too.

So spiritual teachers are on the "up" side of the power differential in this regard. *This is true whether or not a teacher wants power, or whether or not they even acknowledge that they have it.* It is inherent in the spiritual teacher role. A Zen teacher, to stay on track, must take on the responsibility of using such power wisely as a sacred covenant. Just as with therapists (or lawyers, medical professionals, or clergy), *the spiritual teacher, and the teacher alone, is responsible for maintaining the integrity of the relationship.*

Because we want freedom from suffering so badly, as students we will engage in rituals we don't understand. We will listen to talks that don't make sense to us. We may meet with teachers privately and share with them our spiritual struggles. We may open our hearts to them and confide in them things that we wouldn't tell anyone else. Koan work requires that we risk going out on a limb, over and over again. Note the disturbing similarities between a trusting student and a potential member of a cult.

### TRANSFERENCE

As previously mentioned, psychological transference occurs when someone redirects the feelings they have about one person onto someone else. This is another source of relational teacher power.

Transference is not, on its own, necessarily unhealthy. Many people think that it is in fact a necessary part of a process of psychological or spiritual growth. Reacting to a therapist as if they were your mother or father, for example, may unearth those old, stale feelings you carry about your parents or other caregivers. Then those feelings become workable.

Similarly, believing that your teacher embodies Buddha nature, and thus feeling great respect and devotion towards them, might be helpful in the first stages of practice. Exploring Buddha nature as something external to oneself, but also nearby, may help one eventually realize that Buddha nature is also *you*, just as you are. As Zen teacher Robert Aitken wrote, "The teacher of religious practice occupies an archetypal place in the psyches of the students."[76] We may project onto them a whole lot of characteristics that we really want to develop in ourselves. We may need to feel love going outward before we can turn it inward.

Transference may arise in various forms along the path. One common one is when the student comes to believe that they are romantically in love with their teacher. The gratitude and love we feel when finding the Dharma may get transferred onto our teacher as sexual attraction. We may look up to them so much that we idealize them. We tend to overlook their flaws. We may be oblivious to the fact that we wouldn't even consider someone like them as a romantic partner under 'normal' conditions (in which variables like personality, physical characteristics, age, or partnership status are typically of primary importance). I've even heard a teacher in her seventies say that students decades younger professed that they're in love with her!

Or we may be tempted to confuse the teacher, who holds a position with some authority in the sangha, with other authority figures in our lives. We may redirect feelings towards them that were originally directed towards our Daddy, Mommy, or boss. We may find ourselves feeling hostile or rebellious. This can be painful for both student and teacher. While the Zen teacher may be able to work with this, it might also need to be discussed with a good therapist.

There is another type of situation that is along these same lines, but with opposite emotional resonance: We may find ourselves believing that the teacher is, at long last, the perfectly caring parental figure that we missed in real life! We may want to let them make big life decisions for us. That gives the teacher far too much power. Becoming overly dependent on our teacher, we may demand that they be "there for us" at all times. That overtaxes the teacher and may tend to weaken the student's emotional investment in their own friends and family.

An inverted relationship is also possible: We might be tempted to become the "caring parent" *for* the teacher. Knowing that the teacher has some real-world problems (e.g., health, financial, or marital) may bring out our care-taking tendencies. We find we want to protect them, heal them, give them comfort, and make them feel safe. We transfer to them emotions that would be more appropriately directed to a child or lost puppy. We make taking care of them our mission in life, what gives our life meaning.

Such fantasies of sexual or familial love are usually not recognized as such by the student. They operate at a level far deeper than reason or ordinary social life. They are more connected to unhealed wounds and unacknowledged needs than to common sense. Think of it: If I become convinced that I have finally found "the love of my life," or "my mission in life," am I likely to act in a perfectly rational way? Do I tread carefully, weighing pros and cons? It's not for nothing that falling in love is compared to temporary insanity!

### RESPONSIBILITIES THAT COME WITH TEACHING

A well-trained and well-grounded teacher will have learned about transference. They will recognize that it is their job to deal with it, not yours if you are a student, since you are the one who is in a position of vulnerability. They will humbly understand that the student's love and devotion are not directed towards them as an individual but directed toward them because of their role. Responsible teachers will never attempt to use transference to gain a personal advantage.

They will not flirt with you or make inappropriate comments. They will gently but very firmly reject any sexual advances by a student. They won't buy into a lover fantasy. When asked to give specific advice on a life choice, or regularly take your phone calls at 2 a.m., they will refuse. They won't buy into your long-lost-parent fantasy, either.

Trustworthy teachers will not request more time, money, etc. than the professional relationship requires. Going further, they will also refuse any voluntary offers of the same. If you offer to give them substantial personal gifts of money or to take care of them in any personal way, a responsible teacher will decline. Even your caretaking fantasies must be sidelined for the sake of an appropriate teacher-student relationship.

This maintenance of the "boundaries" of the relationship protects both you and them. It is a sign that the teacher is emotionally mature and able to attend to their own needs. It is a sign that that teacher has humbly acknowledged that they can't "be everything" to you. They may suggest you seek therapy if you are depressed or anxious. If you are looking to them to "fix" your loneliness, they may suggest that you enrich your own social network of family and friends. The well-grounded teacher expects to serve the sangha and its members, rather than to *be* served by them.

A Zen teacher's *only role* is to do what they can to help you wake up to your own Buddha nature—to realize *for yourself* the wonder and mystery of this universe of form and emptiness! —and to help you integrate that into your life. Teachers can only help you wake up, not *give* you awakening. I've heard it said that teachers "are selling water by the river."

## ABUSE OF SPIRITUAL POWER

The problem of abuse of power is not only widespread, but also very old. In the Surangama Sutra, after listing delusions that plague those in "mental darkness," at about number twenty of the "demonic states" starts to list those that befall the "good person" who has had some insight. At around the state number thirty, the emphasis changes from states that do damage to oneself to states that do damage to other people. "The good person" who has become convinced (by the demons) of their own superiority loses the ability to see what is going on with themselves. And then, thoroughly convinced of their own goodness and wisdom, and perhaps having gained some unusual powers, they start to gather other people around them and lead them astray. For example,

> The good person...may come to crave the experience of a sustained merging of minds... [People who hear them] all will rejoice in their belief that they have just experienced something entirely new and extraordinary...Their listeners will have such confidence in them that they will be fooled into thinking that they are a Bodhisattva.

The sutra goes on to say that these demon-afflicted teachers trouble, confuse, and profoundly disturb the minds of their followers. It suggests that greed for money (and sex) may be markers of these dangerous leaders. And it suggests that these leaders and their followers will come to bad ends. An eventual loss of the demonic powers and falling into "Unrelenting Hell" are predicted—as well as, on a more prosaic plane, a tendency to run afoul of the local law!

### ACTIONS THAT CAUSE HARM

If we have too simple an idea about how harm comes about we will fail to recognize many forms of teacher-caused harm. It's tempting to try to make a list of specific "thou shalt not" actions that would signal a teacher doing harm. Forcible rape or draining the sangha bank account to go gambling are obviously wrong and damaging (though even these have sometimes been tolerated!). But such a list would only scratch the surface. As psychotherapist Marilyn Peterson has put it, "When violations are defined on the basis of content, those that are seemingly less egregious and visible tend to be ignored, normalized, or dismissed as not serious.... [T]he more fundamental injury...[is] to the core of the... relationship itself."[77]

As should now be apparent, the trust they receive from students gives spiritual teachers a great deal of power. "Boundary violations"—deviations from the proper form and boundaries of the relationship between the one providing guidance and the one asking for it—can be devastating. In particular, it may be tempting to leave off the list of abuses anything to which an adult student apparently "consented." How could it be abuse if the student "consented" to sex? How could it be a misuse of funds if a student "voluntarily" donated the money? If the student "chose" to say yes to a request from their teacher, isn't the student responsible for what follows?

To look at it this way is to completely ignore the vast gulf in power and authority between the teacher and the student who comes to them for guidance. There can be no meaningful "consent" in such cases. In thirteen states in the U.S., for example, clergy having sexual relations with congregants is a violation of criminal law. More importantly, in *all* states professionals and the organizations that employ them have an obligation to provide their services safely and can face civil liability for breaches of trust and other harms.

One group that works with those harmed by clergy sexual abuse offers this insight: "In our work with survivors of clergy abuse we often ask the question, 'Would this have happened if he/she was your neighbor and not your pastor.' Overwhelmingly the answer is 'no'. The witness of survivors underscores the truth that the clergy role carries with it a power and authority that make meaningful consent impossible."[78]

The teaching (or clergy) role itself makes for a structural imbalance in power.

What about the case of single, mature adults with common interests and goals, who *would* have come together even if they were just neighbors? It just *happened* that they discover their mutual sexual attraction while in a teacher/student relationship? While powerful teachers too often try to excuse exploitative relationships with such a cover story, in rare cases the story could actually be true. Well-formulated ethical guidelines generally mandate that an immediate choice must be made: The two can relate as teacher/student *or* as lovers, but not both. If they decide to pursue the relationship, they are required to disclose the attraction to the sangha (or at least sangha leaders), cease relating as teacher/student, and accept a waiting period before starting a new relationship. To do otherwise fails to protect the student: Only with some perspective can the student truly discern whether their attraction is to this particular fallible human individual and not a transference of their love for the Dharma.

Proceeding with a dual relationship also disregards the spiritual well-being of the rest of the sangha. At the very least, the existence of an ongoing "special" relationship between a teacher and a student will cause confusion and raise questions about favoritism. More serious repercussions occur when—as is often the case—the relationship is kept under wraps. Lies, rumors, and subterfuge invade sangha life. Sangha members' trust in the teacher may be severely shaken. The fact that the student in a "secret affair" might not report feeling exploited—or may even say they found the experience beneficial and empowering—is irrelevant. In terms of its effects on the rest of the sangha, the deception itself is a form of abuse of power.

So, we must now ask: *why* might Zen teachers end up causing harm to their students? From what I've read, and what I've personally witnessed, I'd like to outline three modes of teacher misbehavior.

## DELIBERATE MANIPULATION

At one extreme are the teachers who engage in intentional, outright spiritual fraud. Because grateful, trusting disciples make such easy prey, positions of spiritual leadership can be attractive to people who have underlying anti-social tendencies. When they aren't able or inclined to control their selfish impulses, their behavior is called psychopathic or sociopathic.[79] Such a teacher has little or no capacity for empathy, and truly doesn't care about you. They care only about what they can get for themselves.

Such persons often come across as charming, charismatic, caring, and very easy to trust. Making someone feel heard and understood can, after all, be accomplished by using specific techniques of interpersonal communication. While these come naturally to some people, they can also be learned. Communication experts tell you to make eye contact, ask questions, tune into others' feelings, and show respect for what the other person says.[80] Gaining someone's trust doesn't mean that you are trustworthy. Again, there are techniques for gaining trust. Salespeople are encouraged to show warmth, talk slowly, and point to external credentials or play on affiliations, in addition to making people feel heard.[81] If it weren't so, we wouldn't see so many successful frauds, scams, and pyramid schemes in the world.

Such teachers may also come across as very "Zen," and very wise. Simply wearing the robes and holding the ceremonial objects that go along with being a teacher is enough for many people to look up to them as authority figures. If the teacher is intelligent and articulate, they can also learn how to write books and give talks that use (and to some extent, often use correctly and informatively) Zen ideas. This enhances their aura of beneficent power.

To deepen their power over you, they will probably encourage you to rely on them as much as possible. They will cultivate a belief—often more by subtle actions than by explicit teachings—that they, and they alone, hold the key to your enlightenment. They will encourage you to confuse *surrender to the Dharma* (which is essential to practice) with *submission to themselves.* They may also let you believe that they can "fix" your anxiety, depression, money problems, or whatever else is bothering you. They may (while maintaining a veneer of modesty) encourage you to think of them as existing in some special realm of spiritual accomplishment—perhaps as a Fully Enlightened Being—rather than as a human being with the usual limitations. They may convince you that they know *everything* better than you do, and that loyalty to them is loyalty to the Dharma. Even if a student's own gut or moral code is telling them that something is wrong, they may think, "Well, if *the teacher* says it's okay, then it must be, right?"

When the teacher holds this kind of authority, they have all sorts of tricks they can use to get what they want. Asserting authority even in realms where they have none. Lying. Gaslighting (i.e., trying to get the victim to think that they themselves, not the teacher, are acting crazy or irrationally). Emotional blackmail (e.g., "I'll be devastated if you leave"). Actual blackmail (e.g., threatening to disclose secrets shared in private meetings, or to tell the sangha lies about you). Praise. Giving the student special privileges.

Many who seek to "get" enlightenment may need very little deliberate "grooming" (that is, careful preparation to make sure that they will go along with the main abusive events). Unsure of ourselves and in doubt about what we should do with our lives, we may be happy to hand over our power to someone who seems to "know better." We may not notice that we are handing over our power. Or it may be that we actually *want* the teacher to take it.

It is because of these vulnerabilities of the student that the responsibility to keep the teacher-student relationship healthy lies *entirely* with the teacher. We wouldn't say that a child "asked for" a beating from their parent, or that their attractiveness "made" a sexual predator abuse them. Neither should we say that students "brought upon themselves" unhealthy relations with teachers—even if they made the first approach! A fraudulent teacher may want something fairly obvious, such as a fancy car or lots of sex. Or they may feel a need for power and control that goes far beyond what is good for them or the sangha. And, if they are not stopped, they will likely get it.

### SNEAKY OPPORTUNISM

But most abuses of the relationship seem to be far more subtle. The teacher may have real Zen insight, be normally empathetic, and have good intentions, but see an opportunity to fill some desperate or perhaps innocent-looking need or hole. They are unaware or forget that situations often look very different from the side with less power. *Any* time the teacher allows their own needs and desires into this protected space its safety and the exclusive focus on the needs of the student is destroyed.

For example, the teacher may be tempted to use the relationship to satisfy their *own* needs for love and care. After all, they are human beings, too. To be human is to be interdependent and to have needs for love, friendship, respect, emotional support, and physical satisfaction. Any teacher, given the right conditions, can face a strong temptation to let their own desires take precedence over a student's well-being. And, if their resolve to uphold the teacher-student covenant is not explicit, strong, and constantly reinforced, they may give in. This is especially true if they have not made a serious effort to build a family and social life outside of the sangha that (reasonably) fulfills their needs.

This may happen because a teacher meets a student's transference with their own "countertransference." They may willingly take on the role of lover and welcome the student's devotion and adoration. It's amazing how effective the old line "I feel a deep spiritual connection between us" (said with big, moony eyes) is, even now, when coming from a spiritual authority figure.

Yet this does not need to be deliberate or extreme to have harmful effects. Suppose you are a teacher and are having problems in your workplace or your marriage. Suppose you are feeling the sting of being accused of wrongdoing. Perhaps you have just failed at a project that was important to you. Or you're having health problems and are feeling your age. Or life is very stressful right now. A younger, attractive student is looking at you with love and admiration. Wow, that feels good! You aren't going to actually sleep with them or get involved in a romantic relationship. But what's the harm in flirting a little bit? Try to look at this situation from the side of the student: Will *they* be grateful that you "only" messed with their heart and soul?

Or a teacher may really enjoy feeling helpful and effective and welcome you treating them as a wise parent or therapist. Instead of short meetings focused on your spiritual practice, they may encourage you to pour out your heart to them no matter how long it takes. That crosses a boundary. Or they may reverse the proper roles and take on being the lost puppy, making *you* take care of *them*. They praise you for your compassionate nature...and then start confiding in you and asking for *your* emotional support.

They may use any combination of such inappropriate ways of relating. This is not good for the teacher-student relationship, and so is not good for you *or* them. It is the teacher's responsibility to be aware of this dynamic and firmly hold to appropriate relational boundaries. Or the teacher's need could be deep-seated and possibly largely unconscious. We all have shadow sides to our personalities—that is, desires and behaviors we may not even be conscious of, or feel are dirty, or 'unlike us,' and try to deny. We are all prone to spiritual bypassing. Does the teacher have the courage to face into their shadow? If not, do they at least have the courage to ask for appropriate help?

The teacher's need could seem quite trivial: In her book, *At Personal*

*Risk: Boundary Violations in Professional-Client Relationships,* Marilyn Peterson describes the case of a therapist who had organized a conference to be led by a leader in her field. Finding that she was unable to take this distinguished visitor to lunch, the therapist asked others at the conference, including one of her therapy clients (who had expertise in the same field), to do it. While innocently intended, this muddying of boundaries created considerable confusion for the client. The client felt special and validated at a deep level to be so asked when all the therapist had intended was to manage lunch![82] People in power tend to be blind to how their actions will be perceived by those with less power. Ambiguity in roles tends to create uncertainty, confusion, and a resulting feeling of a lack of safety. Even in such a relatively mild violation such as this one, repairing the relationship required serious effort. The therapist had to own up to her mistake. The client had to work through their anger and disillusionment (about the therapist being perfect).

Yes, there are people with recognized psychological disorders who commit abuse serially, deeply, and without remorse. They may make the headlines, especially if the abuse is sexual. But this doesn't excuse the damage we other Zen teachers may do by simply being inadequately aware of our power or our own clay feet. Simply by not being sufficiently aware of our own needs, we could end up *acting,* for all intents and purposes, *as if we were* a manipulative sociopath or psychopath. In terms of the effect on students, it doesn't really matter to what degree a teacher was a conscious manipulator versus a sneaky opportunist. The teacher caused harm.

### THE GOLD RAKUSU EFFECT

Then there is plain old garden-variety ignorance and pride. In my experience, there is a lot of this going around.

I now believe that the training I received in the first lineage in which I was given teaching responsibilities (including private meetings with students) left me sorely under-prepared. *Never* did any teacher tell me that I needed to make a sacred commitment to serving the well-being of the student. I learned *nothing* about teacher power or transference. From what I could tell, I was promoted because I was articulate, had participated in many retreats, and was well along in the koan curriculum. And it did very much feel like a *promotion*, not a taking on of responsibility. While never explicitly talked about, receiving teaching transmission was clearly considered by most within our sangha as something of a public certification of Enlightenment.

In the Dharma transmission ceremony one receives a golden brown (or brown) rakusu that replaces the student's black rakusu. As I practiced for decades with the same group, I saw a number of people I had sat with as humble students make this transition. I saw that many of these same people had seemingly, along with the gold rakusu, received an outsized pride in their own knowledge, accomplishment, and wisdom. Thereafter, when they and a student disagreed about something—often not even on a teaching topic, but perhaps just an issue of sangha finance or communications—they never wavered from their certainty that *they* were correct. They seemed to feel no need to ever learn from the expertise of students, do some reading-up on a topic, or engage with any challenge to their view. They expected students—and the sangha's board of directors—to follow their lead on everything.

Sometimes, this attitude was also carried over to other teachers who they considered to be junior to them in terms of a lineage chart, the date of transmission, or time in a particular sangha. The schoolyard argument of "I got here first" was somehow assumed to carry over to measuring spiritual wisdom and maturity. Given that these senior teachers were actually sometimes ignorant, misinformed, in an emotionally weak place, and/or greedy (i.e., they were human!), this attitude of overbearing authority caused considerable harm. It seems that even if someone doesn't *enter* Zen teaching as a narcissist, becoming a teacher could turn them *into* one!

To my mind, this problem has its roots in taking on teaching as an *identity* rather than a *role*. Zen teaches "no self," and shows us that we are impermanent and always in a state of flux. It warns us against settling down anywhere or becoming attached to anything. To me, this means that one should not settle into an *identity* as "a teacher," either. Rather, I should observe that sometimes I act as a student, sometimes a teacher, sometimes a grandmother, sometimes a grocery shopper, sometimes a patient, etc., as my life flows on. This string of actions, rather than some permanent essence(s), is as close as I can get to identifying a "me." When playing the role of teacher, I take it very seriously. But I consider it a *role*, a part I play in this dream we call our lives, not some solid thing that can be found in my DNA. This contrasts with the position espoused by a recent (now ex-) co-teacher of mine, when they insisted "I *am* a teacher! I am *always* a teacher!"

The problem is that if we take anything as an *identity*, we will naturally feel a need to defend and bolster that identity. The defensive action can clearly be seen in the "I'm right and you're wrong" attitude too often expressed by Zen teachers.

Students should be aware that they play an important role in establishing and bolstering someone's identity as a teacher. One can only teach if one has students! Now that I'm experiencing the culture of the teacher community from the inside, I can see indications of how this plays out. Prestige within the teaching community comes with having lots of students or lots of readers of one's books. Students should be aware that you are the "currency" that makes a teacher rich in status. Greater Boston moved to a more expensive location some years ago, largely due to the then-spiritual director's ambition to expand the membership.[83] Teachers are so protective of their private currency that the Soto Zen Buddhist Association's code of ethics up until late 2022 was largely concerned with tightly regulating the movement of students from one teacher to another.[84] As human beings who like status, it's easy to see how teachers might be motivated to cultivate more students (and in particular, Dharma "heirs") not so much for the students' benefit as their own. It's easy to see how one might be tempted, for example, to teach a more appealing, less risky, "nicer" sort of Zen, rather than risk losing students by keeping their feet to the fire. So if a teacher is very popular, don't take that as a sign that they are trustworthy. If a teacher seems welcoming and eager to take you on, don't automatically assume it is because they are eager to be of benefit to *you*. The motivations may be otherwise, or mixed. Keep your eyes open.

The sharp change in viewpoint I observed when my friends transitioned from student to teacher was so striking that I named it the "gold rakusu effect." I'm terrified that it could happen to me. I hope that thinking through these issues (it's often said that one writes the book one needs for oneself!) and having solid and wise sangha companions will help. I also keep a journal of my own "gold rakusu moments" where I make note of thoughts of pride or ambition when they arise. It helps me not believe those thoughts of achievement and status-seeking. And one of the reasons I like my current teacher is that she teaches at a smallish sangha and *hasn't* written a book.

## REACTIONS TO MISCONDUCT

I mentioned earlier the variety of reactions I observed during Betrayal #1, which resulted in Greater Boston Zen Center splitting away from Boundless Way Zen. It turns out that these reactions are of types that are well-documented in the literature on abuse of power in caring relationships. And, though I didn't know it at the time, I was soon to was to witness them again.

### BETRAYAL BLINDNESS

Psychologist and researcher Jennifer J. Freyd coined the term "betrayal blindness" to refer to "unawareness, not-knowing, and forgetting exhibited by people towards betrayal." She writes that "Victims, perpetrators, and witnesses may display betrayal blindness in order to preserve relationships, institutions, and social systems upon which they depend."[85]

Because students may feel a great deal of dependence on, and trust in, their teachers, it may be that abuses of power are not even recognized, at least at first. Another author elaborates on Freyd's definition: "Betrayal blindness is not allowing yourself to see what is going on, to connect the dots, or to fully engage with reality, because if you did, the information would threaten your relationship with the person who is [very] important to you. What this means is that events or realities that threaten our sense of secure connection to our [spiritual teacher] can feel like life or death to us. Whatever the threatening information may be, we can't let ourselves know about it because it would create such chaos, terror, pain, and confusion that we feel we might not survive it emotionally and psychologically. Instead, we keep the information out, and we don't allow one plus one to ever equal two. By doing this, we keep our world intact."[86]

I believe this was a good part of the dynamic that allowed the two teachers who caused Betrayal #1 to continue to be followed by many of their students. In the fall of 2020, our sangha was still, in many ways, recovering and reorganizing from that betrayal. I, and I think many others in the sangha, tended to believe that those two teachers were just a couple of "bad apples," while *our* teachers (that is, the teachers who split from them and Boundless Way) were the "good teachers." We were not at all prepared for Betrayal #2.

This crisis broke open in the Fall of 2020. I was, at that time, a teacher-in-training at Greater Boston, giving Dharma Talks and holding meetings with individual students under Juin's (then our spiritual director) supervision. We were preparing for the transmission ceremony in which I would receive from him authorization to teach on my own. I was also the sangha's ethics ombudsperson. As the ethics ombuds, I was one of the selected people Juin decided to personally call that November. As I recall, he told me that he had suddenly realized that he'd created a terrible situation. He confessed to having had an intimate relationship with sexual aspects with a student. He sounded devastated. He wanted me, he said, to be part of a discernment group that included a few senior teachers and myself, to decide what to do about his roles in Greater Boston.

It is an illustration of betrayal blindness that I, as his long-time student, initially totally trusted both his words and his judgment. I offered sympathy for his distress. It wasn't until ten days after his call that the thought even occurred to me that maybe he hadn't been entirely truthful, or that perhaps he didn't have the best judgment on this issue. (He hadn't, as it turned out, and he didn't.) I had trusted him completely, for so long! As a professional in my sixties, it came as a surprise to me to see how naïve I had been.

While the story of the abuse itself is the direct victim's story to tell, not mine, let me make brief remarks. In the weeks immediately following Juin's (unilateral) disclosure, this student, like many before her in other sanghas, at first couldn't get her bearings, much less understand the depth of the betrayal. Even though—as it became clearer over time—she had been groomed and suffered severe boundary violations, she initially said that she was feeling primarily pain and (misplaced) guilt. Her initial impulse was to *apologize* to me and other sangha members!

Others in the sangha, including the other teachers, showed considerable and more persistent betrayal blindness, which I will discuss later.

### DEVASTATION

The student, as noted, was initially in a state of great pain and confusion. Think about it: Someone who had claimed to have a great love for her had abruptly cut her off, and now wouldn't even talk to her. Her source of spiritual guidance, of course, had gone out the window at the same time. Having been pressured by him to keep everything secret, she had a lot of ground to catch up on even with her best friends. In an especially cruel complication, the teacher had also been her (paid) pastoral counselor for emotional work. She was adrift and in crisis. The Greater Boston board paid for a good therapist. It took months of therapy for her to recognize how she had been exploited and clarify for herself where her actual responsibilities lay. The literature suggests that, without such support, other victims may never get to that point and can remain wounded and confused the rest of their lives.

Although initially overly trusting when it came to teachers, I was encouraged by others in the sangha (especially Jill Gaulding and Rebecca Behizadeh) to learn more about clergy sexual abuse. So I read up on it. I also listened to the student victim and witnessed the devastating effects that Juin's breach of trust had on her. I talked with other sangha members who also felt destroyed. The effect of the betrayal started to sink in.

The cataclysm our sangha experienced caused me and many others to not only question the wisdom of one particular teacher, but also to question our faith in the Dharma, the sangha, and even in ourselves. I asked myself questions such as:

- How could someone I love and respect so much hurt me (and others) so badly?
- Is everything I learned from him wrong?
- Is my community gone?
- Can I ever trust anyone again?
- Can I even trust myself, now that my own judgment has shown itself to be flawed?
- In hard times, I find sustenance in my Zen practice. When my Zen practice *is* the hard times, where can I turn when my soul hurts?

I heard such questions were troubling others, as well.

Our confusion was further exacerbated by the sense that this particular teacher *should have known better*. He had edited Scott Edelstein's excellent book, *Sex and the Spiritual Teacher*.[87] He had done graduate work that included training in ethics in professional relationships. It isn't that the pain would have been less if we could have attributed the betrayal to naivete. But our attempt to make any sense out of what happened seemed mostly doomed to failure. Even now, I have to resist the temptation to find bitter comfort in an attitude of "Well, it just goes to show you can't trust *anyone*." Boundary violations by spiritual teachers can be spiritually and emotionally devastating.

## DARVO

Jennifer J. Freyd also coined the acronym DARVO. This stands for "Deny, Attack, and Reverse Victim and Offender."[88] It is, the research suggests, a very common way that those who have committed misconduct try to avoid accountability.

I certainly saw plenty of this in Betrayal #1, when the Boundless Way teachers took sole control of the property in which we had all invested. Those teachers denied that they were doing harm. When they met with resistance, they attacked those who were trying to make them accountable.[89] From what I hear, we were accused of lying, exaggerating, and/or being mentally unstable.

I will include in my use of the term DARVO the attacks made on those who witness abuses or dare to advocate for the victims. The main target of DARVO by the spiritual director in Betrayal #2 was the Greater Boston Board of Directors. Juin's view, as he expressed to me, was that the best course of action following his disclosure would be for him to take a short leave. When he returned to teaching, he said, he should be "supervised" by the other teachers. There was nothing in his plan that referred to the board—nor anything in it to address the needs of the victim or the rest of the sangha. While he didn't deny acting with poor judgment in relation to the one student, he, at least at that time, seemed to hold a view that minimized his conduct's harmful effects on others.

The Greater Boston board, however, skillfully led by President Rebecca Behizadeh and VP Jill Gaulding took their "duty of care" for the sangha seriously. The board suspended Juin from Greater Boston roles and tried to start an investigation. They felt that a healing process—for Juin, as well as for the victim and the sangha—could only begin after the full extent of the harm was known and acknowledged. The research suggests that a multi-year plan of supervised and specialized rehabilitation and evaluation is the only way to, with great compassion, assure that someone who has once engaged in sexual misconduct will not offend again. And even then, this can only be started after the person who offended has taken full responsibility for the all the harm they caused.[90]

Juin resigned from his Greater Boston roles rather than answer questions. However, he still tried to exert control over the sangha and over the process of response to the abuse. The victim reports that he attempted to gaslight her when they were in a meeting (in retrospect, ill-advised) arranged by consultants the board had hired. He asked for a meeting with the board and, according to someone who was there, expressed regret for his actions—and then went on to accuse the board of doing everything wrong and having "brutalized" him. A number of others in the sangha then seemed to share the view that the board was overreacting and being vindictive. (There was no doubt that Juin had "punished" himself plenty by messing up his life. But the board's goal was not infliction of more "punishment," but bringing about accountability for the harm he caused to others.) He issued a number of ultimatums as conditions of engaging in a process designed by hired consultants.

In a premature ceremony of apology (another thing *not* recommended in the research) Juin apologized for the initial abuse. Because he had resisted learning from those he harmed, and continued to do harm, a number of us who observed this apology felt it lacked depth. Several months later he returned his robes and documents to his authorizing teacher. From what I understand, though, he has to date refused any supervised rehabilitation. And I have not heard, at this time, of any accountability on his part for the further harms done.[91]

Denying, attacking, and reversing (DARVO) usually works. Is a not-particularly-informed student in the sangha more likely to believe their beloved and esteemed teacher, or some random student with little or no status whom they may have never even met? Similarly, are they more likely to believe their teacher or some board made up of non-teachers?

## CAN TEACHERS WHO ABUSE BE REHABILITATED?

While my concern is mainly with victims and communities—as the leaders of a sangha should be, if facing a case of teacher misconduct! —it is worth looking for a moment at whether a teacher who has abused their students' trust can ever become trustworthy again.

At least for those cases where psychotherapists crossed sexual boundaries, there is research on this. Sadly, there apparently is little hope for rehabilitating those who could be diagnosed with psychopathy or sociopathy, and who are unable or unwilling to control their narcissism. They probably have entered the field precisely because of the opportunities for abuse it provided them. But these types are actually a small minority of offenders. For the rest—for those who probably started with good intentions and then strayed into misconduct—there is some degree of hope.

The sangha must first, of course, have undertaken a full investigation so that the full extent of harm is known. After this, the initial step for the offender is to take complete responsibility for causing this harm. Unfortunately, many offenders never get that far. They often remain caught in defensiveness and DARVO.[92] They never manifest full remorse.

I find this tragic: The teacher has denied himself (it's usually a "him") the undeniably unpleasant but also compassionately supplied opportunity to face what he did, and perhaps go on to live a full and honest life. To the extent that he provided valuable teaching when he *was* trustworthy, the sangha also loses. It is not up to the sangha, though, which road a teacher will take. This is the teacher's choice.

If the teacher can get past that first step, recommendations for both therapists and spiritual teachers prescribe a carefully supervised and probably lengthy (for therapists at least, typically three to six year) program of rehabilitation. [93] The offender must fully participate in, and stick with, this program of psychotherapy, education, restitution, and other possible actions while tightly limiting or ceasing any activities in their professional role. The program finishes with an objective reassessment—not just when the *offender* believes that they have been cured!

Lawyer Carol Merchasin, who has worked with a number of cases of abuse perpetrated by spiritual teachers, reports that successful rehabilitation is rare in her experience. Of the teachers mentioned earlier in this chapter, the only one that I am aware of who sincerely and thoroughly apologized and accepted supervised treatment was, according to his students, Taizan Maezumi.[94] Even then, his later relapse into alcoholism led to his death.

There seems to be far less research on the rehabilitation of spiritual leaders who abuse their power in financial or emotional ways. This may be because such abuse more rarely makes the headlines. It seems plausible to me, though, to extrapolate from the research on sexual abuse.

Investigation, remorse, education, therapy, restitution, and independent evaluation would seem to be appropriate in these cases as well. And, in my experience, the dynamics of DARVO seem to be at least as strong.

## FINAL THOUGHTS

Let me reiterate a point I made earlier. Teacher-caused harm is not a matter of a few "bad" teachers. While I've named many names for informational purposes, I am by no means claiming that these people are all fraudsters. Nor am I denying that anyone I named may also be—in other circumstances and with other students—often valuable and effective in their teaching. Nor do I believe that they are all necessarily beyond rehabilitation. (Zen teaches us that things change!) Nevertheless, there is potential peril in the nature of the teacher-student relationship itself: There is an imbalance of power. One person is trusting another to give them help and the other person—sometimes very consciously, sometimes not—may take advantage of it.

With sufficient education, goodwill, understanding, maturity, and safeguards, I believe that teacher-student relationships *can* actually provide genuine and (largely) safe spiritual guidance. If it weren't possible for relationships with differences in power to also be (primarily) caring, none of us would have survived childhoods in which we were totally dependent on our parents. We'd never summon up the trust to talk to a therapist, hand documents over to a lawyer, or submit to surgery. But it seems to me that education, understanding, maturity, safeguards, and accountability for abuses when they occur are in very short supply in Zen sanghas. To those issues, the rest of this book is addressed.

But first, let's take a careful look at the phenomenon of "teaching transmission," which is what empowers teachers in the first place.

6

# UNDERSTANDING TEACHING TRANSMISSION

OLD CHINESE stories and koans often follow a particular prototypical form:

> A Zen Master, the head of a monastery, is approached by one of the monks. The monk asks a question. The master speaks or makes a motion, and the monk experiences Great Realization. After further study, the master gives the monk Dharma transmission in a solemn ceremony. Now, they, too, are a Zen Master. They leave to start their own monastery or succeed their teacher as abbot after his death.[95]

This is very clean and neat. It "explains" the tidy lineage bloodline shown on many ceremonial Zen documents. This starts with Shakyamuni Buddha in South Asia, then moves on to Mahakashyapa, who is said to have received teaching transmission from Shakyamuni, and so on. As one gets closer to the present, the bloodline winds its way through teachers in Japan or Korea or another Asian country, and then may go on to name people in the U.S., Europe, or other non-Asian cultures.

Ask a contemporary teacher about how they got their teaching authority, and we'll tell you where we fit in our lineage(s). Our bios will usually name our teacher(s) and the dates of our transmission ceremony(s). The ceremonies themselves are elaborate, often including gifts of robes and staffs that, at least in medieval Japan, represented authority. The ceremonies were traditionally conducted at midnight, privately and in the teacher's own quarters, giving them a certain mystique. The final days of preparation often include "secret" teachings or rituals that only transmitted teachers are supposed to know about.

So the ceremony of teaching transmission is a big deal. It's what differentiates those in teacher roles from those in student roles. And, I believe, misunderstandings about what it represents are a main cause of dangerous teacher-student relationships today.

## MYTHOS AND LOGOS

The first point to notice about lineage documents, as well as most of the old stories and koans, is that they are pretty much all made up. For example, you won't find the story of the Buddha transmitting the Dharma to Mahakashyapa in any of the ancient South Asian Buddhist texts. It was invented in China at least in part to defend the practice of monks, in a culture that highly valued family loyalty, abandoning their birth families. Stories about a lineage of ancestors did so by creating a parallel Zen "family line." The first record of the story of Shakyamuni, Mahakashyapa, and the flower dates from eleventh century China.[96]

Or consider Keizan Jokin's *Record of Transmitting the Light*, a volume included in some koan curricula.[97] It purports to tell the stories of all the Zen ancestors in a direct line from Shakyamuni all the way down to what he calls the 52nd ancestor, Keizan's own teacher's teacher, Koun Ejo. The recounting of early generations in South Asia and China appears to be definitive. The lineage appears to get passed on smoothly and cleanly. But as Keizan's account gets closer to his own time, there is a problem: The 44th ancestor did not receive Caodong (Soto) transmission from the (by then, deceased) 43rd ancestor. However, Keizan wrote, a teacher in the Linji (Rinzai) school of Zen had been empowered by the 43rd to act as his surrogate. Keizan spends many pages arguing for this and disputing the arguments of those who said otherwise. And that book only takes us up to about 1300 CE!

Professor of East Asian Buddhism John R. McRae has suggested some "Rules of Zen Studies." One is "Lineage assertions are as wrong as they are strong." Another, regarding the content of stories, is "Precision implies inaccuracy."[98] Studies of the actual documents from which these stories come reveal that many were first written down centuries after the incidents recounted are said to have occurred. In many cases, even the existence of the people populating the stories is questionable. The lineage documents and stories were often composed to justify some view or action, teach some lesson, or establish some presumptive authority. Was Bodhidharma a real person, or a composite of several, or made up entirely? We'll never know.

Scholar William M. Bodiford's research on medieval Zen reveals much ambiguity and conflict about the notion of transmission.[99] It's not at all clear if it was thought to be granted to only one student or possibly to many, or if it was marked by passing on a robe, training in secret rituals, completing a given koan curriculum, bestowal of a succession certificate, or something else. Succession was, in fact, often linked to the need to satisfy wealthy sponsors. Moving along to more recent history, the more one looks around the more one sees that lineages divide, merge, interweave, break, die out, and possibly pick up again somewhere else with great frequency.

But then again, does it really matter? Another of McRae's rules is, "It's not true, and therefore it's more important." Karen Armstrong, in *The Battle for God* explains how premodern people "evolved two ways of thinking, speaking, and acquiring knowledge...mythos and logos. Both were essential; they were regarded as complementary ways of arriving at truth, and each had its special area of competence. Myth was...not concerned with practical matters, but with meaning. Unless we find some significance in our lives, we mortal men and women fall very easily into despair. The mythos...was also rooted in what we would call the unconscious mind...embodied in cult, rituals, and ceremonies which worked aesthetically upon worshipers...enabling them to apprehend the deeper currents of existence."[100] These old stories, ideas of lineage, and ceremonies, then, belong to the realm of mythos, not logos or reason. They are not meant to be a precise recounting of facts, but (ideally) to inspire a spiritual and religious sensibility. They deal with the mysterious, the magical, and the unconscious. They are meant to inspire awe, connection, and compassion.

I love the symbolic meaning of the lineage chart as signifying a connection between our minds and hearts and those of many others distant in space and time. *And* any literal interpretation is extremely shaky. Lineage claims do not, and never have, actually provided any sort of iron-clad legitimation of authenticity. Unfortunately, what often happens in many religious and spiritual traditions is that fundamentalists try to assert that the myths of their faiths are actual facts. Christian fundamentalists, for example, do this with the story of creation in the book of Genesis. In recent decades they have, in the U.S., increasingly sought to enforce their views on this and many social issues in this-world political and educational realms. Claiming that God is on your side is a powerful tool of persuasion!

I believe there is a similar problem in Zen. Instead of letting the *mythos* of lineage and ceremony take us deeper into the great mystery, they are taken as *logos*. They are used to establish temporal structures of power. Both teacher and student are tempted to give great weight to the "fact" of the teacher's transmission, and the "fact" that the student is not yet "there." Attention to the dynamic, mysterious, and sacred relationships of the here and now (and all space and time) is lost in the rush to establish a supposedly concrete basis for claims of authority.

## WHAT TEACHING TRANSMISSION IS NOT

So it is worth spending some time thinking more about what Dharma transmission really represents. There are a number of common understandings which, to my mind, don't hold up to closer examination.

### NOT ENLIGHTENMENT

Bodhidharma, the (mythical) first Chan ancestor in China, is said to have written:

> A special transmission outside the scriptures,
> Not founded upon words and letters.

> By pointing directly to one's mind,
> It lets one see into one's own true nature and thus attain Buddhahood.

So a good first guess at what a "transmission" ceremony means is that "transmitted teachers" have "seen into their true nature" and received "enlightenment." And one may then conclude, that if one is a good enough student your teacher may someday "transmit" enlightenment to you.

I see four major problems with this equation of "transmitted teacher" with "enlightened person." First, enlightenment is not a matter of one and done. The possibility of awakening is in every moment. Once one has experienced a profound opening experience, one is unlikely to ever forget it completely. But one does *not* then walk around as a permanently enlightened person. One has not entered a new ontological state; realization is not a culmination. You walk around as a person with a particular *memory* of insight, which is different from the insight itself. The path merely starts here, as the lifelong work of integrating such insights into our lives begins.

Imagine a situation in which we all wore spiritual mood rings.[101] Suppose they appeared yellow when our small self was in charge and blue when our thoughts and actions were guided by the Dharma. We would be more likely to realize, then, that *each* moment is an opportunity to turn yellow to blue.[102] We'd never see a human being wearing a steady blue. A gold-brown rakusu along with a yellow ring would signal "Danger!" And we'd observe directly that getting a flash of blue is just the beginning.

After an awakening we must throw away thoughts of having achieved something, raise our aspiration for enlightenment afresh, and get back to practice. Eihei Dogen, the founder of our Soto School of Zen, described this as the "circle of the way" which we travel in "continuous practice."[103] He also wrote,

> The Great Way uniquely transmitted by buddhas and ancestors is confirmation.... It is usually thought in

> the world that a person is confirmed when the merit of the practice is complete and becoming a buddha is determined; but it is not so in the buddha way... Attaining buddhahood spoken of here is always successively. As part of successively you attain buddhahood. Confirmation turns this attaining buddhahood. This turning keeps on continuously, moving on to the next turning. It continues happening...It is not concerned with self and other in the past, present, and future. It is just hearing from the Buddha.[104]

Students and teachers would do well to remember that *all* of us are still on the path. None of us are at its terminus. There is no terminus.

Second, one may have a great deal of insight, and many successive awakenings, and yet not become a teacher. In Soto Zen, students learn that Dogen had a great awakening upon hearing about "body and mind dropped away" from his teacher Tiantong Rujing. Dogen subsequently received teaching transmission from him. Yet in Keizan Jokin's *Record of Transmitting the Light* we learn that Rujing also confirmed that his temple's illiterate gardener had "clarified the way." Keizan comments, "Truly, in a community where the Way exists, there are many who have the way and are committed to it."[105]

I have certainly seen this in my home sangha. Many have great insight and have matured greatly in integrating this into their daily lives. Engaging in formal teaching, however, may or may not follow. Teaching requires a certain amount of time and energy to study and to engage with others. Not everyone busy with work and family can do that. Teaching requires some communication and relational skills that not everyone has. Yet people who have awakened and are following the way may powerfully serve the Buddha, Dharma, and Sangha in a whole variety of roles and occupations.[106] There is plenty of pain and injustice in the world, and many ways in which sentient (and insentient) beings need our wisdom and compassion. How limited our effect would be on the relative world if all of us devoted our time to preparing Dharma talks! I believe the most advanced Zen practitioners might very well be found driving for Uber or teaching kindergarten.

Third (as mentioned in chapter 4), while enlightenment experiences may come about in relationship with one's teacher, they may also come in relationship with someone or something else. In *The Record of Transmitting the Light,* Keizan asks, "Xiangyan was awakened when he heard bamboo being struck, so why didn't he become a successor to bamboo? Lingyun was awakened by peach blossoms, so why didn't he become the successor to peach blossoms?"

Keizan thus distinguishes awakening, which may be precipitated by a conversation with a teacher—or by bamboo or blossoms, a honking car, or a sneeze—from the issue of teaching succession. He continued (about a teacher he was criticizing), "It is a pity that Cheng-gu did not realize that succession takes place in the quarters of Buddhist patriarchs…it seems that he did not know of the mutual recognition there in the room." It appears that *teaching* transmission *does* always happen between a teacher and their successor. When Bodhidharma wrote about "transmission' outside the scriptures," it seems to me that he was using the term to mean something other than authorization to teach.

Lastly, the story of the teacher "transmitting" enlightenment suggests that the teacher is somehow in control of the timing and depth of the opening process. Students who report being suddenly awakened during an encounter with a charismatic teacher may be particularly prone to see enlightenment as "coming from" the teacher.[107] But that attributes power to the teacher that is not theirs at all. We are already Buddha Nature, and its cultivation in our lives comes from Buddha, Dharma, and Sangha.

For most of us, the timing of our ripening for an opening is mostly uncontrollable and unpredictable. I first experienced "the bottom falling out of the bucket" at age ten at the sound of an airplane flying overhead. This was decades before I even heard about Zen. Others work with a teacher for years without any real shift in perspective. (Recall that Ananda, in spite of sitting right next to Shakyamuni Buddha, didn't awaken until after his death!) I have no idea why the timing is so unpredictable, and I don't think that faster or slower makes any person more or less "special" than another. Recall that occasionally those old stories or koans end with the student still being clueless in spite of the teacher's best efforts. I'm sure we would be reading many more such stories had those who crafted the chronicles thought they would be more inspiring than discouraging.

The opening of the Dharma Eye, while presumably necessary for teacher status, is not sufficient. It is not one and done. It is not a merit badge. Nor are teacher successors the only people who have had openings. Not all openings take place in the context of teacher-student relationships, nor do teachers cause them. But *teaching* transmission apparently does take place between teacher and student.

### NOT A SPECIAL MYSTICAL POWER

Zen teachers are said to have received "mind to mind" transmission of the Dharma. This can be confusing. I remember hearing that a rumor circulated among the students of a well-known contemporary abbot: The act of teaching transmission, supposedly, involved the teacher pouring something special into the successor's brain by means of them sitting for a long time with their heads pressed together!

Even if we aren't as literal-minded as that, we may still have the impression that some *thing* in the mind has been mysteriously transferred. The transmission ceremony, which is nowadays often witnessed by one or more students, usually includes a ceremonial "transfer" of Dharma wisdom from the teacher to their student via water and a pine branch. I believe we are meant to interpret this in a *mythos* sense. That particular water ritual, we might note, is part of the precepts-receiving ceremony as well. Yet those receiving the precepts are not then authorized to teach. Dharma wisdom is everywhere if we are open to it.

The education in secret rituals may also encourage the belief in special powers. Yet, from what I can tell, these special mudras (hand positions) and chants probably have less to do with the Dharma and more to do with South Asian or East Asian indigenous traditions. They are steeped in *mythos*. I am open to the idea that they have some kind of energy that we can't rationally understand; I know that rituals, chanting, and drumming can often reach us in ways that words cannot. Yet anyone who joins one of our sitting practices is also immediately taught mudras for sitting and walking practice. They also join in chanting a magical incantation (*dharani*). I have yet to see any student (or teacher) walk on air or see through walls as a result. Any effect is subtle. I suspect that a significant reason for keeping some rituals "secret," historically, has been to maintain the mystique of power.

Much more helpful and important is Keizan's phrasing of "mutual recognition" in the room. In modern lingo, we might say that the teacher and student have found themselves to be "on the same wavelength" and that transmission involves formal recognition of this. The mystical elements evoking ideas of secret knowledge involved in the transmission ceremony are part of its *mythos*. It is not a literal, *logos* transfer.

In *Zen Sand*, Victor Sogen Hori uses the phrase "mind to mind" in explaining the history of koans. He explains that koan practice has its roots in a very old Chinese literary game. One person would state a line of poetry, laden with allusion and analogy. The next player was challenged to "recognize the hidden meaning of the other person's allusions and…thrust back using a similar allusion with some other hidden meaning."[108]

In Zen koan work with a teacher, the curriculum makes the first move by providing a passage. The student, rather than being asked to explain the hidden meaning (i.e., intellectually discoursing about "form," "emptiness," "non-duality," etc.) of the passage is invited to become one with the koan, to be (for example) the sound of one hand. That is, the student is invited to express an opening that cannot be described in ordinary language. In some traditions, Zen teachers require that the student come up with a literary or original "capping phrase," even more closely mimicking the Chinese game.

Joan Sutherland, in *Through Forests of Every Color*, also talks about koan work communicating experiences "incommunicable in ordinary ways." She writes about koans being "precisely accurate, a language native to" the place to which one has opened. "As we gradually rejoin a life already in progress," she writes, "the koans are a kind of traveler's phrasebook for the journey back into a familiar world seen with new eyes."

What Hori and Sutherland write about koans, which are more commonly used in the Rinzai school of Zen, also rings true regarding studying the teachings of Eihei Dogen, founder of the Soto school. Dogen's writings tend to be dense, obscure, and confusing. Our sangha's periodic Dogen study groups have been familiarly known as "Dogen Support Groups." Yet I have had the experience of finding a particular passage of his suddenly "opening up" for me accompanied by the thought, "He couldn't possibly have expressed things more clearly!"

Understood this way, "mind to mind transmission" is not about the teacher passing something on to the student. Instead, the teacher, by prodding and coaching, helps the student come to their own experience of the mysterious dark vastness of our interdependent, lively, and vital existence. The student then, by their presentation of a koan or other means, demonstrates that their candle is now lit. The student recognizes the lit candle of the teacher, and the teacher the lit candle of the student.

To use a modern metaphor of radio transmission, the "mutual recognition in the room" is not a matter of the teacher actively broadcasting and the student passively receiving. A better image is two people listening to music on the radio, each through their own earbuds. They can't hear what the other is hearing, and neither is allowed to name the piece or give the call numbers of the station. But as they individually dance to the music it becomes apparent that they are both tuned into the same Dharma "station."

Yet, as mentioned earlier, opening experiences by themselves don't make teachers, nor does a teacher's confirmation of a student's opening experience.[109] So the question of "What is transmitted in teacher transmission?" is still unanswered.

### NOT PATRIARCHAL AUTHORITY

Lineage charts play important roles in Zen ceremonies. Traditionally, receiving teaching transmission means that one becomes the "Dharma heir" of one's teacher. If one then conveys teaching authority on to further "heirs," one's name is added to the list of Zen "patriarchs." The word patriarchs, from the Greek for "ruling father," was traditionally synonymous with "ancestors" since all but some very recently recognized ancestors have been men. Objects traditionally given as indicators of transmission are variations on the robes and scepters associated with kingly authority since ancient times.

This probably made perfect sense to people in cultures structured around patriarchal lineages and that stress filial duties and the honoring of (primarily male) forebears. One sees a similar pattern in the scriptures of the Abrahamic traditions, with long lists of who begat whom. In such a culture, the fathers are indeed expected to rule—not just over their wives and daughters, but also over their sons. Elder males are to be *honored, served, and obeyed!* Often this is justified in religious terms as consistent with an imagined natural hierarchy of the divine to the emperor or pope; the emperor or pope to fathers and priests; and fathers, whether familial or religious, to everybody else.

Yet the emphases on fatherly authority, distinguished ancestry, and obligations of obedience and service don't make much sense when transplanted to the contemporary West. The idea of royal or noble bloodlines has largely gone the way of the dodo. Western feminist activism has made inroads on patriarchal thinking and oppressive patriarchal structures. At our ceremonies of receiving the precepts (Buddhist ethical teachings), I started giving a Women Ancestor's Chart along with the patriarchal one. I am considering introducing a nonbinary one—probably featuring Avalokiteshvara/Guanyin—or a less linear one that includes communities, places, and individuals not usually recognized as ancestors. Western cultures tend to emphasize individualism and independence over filial duty, and the future over the past. In fact, becoming a Zen student here often means breaking *away* from the spiritual practice (or lack thereof) of one's actual ancestors.

The notion that transmitted teachers are authoritative figures who must be revered, served, and obeyed is still alive, however. Forms, ceremonies, and honorifics (e.g., Zen "master") that treat teachers as extra-special can add to this impression. In terms of the this/that and yin/yang images introduced earlier, this notion of transmission would be illustrated by the white circle (active teacher yang) dominating the black circle (receptive student yin) until the black circle "graduates" to being white. And, I believe, this image is behind a lot of the troubles and scandals affecting U.S. Buddhist communities.

Teachers who expect to be honored, served, and obeyed, and students who go along with this, may perpetuate the notion that teachers are somehow god-like, with a direct line to the absolute. It may reinforce students' desire to believe that the people we are turning to for help in figuring out our own lives already have their lives all figured out as a result of their specialness. Students may then hand over too much of their own power to these teachers in hopes that they will someday "inherit" that "thing" that the teacher has. It's easy to see how inflated teacher egos and abuses of power could readily follow.

I have certainly held idealized images of my teachers. For example, I remember my very first teacher giving a talk about our Zen vows and our intention to keep them. Being newly divorced at that time, I felt bad about breaking my marital promise of "till death do us part." Surely, I believed, this teacher and his wife (who was also in the sangha) were doing better than I! When I mentioned my distress during the discussion after the talk, the teacher gave a vague reply. I think I would have had a more realistic view of Zen and Zen teachers had I known, at that time, that even though this teacher had begun Zen practice at a young age, he had had two earlier marriages that ended in divorce.

Even if a teacher manages to maintain appropriate humility in spite of student idealization, too much emphasis on "family line" talk may still, I think, contribute to problems. Framing teacher/student relations in parent/child terms seems like a recipe for encouraging psychological transference and countertransference. Neither teachers who treat students like children, nor students who make teachers into players in their unresolved childhood dramas, make for a healthy sangha.

A teacher's job is to help students find what they themselves never lost: Buddha nature. We are, as I mentioned earlier, engaged in "selling water by the river." Teachers are students who are a bit further along this spiritual path who may be able to help those coming behind avoid some of the distractions and traps that commonly lie along the way. However, we are still human and have clay feet. We may, unfortunately, not be further along than our students in psychological, social, intellectual, or moral development. We are *sure* to be less informed and skilled in some areas. We should be very wary about having loyal, blindly obedient "followers" lest we lead them off the nearest cliff!

There are probably both advantages and drawbacks to granting formal authorization to teach via a lineage-based (teacher-to-new-teacher) system. Alternative systems such as seminary training may give more comprehensive education yet be more dry and rigid. Self-proclaimed teachers may be very good, or they may be quacks. However, we might structure the approval of teachers, there are good reasons to be leery of thinking of it as inheriting the right to be served and obeyed.

Beware of teachers who take their place in a lineage overly seriously. Some, for example, are proud of being a second rather than fourth generation descendent from some particular forebear, as though second is clearly better and more authentic than fourth. First of all, the tradition teaches that the student should *surpass* their teacher, which would make the fourth generation better. Second, this emphasis on generations draws attention away from *what they do*. Third, I believe that over-concern with lineage can feed into "betrayal blindness." Any acknowledgement of abuses perpetrated by one's teacher, or their teacher's teacher, may seem to threaten the validity of a teacher's *own* authorization. I suspect that this is a substantial factor in some of the vicious blowback that gets directed at people who raise the issue of teacher abuse of power.

### NOT LEADERSHIP OF THE SANGHA

Zen teachers are looked up to as spiritual leaders and guides. Does a teacher's authority extend to all decisions affecting the community?

In the Asian monastic traditions, the question of teaching succession often included the question of who would be the next abbot of the monastery. The abbot was the head of the whole shebang. They were not only the top spiritual teacher but also the top authority regarding the day-to-day functioning of the institution and planning for its future. Yet this model is problematic, even in the cultures in which it originated.

For example, many Soto Zen students know that Dogen and his Dharma descendent Keizan are considered the first founders of the Soto school: Dogen for bringing the tradition to Japan from China and giving it initial formulation, and Keizan for spreading it throughout Japan. But Keizan wasn't even born yet when Dogen died. We usually don't hear about what went on in between.

Bodiford's book recounts a series of conflicts—and even conflicts about whether there *were* conflicts.[110] Dogen gave teaching transmission and the abbacy of Eihei-ji temple to Koun Ejo. Ejo had been a talented editor of Dogen's writings. But, at least by some accounts, he was less charismatic and less talented as an administrator. Ejo in turn gave transmission to four students. One of them, Tettsu Gikai, was his successor as abbot of Eihei-Ji for about five years. Gikai was reportedly a talented cultivator of donors and manager of building projects, but his abbacy was apparently disputed. He eventually left Eihei-Ji and moved to another province (whether voluntarily or not is unclear). Some of his students went along. These included Keizan, to whom he later gave transmission. The teacher who ultimately prevailed in becoming the abbot of Eihei-ji has become known in history only for becoming the abbot.

So, must a transmitted teacher be an inspiring spiritual leader? An influential writer? A poet? Fluent in at least a couple Asian languages? A careful custodian of tradition? A visionary innovator? A great editor? Disseminator? Effective manager of the daily functions of an organization? Skilled manager of building projects? A talented fundraiser? Good at winning in struggles for power? All this, of course, in addition to being a Zen adept? Perhaps you would also like them to take the lead in social justice projects? And also head a pastoral care group that visits those who are ill or grieving? It can't be reasonable to expect one person to do all these things well.

Yet this model of single-pointed leadership seems to have been transferred to Western Zen sanghas. The U.S. sanghas I know of were mostly started by individual teachers who gathered students around themselves. Small sanghas may be unincorporated, with the sole teacher making all the decisions. Larger sanghas are often incorporated as U.S. nonprofit organizations and have a board and perhaps paid staff. Yet often the board president, or sometimes all of the board's officers, are teachers and/or devoted students of the lead teacher. It seems common to refer to sanghas as "Teizan's sangha" or "Jane's group," naming the top-ranked (or sole) teacher as the community's clear leader. Sometimes this works out fine. Too often, from what I've seen, it does not.

Among the possible consequences of this model are stress and burnout on the part of an overworked teacher. Another is disappointment and frustration in the sangha when some of a teacher's skills are subpar. And there is a third and devastating problem: An environment ripe for abuse of power. Because students look up to them, spiritual teachers have considerable interpersonal, influential power, as discussed earlier. If a sangha unquestioningly accepts a teacher's authority over all things sangha related or has a puppet board whose main focus is serving and protecting *the teacher(s),* the teachers have virtually no checks on their behavior.

For good reason, then, boards of U.S. 501(c)(3) organizations are charged with clearly laid-out duties to care *for the organization*, be loyal to its mission, and make sure that civil laws and regulations are obeyed. Independent boards can potentially provide checks on teacher power as well as expertise in those areas of organizational management that a spiritual teacher may lack.

### NOT A SET OR STYLE OF TEACHING

While one might think that, since Buddhist teaching was first passed along as an oral tradition, and since the word *Dharma* is often defined as "the Buddhist teachings," that "transmission of the Dharma" meets the passing along of a set of oral or written teachings.

The passing along of secret teachings in transmission ceremonies has, indeed, been part of Zen teaching transmission. "The Song of the Precious Mirror Samadhi," for example, was passed along only in transmission ceremonies until the twelfth century.[111] Perhaps this was intended to reserve the more difficult teachings only for those more ready to understand them. Or perhaps it was meant to deliberately create an aura of mystery to enhance power. Even in 2023, the documents I copied as part of the transmission process included a list of "secret books." Yet all of the works mentioned, including "The Song of the Precious Mirror Samadhi," are now publicly available. So transmission can't be said to revolve around such writings.

More importantly, Buddhism as a whole frowns on thinking of the Dharma as something that can be memorized or written down. According to the oldest stories, Shakyamuni's disciple Ananda, apparently having a great memory, was able to remember every talk the Buddha gave word for word and so preserve and pass on the teachings. But, the Zen story goes, transmission did not go from Shakyamuni to Ananda. The next successor in the lineage was Mahakashyapa, who smiled when the Buddha held up a flower. Mutual recognition occurred between Shakyamuni and Mahakashyapa, and it was Mahakashyapa who led the community after Shakyamuni's death. As the passage attributed to Bodhidharma above said, it is a "special transmission outside the scriptures, not founded upon words and letters."

Other stories illustrate how mere scholarly knowledge of the sutras is disdained. The young Deshan thought he was an expert on the Diamond Sutra. But he burned all his commentaries not long after a woman selling tea by the road took him down several pegs. So teaching transmission isn't about the transfer of verbal or written teaching materials.

Or possibly what is transmitted is a *style* of teaching? To some extent, this is true. Soto Zen teachers tend to have Soto successors, Rinzai Zen teachers, Rinzai ones, etc. Particular forms and rituals, ways of using koans (if used), and even styles of dress tend to follow the paths of succession. If this is emphasized, it may be thought that transmission is complete when the student has become a clone of the teacher.

But Dharma successors seem to have a habit of not quite following their teachers' style—which is to the good. A student who merely imitates a teacher cannot be said to be fully fledged. A student is supposed to *surpass* their teacher in understanding. Follow the example of Juzhi Yizhi's "one finger Zen" too closely and you are likely to end up with only nine digits! Authentic teaching can only come when we each manifest in this universe as ourselves.

The history of Zen is full of stories of teachers and students who combine different traditions, who innovate, who take Zen practice out of the context in which they learned it and adapt it to new places and times. This is always surrounded by controversy, of course. But the Dharma is vast and alive, not something that can be confined in some particular box.

Considered as "skillful means," and as connecting us with practitioners from other times, the traditional written teachings, and the variety of our styles of practice, are important and merit study. Yet these still do not fully capture the "what" in the question, "What is transmitted in teaching transmission?"

## TRANSMISSION IS ENTRUSTMENT

If Zen teaching transmission is not synonymous with enlightenment, and not centrally about mystical power, authority, leadership, or the content or style of teaching—what, then, is the key feature? In the final analysis, Zen teaching transmission is primarily an *entrustment.* The teacher giving transmission believes that the person named as a successor can be trusted to continue to manifest the Dharma and to open the path for others to the best of their ability. Transmission entrusts the recipient with putting the teaching of the Dharma and the well-being and development of students above their personal interests. It is a signal that this particular human being, in the view of the elder, will be able to serve as a reliable spiritual friend. The granter should be confident that the grantee can be trusted to serve the Buddha by serving the sangha in a teaching role, safely and effectively. The successor *merits* such trust when they truly take on and fulfill these responsibilities.

Recall the yin/yang diagrams for healthy teacher-student relationships introduced earlier, and its difference from this/that thinking. The roles of teacher and student are different, as illustrated by white and black. And there is an interdependence: without a student there is no one who teaches, and without a teacher there is no student who learns. The relationship is intimate, not arm's length peer-to-peer. The teacher is also still open to learning and the student has some things to teach (the polliwog "eyes"). And the relationship is dynamic—the diagram is spinning, each polliwog chasing the other. Let me suggest, as an image pointing to what transmission means, that we also think of this as a Dharma Wheel rolling forward in time. When one commits to fulfilling the duties of the teaching role, including maintaining the appropriate boundaries, one *commits to keeping the Dharma wheel turning.*

Recall as well the psychology research I cited earlier: teachers who understand their power in terms of *responsibility* and *social* aims (rather than opportunity and individual goals) are likely to do much better by their students and sanghas. The part of the transmission ceremonies I found most touching was a ritual in which my teacher rubbed my head—an act that reminded me of the "grandmotherly care" referred to in some of our old Zen stories. In our patriarchal culture, it is easy to think of the (kingly) staff given to transmitted teachers as a sign only of hierarchy and potential brutal tyranny. I think we might do well to borrow an image from a Christian source: The word "pastor" comes from the Latin word for "shepherd." The staff might also be seen as shepherd's crook, helpful in *caring for* the flock.

To my mind, the point of invoking the ancestors is not to praise the recipient of transmission but to make it clear that these responsibilities are serious and heavy. For 2500 years teachers have kept that wheel turning as each generation passes on to the next, *and now all their eyes are on you.* This isn't just a hobby. Nor is it an identity you can rest in, or a qualification you can add to your list of personal achievements. It is a charge. The Three Treasures have come down to us from ancient times. Will I keep them, guard them, and pass them on? Or will I, because of my beginningless greed, hatred, and delusion, screw it up?

Consider how well our current generation has done with the entrustment to us of literally billions of years of development of biodiversity on this earth. We have squandered that and are continuing to do so. We are destroying what used to be a relatively stable climate and relatively abundant resources of fuel and clean water. This does not give a lot of grounds for confidence in human beings. But we carry on anyway.

I think you have to be a little bit nuts to want to be a teacher. The old sutras are full of graphic descriptions of the sorts of hell that are reserved for those who lead followers astray. Even if you don't take that literally, the implied obligation should be daunting. A sangha member recently asked me when I decided I wanted to become a teacher. I laughed! I love my sangha, and the Dharma. I have more or less fallen into teaching because it seemed to me that my home sangha, as well as perhaps the *mahasangha* (the broader Buddhist community), needed me to do that. Wanting has not really been part of the picture.

I also don't feel that I have become a teacher in some permanent sense. It is a major mistake to identify with being a teacher. That is just another form of selfing, and attachment. Instead, I think of Zen teaching as a role that I have taken on, aware of the responsibilities that come with it. Here the symbolism of putting on a different sort of robe at the time of transmission is useful. I haven't changed at some molecular level from "mere student" to "enlightened teacher": I'm still the same human being. I take on the robe and the staff and hope to pass them on before I die, or before illness or circumstance tells me that I must set them down.

And I'm writing this book mainly because I'm scared to death of screwing it up. I've seen so many lovely, caring people who I've known for decades end up causing division and damage. I know that I carry the same seeds of harm in myself. I need the support of—and accountability to—a healthy sangha. I need the same from other institutions and structures that up to this point have seemed to be failing badly in assuring safe practice.

## THE DANGER OF SELF-INFLATION

My experience in talking with Zen teachers is that most believe that, while *others* may have inflated egos, they themselves are humble. This is often a delusion. Please consider the following:

> Often we don't notice the buildup of pride, which grows out of commendable self-confidence, but then climbs unnoticed until we find that we are stiffly defending our position and our patch. An old Hasidic teacher compared the unnoticed inflation of pride to taking a journey by carriage. We look out of the window and swear that the country-side is level. Only when we begin the sharp descent do we realize the preceding slow climb of our pride.[112]

To some degree it's probably inevitable that students will hold a somewhat idealized image of teachers, at least early in their practice. Some Buddhist writings seem to encourage reverence and an attitude of subservience. When we are new students, we may also need to project onto teachers our own confused intellectual understandings of what it means to "be enlightened," simply to bring those beliefs to the surface. (Seeing through them, we hope, develops with greater spiritual maturation.) But when students treat us as exceptionally wise and special, this creates a feedback effect on unwary teachers. If we don't recognize what's happening we will start, as one of the other participants in a Buddhist Healthy Boundaries course I took put it, to "believe our own PR."

As I mentioned earlier, I've started calling this trap the "gold rakusu effect." Having only transitioned from wearing a black (student) rakusu to a gold one a few years ago, I think I now have a good visceral sense of how the slow creep of pride comes about. Almost immediately people who always before had just been my fellow students started to demonstrate respect, deference, and gratitude in a thousand tiny but cumulatively important ways. In general, sangha members started to listen more to what I had to say. I noticed one apologizing in a situation where I was at fault. A few started to stand back as I pass by.

Some acts of deference seem spontaneous, while others (such as standing back) may actually have been taught as part of a sangha's culture. Unless you are very aware of this going on, it's easy for it to go to your head. Admiration, gratitude, and reverence directed towards the Dharma can be easily confused with admiration of the teacher themself in the minds of both students and teachers.

Also, importantly, after my initial transmission I was admitted to the meetings of my home sangha's other transmitted teachers (who had not yet left). In such meetings I could see interpersonal bonds and shared opinions being formed and reinforced. When teachers (who may often be old friends, even spouses, and at least respected colleagues) mirror attitudes of confidence and superiority back and forth among themselves, the feedback effect compounds mightily. And it's insidious. I could talk about appropriate humility all day and could sincerely believe that I personally have not become proud…as long as my favorite "mirrors" keep telling me that I'm doing just fine.

Finally, the widespread notion that teachers lead the sangha, mentioned earlier, can add to ego inflation. Teachers may feel obligated by the example of ancestor abbots and the needs of the sangha to display strong leadership, confidence, and decisiveness. Both teachers and students may expect that the teachers be consulted, trusted, and followed on all sangha decisions—whether or not these are anywhere near the teachers' actual areas of wisdom, expertise, or responsibility. During Betrayal #2 our transmitted teachers considered themselves to be experts not only on the Dharma, but on teacher misconduct and other matters of board business. They mostly declined opportunities to learn about the experience of the students or the effects of abuse.

This failure to learn did not come about, I believe, because they are bad people. They were and continue to be, by and large, very good people in most regards. They generously volunteer time from their otherwise busy lives to try to guide others in the Dharma. But the culture of our sangha and the resultant feedback set them up to fall into the very human trap of ego inflation.[113] They were (over-)confident that they "knew best."

Is the only solution to erase the teacher-student distinction? I don't think so. While students often teach and teachers must always continue to learn, I believe there still is a role for specialized teacher training and teacher-only activities. But I think that creating sangha cultures and other institutions that remind teachers of our limitations and the reality of the temptation to pride may offer a better path.

## TEACHER TRAINING

To be more specific, the expectation of what it takes to become a teacher includes "mind to mind transmission" in the sense of mutual recognition "in the room." Prospective teachers have also likely engaged in some study of the scriptures and displayed some proficiency in rituals and form. Completion of a koan curriculum may also be required. The transmitting teacher probably has some idea that their successor is articulate enough to deliver Dharma talks and has sufficient interpersonal skills to be able to give guidance to students in individual meetings. One hopes that the teacher-to-be has also substantially integrated their insight into their life in the relative world. And the transmitting teacher probably needs to believe that the teacher-to-be is not using Zen to bypass major psychological developmental tasks.

While these seem to have been the prevailing criteria for the training I experienced, I don't believe they're sufficient. These criteria, alone, may tend to build up the recipient's ego and confidence. Public acknowledgement of one's accomplishments in these areas may make teachers prone to believing that they are more advanced, and more deserving of authority (or money, or emotional support, or sexual gratification, or trust, or deference), than is healthy. Teachers are then ripe for being tripped up by our own clay feet and doing tremendous harm. While teachers still must be held personally accountable for their misconduct, I believe that widespread misunderstanding of transmission and deficient training are also doing no one any favors. There needs to be investigation and real accountability at the training level as well.

I can think of a few things that could, it seems to me, work to help create more trustworthy authorized teachers:

- An extended program of education about the spiritual power that students inevitably project onto teachers, and about student vulnerability, transference, countertransference, teaching ethics, and possible ill effects of meditation. The teacher's absolute responsibility for maintaining appropriate boundaries must be stressed.

- A requirement that one make an explicit, detailed, and public commitment to putting students' and the sangha's needs above one's own, before beginning to teach.
- A careful evaluation, undertaken with feedback from others, of one's strengths and limitations, and formation of a realistic idea of what one can (and what one can't or shouldn't) offer while in the role of teacher.

Those may seem pretty obvious given earlier discussion. My last suggestion is a bit more speculative, though I think it may be important:

- An expectation that one will regularly take sabbaticals from teaching, returning during these periods of time to an entirely student role. We tend to see the workings of power much better from below than from above. A few months away from our accustomed position of status—perhaps even sitting as a beginner in a different tradition—may, I believe, help us keep the humility we so desperately need, yet so often leave behind.

Still, just working on teacher preparation is not enough. Though I was a career educator, I have come to see education's limitations. Some of the people who betrayed students most harmfully in my home sangha had plenty of book knowledge! Some even had advanced degrees in psychology, counseling, or law. They had certainly learned about (or even taught) professional ethics and/or fiduciary duty. We also need to examine other structures at the sangha level and beyond that have led to harm, and how these might be changed to help prevent it instead.

## FINAL THOUGHTS

At the heart of Zen practice is a mysterious, mystical power. It can free us from being trapped in our limited karmic selves and open us up to our participation in the vast, wonderful, terrible, immediate present world in ways that we could never even imagine. This Buddha nature is our birthright. This mysterious power is not something that only teachers have, and which they will impart to us if we obediently follow their instructions. We need to have faith that *we*, ourselves, are Buddha, Dharma, and Sangha.

Yet most of us could also benefit greatly from a safe sangha environment and, perhaps especially in our earlier stages of practice, interactions with a trustworthy spiritual friend. "Trustworthy" is the important word.

7

# SANGHAS ARE IMPORTANT

TEACHERS CAN be helpful or lose the Zen Way and do harm. Local Zen communities can also be critical aids, or veer away and do harm themselves, compound the harm caused by teacher misconduct, or create environments in which harm is more likely to occur.

Convert Buddhist sanghas in non-Asian cultures come in a great variety. Some are huge and thoroughly institutionalized, while others are small and informal. Some have one teacher, others many, and some none. They are subject to different laws depending on location and level of formality. Even within Zen, they differ depending on the national origin of the ancestral teachers, and within that, the sects that formed within those nations. Unlike in Asia, they tend to be mostly populated by lay people living in their own homes and often with families. And the move to lay practice is only one of the many adaptations made in the transition.

I write mostly from the experience of the Sanbo Kyodan and White-Plum-related sitting groups and organizations in which I've practiced. These have varied from tiny and teacherless to large with ambitions to create a uniquely American "school." In these, I have had recent cause to think about how Zen sanghas can create, add to, or become fertile soil for damage. And I've thought about what could be done to help sanghas stay healthy.

## THE HEALTHY LOCAL COMMUNITY

In a very old Buddhist story, Shakyamuni's cousin and attendant Ananda one day says to him, "I think that half of the spiritual life is spiritual friendship." Shakyamuni Buddha corrected him saying, "Do not say this, Ananda! Spiritual friendship is not half the spiritual life. It's the entire spiritual life!"

My practice isn't just about me and getting my head on straight. Nor is it limited to the relationship between me and my teacher, if I have one. We say that the whole universe is interdependent and that we save all beings. The multiple face-to-face relationships we have in our local Zen communities are our first opportunities to both strengthen our practice and put it to the test!

Healthy communities create opportunities for formal practice such as weekly sits and less frequent retreats. Most also offer classes or discussion groups for learning more about Zen or studying the precepts. When they function well local sanghas become systems of beneficial mutual support. By participating in a healthy sangha we are reminded again and again to wake up...and wake up again...and wake up again. Others can often see our stuck spots and delusions more easily than we can ourselves, and we can often see theirs. Lifelong friendships can develop as members sit and work together. Sanghas can also engage in organized service projects in their local areas or coordinated work on social, racial, or environmental justice at a larger scale.

All this takes organization, labor, and often at least some amount of monetary support. Sanghas are supported by giving (*dana*) which may take many forms. If you really want to be part of a sangha, and not just use the sangha by showing up when you feel the need, you should expect to contribute, too. There are many service and leadership roles.

A sangha is, nonetheless, a group of living, breathing, flawed human beings. Just as we may idealize our teacher, we may hold the illusion that our sangha should somehow be a place outside of normal life. Given that it is populated by people who are either enlightened or well on their way, we think, what could go wrong? We may read about the "harmony of the sangha" and think it means that everything should be peaceful and calm. We come and chant together and sit in silence. We imagine that meetings of the leadership are characterized by mutual respect and happy consensus. I sure wore those rose-colored glasses for much too long!

But real Zen is about *our lives*, right here, not about escaping from their messiness and complications. We can be assured that disagreements will arise. We can count on there being a difficult personality in the mix (or two or three). Some projects will fail or go off course. There will be difficult decisions to make. Mistakes will happen. Achieving coordinated action as an organization usually involves developing some level of specialization and hierarchy. And then there is no escaping the fact that someone might be tempted to abuse their power, however broad or limited it might be.

If we really trust that everything is included in the Buddha Dharma, that even *this* is "it," then we can see that even dissonance is "harmony." And that these sorts of very human behaviors aren't actually problems. They are just more of the universe universing, and occasions for us to try to respond (with wisdom and compassion) rather than react based on our old patterns. A healthy sangha will likely have developed robust ethics codes, governance structures, and policies in advance of disagreements and misconduct arising, so as to be prepared. It will make every attempt to assure that all its leaders and members understand their respective responsibilities. When someone fails in their responsibilities, the healthy sangha will provide a path to accountability and repair. It will seek to develop a culture of inclusivity, openness, and transparency. It will seek to develop structures of communication that allow all voices to be heard and the wisdom of the sangha to come forth. Many sanghas have adopted authentic practices of "council" or "circle practice" for this purpose.[114]

I will say more about some of the particulars of structure and culture later in this chapter. But you will be more motivated to pay attention if I first describe how badly things can go wrong!

## HOW SANGHAS CAN CAUSE HARM

The societies we live in are rife with beliefs that say that some people are worth less than others. The dividing lines include gender identity, sexual orientation, race, national origin, age, and so on. Sanghas may—whether due to inexperience, unconscious biases, or outright intent—harm those not in the dominant group. For example, do we honor or simply appropriate the Asian traditions that inspire us? Yet, at the same time, some of those traditions, such as bowing and serving food, may resonate poorly with people who associate these with submission of their group in the past, often enforced by violence. I don't have answers for how to negotiate these issues, but I do know that we have to be involved in doing so.

I've also seen that sanghas, even non-cultish ones, may do harm by asking for too much from people. Just as it may be hard to say "no" to a teacher, a sangha member who loves and trusts the sangha may be tempted to overcommit their personal resources to the organization. While requesting excessive financial donations can be part of the problem, I've particularly witnessed overtaxing in regard to *time and energy.* While I will be eternally grateful to the courageous board members who brought Greater Boston through Betrayal #2, there is no doubt that they suffered personal harm in the process, beyond the direct betrayal trauma of the misconduct. They put in endless hours dealing with the crisis at the expense of their jobs, the health of their marriages, their moods, and their sleep. The work of the boards previous to them (when we split from Boundless Way and moved the zendo), and after them (Betrayal # 3, coming up in the next chapter), also put enormous stress on those who volunteered for board service. We are still struggling with the issue of how to get organizational needs met without burning people out.

But, as with teachers, a very deep spiritual harm is brought about when sanghas fail to adequately prevent or address abuses of power.

### INSTITUTIONAL BETRAYAL

Psychology professor Jennifer J. Freyd, who coined the term "betrayal blindness" (discussed in chapter 5) also coined the term "institutional betrayal." This refers to "the failure to prevent or respond supportively to wrongdoings within the institution when there is a reasonable expectation of protection."[115] She and her colleagues have studied this in workplaces, schools, health care organizations and courts. Institutional betrayal often has *more* harmful and long-lasting effects than the initial abuse. While the initial wrongdoing might be attributed to one errant individual, institutional betrayal signals that whole communities and systems are stacked against the victim.

Zen teacher and psychoanalyst Barry Magid similarly describes institutional silence as the community-level equivalent to a scenario that often comes up in therapy. When, for example, other family members fail to prevent or respond to child abuse the child grows up experiencing "the world…as a passive, unresponsive bystander to their suffering." While the therapist can't undo the original harm they can help it be spoken about and named. This restores the client's sense of agency. "Sadly," Magid notes, "there has too often been a repetition of the scenario of the failed witness in Buddhist communities where abuse has taken place."[116]

I can testify that these insights are highly applicable to the institution of the local sangha. If Zen sanghas *were* effective at preventing abuse, most of this book would be unnecessary! And there is a marked tendency for sanghas to respond to abuses with their own repetition of "Deny, Attack, Reverse Victim and Offender."

If one studies the history of responses of sangha leaders and sanghas to the abuses of power by teachers, one tends to overwhelmingly see just such a pattern. The abuse is denied or minimized. The victim is accused of lying, or of causing disruption in the sangha, or of being insufficiently spiritual. The teacher stays on in their spiritual leadership role while the victim silently leaves the community. This pattern may repeat itself over years or decades as student after student is exploited. It may take major scandals involving lawsuits and national press coverage to make sangha leaders pay even the most minimal attention to misconduct within their group. And then the response may still be one of denial or countersuits. If you look into the histories of the abuses mentioned in chapter 5 and their consequences, you'll see this pattern over and over again.

Why does it happen? Senior teachers and those in their inner circles have built strong bonds of trust among themselves. When presented with an allegation that one of your long-time friends or honored teachers has committed an abuse one may naturally find it difficult to believe that they are capable of such bad behavior. Such loyalty may be considered a good thing because it creates and sustains bonds among people. Yet it also creates a dualistic separation between the trusted "in" group" and the distrusted "out" group.[117] When the out-group is less powerful, dismissing their concerns preserves not only the harmony of the in-group but also its power and authority.

How can you really tell whether there is abuse going on, and if so, who is causing the abuse? Relying on feelings can be misleading. If you rely only on feelings, and especially feelings of trust, you will likely act in a biased and unfair way. Perhaps you trust a person because they have a long history of trustworthy behavior. But isn't it still possible that they screwed up *this* time? Or, more dangerously, perhaps the person gained your trust by using the manipulative "how to get people to trust you" communication techniques I described earlier. While the closeness of a community encourages the morality of loyalty, enacting the ethics of fairness and care for the vulnerable requires that such interpersonal loyalties be set aside.

Either way, when there is a difference in power and a chance that power is being abused, the next step must be some actual fair-minded and reasonable investigation of the facts. What were the actions involved? What words were said? Is there written evidence? Are there witnesses? Which story is more consistent and credible? While it is difficult if not impossible to fully discern someone's inner intention, advice such as "follow the money" encourages a fair investigator to look into probable motives.

Besides appeals to feelings and in-group loyalty, there are related manipulative techniques for avoiding fair-minded investigation. One is to encourage adjudicating bodies to immediately regard allegations of abuse as unverifiable differences in verbal claims—as "he said, she said." Yet it's impossible to know if a claim is unverifiable until *after* you've made a serious attempt to verify it. Another technique is to imply that to investigate would be to give in to disreputable desires to finger-point and blame and in itself would be an offence against the teacher. Mediation of a "problem in interpersonal relations" may be mis-prescribed as a substitute. Yet another avoidance strategy is arguing that to investigate would be "to stay mired in the past." While it can seem wise and progressive to stress being forward-looking actions, such advice drops an impenetrable curtain over the abuser's harm-causing actions. Lastly, a group may say it will do an investigation, but then do it in a way that is far from fair-minded.

A fair investigation would allow a sangha (or teacher group, as will be discussed in a later chapter) to apply *good judgment*. Good judgment is not judgmentalism, but rather combines wise discernment with compassion. It is not harsh, vengeful, or blaming. It is not based on personal loyalties to either the perpetrator of harm or to the victim. And that good judgment should continue on after the investigation into the prescription of effective remedies. Follow-through to make sure these are implemented is necessary as well. Those with responsibility of caring for the sangha should seek the truth, name harms, call for accountability, and—above all—seek the healing of those harmed.

### AND THE PRICE OF INSTITUTIONAL COURAGE

My home sangha, Greater Boston, has thus far been an outlier in terms of the ultimate result regarding Betrayal #2. In our case, the teacher left, and the student stayed on. But this doesn't mean that institutional betrayal didn't occur at all.

At the time of the abuse, we had two parallel power structures. The board of directors, which had no transmitted teachers as voting members, was in charge of the "business" end of the sangha. The transmitted teachers (actually, only a subset of them according to the bylaws) were in charge of guiding spiritual practice. But the specifics of this division were not very clear. We had an ethics policy that was vague and outdated. A marked difference of views arose.

The board members, as well as some others of us, studied the literature on clergy sexual abuse and the legal obligations of boards. As a result, we realized that our first responsibility was to come to the aid of the injured student. Next in priority was the well-being of the sangha at large, with our former spiritual director, Juin, included in this concern for healing. We felt that true compassion for him would include requiring real accountability. If he could also be encouraged to engage in a serious, supervised program of rehabilitation, a future as a Zen teacher would not necessarily be lost. We knew it was the board's responsibility to deal with the misconduct. As mentioned earlier the board suspended Juin, later accepted his resignation, and even later put up a very brief note about the misconduct on the sangha website.

The other transmitted teachers at Greater Boston (by the time of the disclosure there were six), however, saw things differently. I believe that they, like me, had never been asked during their training as teachers to make a commitment to the well-being of students. Nor were they educated in how to recognize and safely use the power that students attribute to them in order to merit students' trust. There was no apparent effort on their part to learn about power and abuse, or about the legal responsibilities and authority of nonprofit boards.

In fact, they talked down to anyone who attempted to inform them. I witnessed them treating intelligent and well-informed board members as if they were unruly children. It was implied that the board members' commitment to the care of the sangha, rather than to carrying out the teachers' orders, was a sign of disrespect.

Ironically, the only non-teacher they appeared to regard as a well-informed and independent adult was the student victim. They seemed to ignore the fact that it was precisely the student's trust and respect for the spiritual director that had made her vulnerable. They tended to view the student as a consenting adult. Some of them said that the primary moral injury was adultery, that the primary victim was the spiritual director's family, and that the victim was co-responsible for the harm. Some resisted using words like "abuse," or even "misconduct," to describe what he had done, preferring to refer to his "mistake." The teachers seemed to think that the fact that he sought therapy (with someone of his own choosing), along with speaking at a premature ceremony of apology (that they arranged), pretty much resolved the problem.

Because they couldn't understand why the student victim and many others of us were so upset, they offered little or no support. "You need to move past this and get back to the Dharma," we heard from some. The few formal Dharma talks that might be taken as vaguely alluding to the abuse seemed to imply that it was students' understanding that was the source of our continuing distress. For example, one was on the precept of "not finding fault with others" and another on a koan in which a "delightful" teacher knocks the chair out from under a student.[118] Some of us were told in private interviews with teachers that it was not appropriate, in that context, to discuss the abuse. More than one teacher told me that they did not consider the spiritual and emotional distress of students—especially any student who was not "theirs"—to be their concern. Nor did any seem to think they had the least bit of responsibility for the misconduct in spite of it being caused by their teaching peer.

And they attacked. The transmitted teachers accused the board of being too harsh on the offender. And because we were (in their view) being insufficiently deferential to their opinions, a number of us were subjected to various sorts of accusations and verbal abuse. Various of us were accused of being mentally unbalanced, or of drowning in a victim mentality. One teacher accused me of being interested in getting "the salacious details" because I let the student talk to me.[119]

One by one, these transmitted teachers all abandoned Greater Boston over the next year, taking their sitting groups with them. While many of them initially claimed they did this because they only wanted to work with their own small groups, they soon created a new overarching group. Because they had minimized the abuse, their students also tended to remain betrayal-blind. Many friendships of years and even decades were cracked or broken as those of us aware of teacher power fought to create a safer sangha, while our old friends followed their teachers in departing.

Let me describe to you what this felt like from the student side. It was as if our spiritual director were a bus driver and crashed the sangha vehicle into an embankment at high speed. We passengers lay broken and bleeding on the side of the road. The most-harmed student needed immediate intensive care. We expected that health professionals (read: our Zen teachers) would arrive and help us out. But some of them drove right by. Others stopped and offered us advice on nutrition and exercise.

Some got in the way of us trying to bind up each other's wounds. Some, believing we were overreacting, tried to get us to move on by kicking us. Eventually, they drove off to have breakfast together.

Living through this didn't just feel like Betrayal #2, as I have labeled it for the purposes of this book. It felt like Betrayal #2 (the spiritual director), #3, #4, #5, #6, #7, and #8 (the other teachers) spaced weeks or months apart. This was exhausting. So while the board side of sangha leadership held fast, the teaching side of the institutional leadership only compounded the initial harm. It was in this environment that I became, just weeks after receiving the first stage of teaching transmission, the interim spiritual director. Everyone else with transmission had left or was thinking of leaving.

What does an institution look like when it *doesn't* betray the victim? Faith Trust Institute's *Responding to Spiritual Leader Misconduct* is a guidebook written in conjunction with a number of Zen teachers. It outlines seven "Elements of Justice-Making":

1. Truth-telling
The victim-survivor needs to give voice to the reality of the abuse.

2. Acknowledging the violation
Someone who matters, like the governing body or board, needs to hear the truth, name the abuse, and condemn it as wrong.

3. Compassion is to suffer with the victim
The powers-that-be need to listen to and suffer with the victim. Wait until later for problem-solving.

4. Protecting the vulnerable
The powers-that-be need to take steps to prevent further abuse to the victim and others.

5. Accountability
The powers-that-be need to confront the perpetrator and impose negative consequences. This step makes repentance possible for the abuser.

> 6. Restitution
> The powers-that-be need to make symbolic restoration of what was taken, to give a tangible means to acknowledge the wrongfulness of the abuse and the harm done, and to bring about healing (e.g., payment for therapy).
> 7. Vindication is not vengeance
> It means to set the victim-survivor free from the suffering caused by the abuse. Some experiences of justice can vindicate the victim-survivor and free them to even consider "forgiveness."[120]

Sanghas would do well to follow these guidelines. Such sanghas display institutional *courage*.[121]

## CRITICAL STRUCTURAL ELEMENTS

As I look around, and at our experience in Boston, I've seen how weaknesses in some critical structures significantly contribute to difficulties in addressing abuses of power.

### ETHICAL CODES

Very rarely do sanghas spell out what kind of behavior they expect from teachers, other sangha leaders, and other sangha members. Some sanghas never get around to creating an Ethics Policy at all...or perhaps deliberately avoid it. Looking at the websites of Zen groups, you sometimes find that their "policy" is simply a list of the sixteen Zen precepts. While the precepts form the ethical foundation of our practice, they don't provide much guidance when cases of abuse arise.

Buddhist ethical precepts are often said to be practiced on three levels:

- At the literal level, a precept is simply a rule to be followed. Do not kill, speak falsely, misuse sex, etc. But that doesn't always help much. We "kill" every time we step on a bug or take an antibiotic. It's impossible to never kill.

- At the compassionate level, we consider the particular circumstances and the relative importance of the different precepts before acting. But we aren't told *which* precept is most important right here and right now.
- At the absolute level, there is no longer any talk of "good" or "bad." Contemporary Zen teacher Nancy Baker writes about having learned this to refer to a level of "nondual moral freedom" that arises when "the precepts are no longer separate from us." It might be thought that this applies to a person who is very advanced—is so advanced that they follow the precepts simply by doing what comes naturally. Baker quotes St. Augustine, "'Love God, and do what thou wilt.'"[122]

So how we actually *live* the precepts is a complicated, life-long exploration!

It is possible for the precepts to actually be weaponized to *suppress* attention to abuse and to facilitate betrayal trauma and DARVO. People who try to speak up about misconduct may find themselves quickly silenced by a literal interpretation of the sixth Grave Precept which says that one should not "find fault with others." Or letting outsiders know about abuses in Zen might be labeled, out of concern for institutional reputation, as violating number ten, "defaming the Three Treasures." When one works with the precepts at the compassionate level, it may not be clear that, when someone is doing harm (in the name of the Dharma!), prioritizing a literal interpretation of "speaking truthfully" (number four) is what is necessary.

The absolute level of the precepts can also be weaponized. Someone who believes they've really "arrived" may be convinced that they no longer need to follow the precepts because they are one with them. In fact, they may believe that the precepts follow *them*. If someone perceives themselves to be thoroughly good and spiritually elevated, then it follows that *whatever* they do is, by (their) definition, good and spiritually elevated. And if a student idealizes them and (over-)trusts them, the student will go along with this ruse. Given that we all engage in at least some degree of spiritual bypassing our very human shadows, this often leads to big trouble. Any cruelty can be rationalized by such an appeal.

While Baker quotes St. Augustine in the introduction to her book, later on she makes an important clarification. The absolute level of living the precepts is not some permanent state. Rather, it arises in "moments" and must continue to be developed through lifelong practice. Any of us may visit it from time to time, but nobody—even the most esteemed teacher—lives there.

Which of the precepts and which level is most important for ensuring safe practice? I'd suggest that this sign be printed in red and posted on the inside of every Zen teacher's private meeting-room door:

While "f*" could be taken literally (Grave Precept three, "not misusing sex") or metaphorically (any of the other precepts), the level of interpretation in this case is easy. It's literal. Do not screw, or screw up, your students. Sometimes we just need a giant stop sign.

Creating a safer environment means spelling out clearly what sorts of relationships and behaviors are appropriate and healthy, which ones are not (i.e., are f*ing), and which may need to be subjected to a more extensive discernment process. Most of these rules should focus on the teacher-student relationship because of the wide differential of power. The code should require that teachers undergo training concerning abuse and healthy boundaries. (Greater Boston's revised policy required completion of the Buddhist Healthy Boundaries course.[123]) It should forbid sexual involvement with students by teachers and advise at least high caution about teachers taking on dual roles. It should spell out what sorts of gifts and payments can, and cannot, be accepted by teachers.

Other parts of the code may apply to other sangha leaders, or to sangha participants in general. Ideally, a mediation-type process may be outlined for cases where there are disagreements *between people of relatively even power*. Such disputes are often referred to as "interpersonal conflict," and the mediator is expected to take a position of neutrality.

A more serious plan of investigation, consequences, and remediation, however, must be spelled out for dealing with complaints about *abuses of power*. It should *not* tell victims of such abuse that the responsibility to report belongs to *them*. Mediation should *not* be prescribed for difficulties in which there is a substantial power differential. When abuse is believed to have occurred the sangha board *cannot* be neutral. In order to carry out their "duty of care," they need to prioritize healing for the victim and accountability for the offender—even if that offender is their own teacher.

What about if a student and teacher claim that their sexual attraction is mutual? It is still unethical for them to act on the attraction, at least right away. As mentioned earlier, good ethics policies will prescribe breaking off the teacher-student relationship and observing a waiting period before beginning the romantic relationship. If the teacher-student relationship has been long-term, a substantial "cooling off" period—I've seen two or three *years* mentioned in some literatures—will be necessary for the student to get out from under any spiritual thrall.

But what if this particular teacher and student only met privately once or twice? Or the student only heard a Dharma talk given by the teacher? And perhaps the two only differ slightly in their status as clergy or spiritual teachers? One factor the board should consider is the emotional and spiritual maturity of the parties. A less mature student may be star-struck after only the most minimal contact with a "Zen master." A more settled person, on the other hand, might initially relate to a teacher more as a fellow human. If the two are of similar and mature ages, have many common interests outside of Zen, are similar in other types of status, and are both unmarried, a brief teacher-student encounter could be barely relevant. The waiting period in this case might only be a month or two. The cases I've heard about, unfortunately, generally bear little resemblance to this special case.

An ethics policy should also include a process for starting an investigation. It should indicate which ethical concerns can be brought to an ethics ombudsperson, committee, or circle, and which (including cases of abuse) should go directly to the board. Many plans then also spell out how the investigation is to be conducted. In order to have a fair investigation, boards should strongly consider hiring a neutral outside investigator to dig up the facts. Even if sangha members are able to overcome their personal loyalties and seek out the truth, their findings could be later discredited by accusations of bias. Plans to make the ethics policy a living practice through discussion and activities that include all sangha members should also be put in place.

Putting together such an ethics policy is not an easy task. The ethics document written for the Zen Center of Los Angeles, in the wake of very serious misconduct crises in both 1983 and 1997, is exemplary. It runs to fifty-one pages. At Greater Boston, we revised our ethics policy substantially in the wake of Betrayal #2. While, at only eight pages, it could benefit from greater elaboration, it would have been invaluable to have had something even this clear in place when the crisis hit.

Making ethics part of the living, breathing culture of the sangha is even harder. At Greater Boston, we had all teachers and other leaders read and sign our policy. At our 2022 annual meeting we held a covenant ceremony at which each group (teachers, board members, practice and working group leaders, and general members) read out loud a summary of our practical and ethical commitments to each other. However, the ethics council, charged in our policy with organizing programs of preventative education, fizzled out quickly (for reasons including a health crisis in the family of its leader). When we hit Betrayal #3 (yet to be described), it was clear that, covenants or not, we still weren't all on the same page.

## BOARDS

Many sanghas start out with just a few members. There may not be many decisions to be made. Concerning questions of formal practice and ritual, the teacher (or in the absence of a teacher, the most experienced student) usually takes the lead. But as they grow and look to rent or buy spaces for sitting groups and retreats, or pay stipends, things like funding and insurance start to be important. In the U.S. this often involves getting incorporated as a 501(c)3 nonprofit organization. The organization then is a legal entity separate from the individuals in it at any given time. It can then accept tax-deductible donations and enter into contracts. Such organizations are required to have a board of directors.

The board is legally entrusted with the well-being of the sangha. Board members have "duty of obedience" that requires them to follow the law and carry out the organization's stated mission. They have a "duty of loyalty" that requires them to place the organization's interests above their own at all times. Finally, they have a "duty of care" that requires them to take their board duties seriously: they need to be active in looking out for the organization's interests. I created the following figure as an illustration of this for a Greater Boston membership meeting.

**Legal View of GBZC**

Mass. Laws for Nonprofits and other laws (e.g. about harassment, etc.)

### GBZC Articles of Organization

- Stating our purpose, directors, and address
- Approved by a ⅔ membership vote

### GBZC Bylaws

- Details of organization (**including existence of Practice Groups, a Senior Teaching Community, and Committees within GBZC**)
- Details of member and director meetings and voting
- Approved by a two-thirds majority membership vote

### GBZC Board of Directors

Elected by the membership by majority vote.

1. Duty of Care: Take care of the nonprofit by ensuring prudent use of all assets, including facility, people, and good will;
2. Duty of Loyalty: Ensure that the nonprofit's activities and transactions are, first and foremost, advancing its mission; Recognize and disclose conflicts of interest; Make decisions that are in the best interest of the nonprofit corporation.
3. Duty of Obedience: Ensure that the nonprofit obeys applicable laws and regulations; follows its own bylaws; and that the nonprofit adheres to its stated corporate purposes/mission.

Yet sanghas often continue to be, in practice, led entirely by the teacher or teachers. Teachers may serve on the board or have such influence on the board that they might as well be in charge. The case where the teacher(s) have the necessary skills, devotion to the well-being of the sangha, and humility to do this well seems to be rare. Sometimes in small sanghas, though, this level of teacher leadership may be unavoidable.

Teacher dominance can cause boards to ignore or neglect their responsibilities to the sangha. Perhaps accustomed to deferring to the teacher in spiritual practice, board members may carry this over to prioritizing the teacher's interests in other areas. In some cases, the board may neglect its duties because "the law" is demonized and seen as conflict-oriented and stodgy, in contrast to ideals of infinite empathy or "crazy wisdom." Or neglect of the legal duties may come about simply because board members are usually unpaid volunteers who have busy lives and other responsibilities. It's just easier to assume that the teacher knows best!

From my experience, it seems common for board members to believe that their responsibility is to *serve their teacher* and that their jurisdiction is limited to matters of finance and logistics. Both of these beliefs are incorrect, and both lead to disaster in the case of teacher abuse of power.

Board members have both an ethical and legal responsibility to make their community a safe place to practice—to take care of their people. It is their responsibility to take steps to try to prevent misconduct and to address it when it happens—even if the misconduct was committed by the sangha's founding teacher. It is *their* responsibility to do this, whether or not the victim(s) bring a lawsuit against the organization or the teacher. It is *their* responsibility to do this, even if teachers or outside consultants try to dominate the process.

Thinking that their responsibilities are primarily financial, some boards believe that dealing with reported abuse is mostly about protecting the sangha from expensive lawsuits, especially in cases of sexual abuse. Really? Losing some cash (or having one's insurance company lose some cash) is more important than remediating the devastating harm that such abuse can cause the victim and witnesses? Financial concerns should trump ethical ones? A sangha that doesn't prioritize doing the right thing in the aftermath of abuse is confused in its understanding of Zen. However, in terms of preventing *future* abuses, both ethical and financial concerns point in the same direction: preventing abuse prevents both future harm to students *and* future possible lawsuits.

Everyone on the Greater Boston board at the time of Betrayal #2 erupted had been a long-time student of the spiritual director. This is actually not a strong structure. I've heard it suggested that a board should include a member or members from *outside* the sangha who might be more willing to call out bad behavior by a teacher. Our board was extremely fortunate to have some members familiar with both the law and the dynamics of abuse, and the other board members were willing to listen and read up on these topics.

More prosaic matters may also indicate a board's neglect of its duties. Lip service may be given to the ideal of transparency in decision-making, but what this means practically may remain opaque to the membership. A board may have no way to oversee subsidiary sitting groups or activities even though they are legally accountable for them. A board may never get around to keeping track of its votes, or writing down its policies, or setting up an ethics committee. These may all seem unnecessary in a "one happy family" sangha, but neglect of them will be seriously regretted if someone complains of harm.

## BYLAWS AND POLICIES

Mention bylaws and you are sure to evoke yawns of boredom and disinterest. But the bylaws, along with the articles of incorporation (that were filed with the state if you are incorporated as a nonprofit) are critical. The Articles state your mission; the Bylaws state the allocation of powers and responsibilities. These should be codified in formal policies and procedures documents. You will rue their absence or vagueness should abuses of power occur in your sangha!

I remember that there was a lot of talk about prevention of abuses and democratic governance when Boundless Way was created. Like Greater Boston later on, Boundless Way had two parallel power structures: one of senior teachers to govern the "spiritual" aspects and another of mostly non-teachers to run the "business" aspects. The teacher group was, among other things, supposed to provide a check on abuses through mutual monitoring. One of the three founders wrote publicly that when a fourth teacher was added to the teaching group, he came on as a "full equal."[124] Yet, when push came to shove, it turned out that there was nothing in the bylaws that set out decision-making rules for the teaching group. Instead, after that particular founder retired, the remaining two founding teachers, from what I understand, insisted on what they called "consensus" decisions. Another teacher told me that this was double-speak for "you all can't change anything unless the two of us agree." Such was the underlying dynamic behind Betrayal #1.

Greater Boston had to quickly change its own bylaws when it morphed into an umbrella group for the sitting groups led by the teachers who left Boundless Way. While a good attempt was made, there were still parts that were vague, especially about the division of responsibilities between the two leadership groups. The transmitted teachers seemed to have the impression that they were in charge of everything they cared to opine about. Nothing was written down about how a lineage-authorized teacher might be judged worthy of being a teacher in our community, or how they might be expelled from it. These lacunae, along with the vagueness of the existing ethics policy, meant that the Greater Boston board had to wage even more of an uphill battle when responding to abuse.

After Betrayal #2, we put together what we thought would be a more adequate set of bylaws and policies. These spelled out the responsibilities of the board (i.e., including the responsibility for dealing with misconduct) and of the senior teachers (at the time, myself and one other teacher who was giving individual advice under supervision). I created the following figure as an illustration of the proposed bylaws and policies for a special Greater Boston membership meeting in March 2022. It was, except for a few small details, what we ended up adopting.

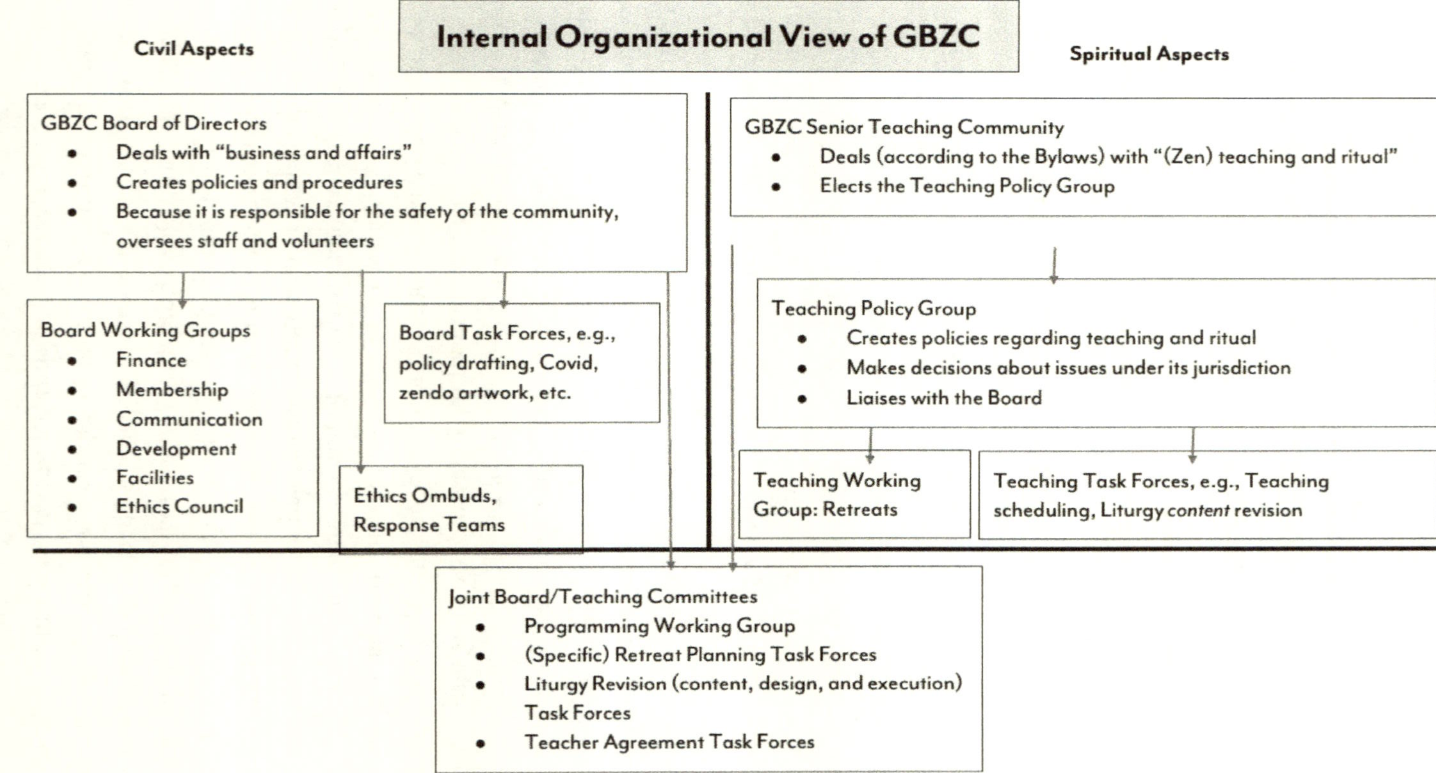
Internal Organizational View of GBZC
Civil Aspects
Spiritual Aspects
GBZC Board of Directors
• Deals with "business and affairs"
• Creates policies and procedures
• Because it is responsible for the safety of the community, oversees staff and volunteers
Board Working Groups
• Finance
• Membership
• Communication
• Development
• Facilities
• Ethics Council
Board Task Forces, e.g., policy drafting, Covid, zendo artwork, etc.
Ethics Ombuds, Response Teams
GBZC Senior Teaching Community
• Deals (according to the Bylaws) with "(Zen) teaching and ritual"
• Elects the Teaching Policy Group
Teaching Policy Group
• Creates policies regarding teaching and ritual
• Makes decisions about issues under its jurisdiction
• Liaises with the Board
Teaching Working Group: Retreats
Teaching Task Forces, e.g., Teaching scheduling, Liturgy content revision
Joint Board/Teaching Committees
• Programming Working Group
• (Specific) Retreat Planning Task Forces
• Liturgy Revision (content, design, and execution) Task Forces
• Teacher Agreement Task Forces

The idea was that teachers should be respected for their teaching, guidance of ritual, and—one hopes—modeling of wisdom and compassion, but that their opinions on matters such as budgeting, real estate, or misconduct should hold no more weight than that of any other sangha member or board member. The new bylaws specified that, while teaching authorization would still be done via traditional lineage lines, teachers would become *Greater Boston* teachers only after vetting by a committee, a vote of the board, and the signing of an agreement. It specified removal processes for teachers as well as for board members and sangha members.

I put a lot of work into drafting those bylaws myself, and then they were reviewed and revised by a committee and voted on by the membership. My hope was that these would put our sangha on solid ground organizationally. Such a shared leadership model would, I hoped, reduce stress, unreasonable expectations, and the potential for abuse. I believe the new bylaws and policies were a big improvement over what we had before, and I think this kind of model could likely work well in many sanghas. But I underestimated the level of punishment that comes with speaking out about abuses of power. What actually happened at Greater Boston, after the adoption of this new structure, is a topic for the next chapter.

## SANGHA CULTURE

Individual sanghas tend to have their own individual cultures. Especially in non-Asian contexts, where many adaptations have been made to practices that were standard in Asia, Zen culture shows up in a diversity of social forms and external representations. Can these be harmful? Are some forms better than others at preventing damage?

### FORMS AND RITUALS

We've had considerable discussion in our sangha recently about the Soto forms and rituals we've adopted. Of special concern are the ones that seem to delineate and reinforce hierarchical levels of status and authority.

Transmitted teachers, for example, wear special rakusus and robes and may carry various sticks and other props, none of which students are allowed to use. Students in our sangha until recently were expected to defer to teachers when, say, passing on the stairs, and to wait for them to take the first bite before eating during formal meal practice. There may be special processions and bows associated with teachers. Special titles and places in the zendo are further signs of distinction. Various rituals, such as morning bows and certain offerings of incense at sesshin are done only by teachers. Ceremonies such as those for receiving the precepts, and certainly those of teaching transmission, are only officiated by teachers. Only teachers give formal talks (*teishos*). Only teachers meet privately with individual students to give guidance. The roles of Zen priest or monk may carry other signs of distinction. Yet even among students there are some hierarchical distinctions: those who have not (yet) received the precepts do not wear a rakusu at all.

To the cynic—as well as to some of those who have been wounded over and over by teacher arrogance—the special stuff that attaches to teachers can seem to be nothing other than symbols designed to establish their power and protect their privilege. And there is no doubt that, even if a teacher is initially humble, such distinguishing and deferential practices could "go to their head" and inflate their ego. When that has happened, the tradition of teachers meeting privately with students becomes particularly prone to abuses.

The solution may seem to be a radical form of democracy—the equality of peers. Or perhaps teacher status and one-on-one meetings should be abandoned entirely in favor of group practice alone. At Greater Boston, we experimented with adding forms of group practice, such as Koan Salons and discussions modeled on *lectio divina* (Latin for "divine reading," a Christian monastic practice), from late 2021 to early 2023.

While I would not at all discourage group practice, I disagree with the idea of throwing away the teacher role and offering *only* group practice. This not only tosses away all titles and robes, but also endangers the *mythos* of Zen. It characterizes the teacher-student relationship as nothing more than a *logos*-based weighing of relative power. It runs the danger of reducing Zen practice to only a discussion group, disconnected from a wisdom tradition going back to ancient times. It doesn't so much rid the group of power dynamics as paper them over with a false equality. Even in a circle of peers, some will be more articulate, more charismatic, or maybe simply louder than others. They will be able to influence others (for good or ill), with or without a highfalutin title.

And because, as Aitken said, "The teacher of religious practice occupies an archetypal place in the psyches of the students,"[125] if one of the "peers" is an authorized teacher, power will present anyway. Since I consider teaching to be a role rather than an identity, I often wear my student rakusu rather than my teacher one when I'm not on duty—that is, not offering dokusan or a Dharma talk or conducting a ceremony. I need to stay aware, however, that I may still be on duty in a student's mind, and still be the target of their projections. And I think that too much of a buddy-buddy feeling could actually dilute the effectiveness of the forms. As I mentioned earlier, sometimes a student may need to temporarily idealize the person in the special robes on the way to recognizing the Buddha nature that they already are. Also, more dangerously, a teacher's pretense of humility may serve as a cover for pride and abuse.

Wouldn't it be better if inequalities were explicitly recognized, and those entrusted with power were thoroughly aware of (and kept in line with!) the responsibilities that come with it? That is the spirit of the yin-yang diagram introduced earlier. Holding this dynamic, ever-shifting, non-dominating, caring, potentially-enlightening-for-both-student-and-teacher relationship is not easy. But I believe it's our Zen way.

I just recently received the gift of a fresh view of "ancestral" traditions from reading Zenju Earthlyn Manuel's *The Shamanic Bones of Zen.*[126] I've long been aware that ritual and ceremony affect us at levels unreachable by our rational minds. However, my view of ancestors had been fairly cynical. (Perhaps you noticed this when I was discussing patriarchal lineages in chapter 6!) Manuel draws a link between Zen forms and even more ancient indigenous shamanic rituals. In a number of countries, including Japan, the shamans were traditionally women. Keizan, one of the founders of Soto Zen, put a great deal of faith in the ancient indigenous shamanic practices of Japan (as well as in women).[127] In this sense, honoring our ancestors and honoring the earth are ways of touching the sacred, the fullness and flow of life.

In Zen rituals and ceremonies, the officiant is playing the role of the traditional shaman. Manuel writes, "The trouble comes when those who are not aware of the spirit of the forms use them without understanding or to show achievement. It comes when the forms are used to establish authority or to sustain a hierarchy rather than as a portal to depth, insight, and wisdom for the sake of humanity.... It can seem as if the purpose of the temple and aspirants is to support the hierarchy whereas, in truth, the purpose of the hierarchy is to support those who are participating."[128]

It is not that *only* the teacher/shaman is in touch with the magical, mystical power, and everybody needs to rely on them, or get some of that "from" them. Manuel writes, "While in the wilderness of zazen, *we* are the shamans of our lives."[129] But because it *is* a wilderness, and so not very safe, it is good to have a guide. A guide is equipped with a "medicine bag" of experiences and teachings to help you find the way and avoid the traps.[130] That's the teacher role: to be a fellow human being who is more familiar with the Way and so able to provide some guidance. It's not clear to me, however, that one's spiritual guide needs to be a formally authorized Zen teacher. For some people, though, I think that will be true. For this reason, I believe that teachers and the forms pertaining to teachers need not to be discarded but to be re-enchanted with their deeper and truer meaning.

## TEACHER CULTURE

Most teachers I know are part of some sort of group. Boundless Way was structured with a teachers' council and Greater Boston followed suit. Even when there is only one teacher in a sangha, the ones I know at least have teacher friends from when they trained.

These groups create their own teacher culture. Ideally, they could be locations of continuing education, emotional support, collegial critique, and monitoring for the effects of personal shadow. One might fear that solo teachers might be more prone to ego inflation, being "one of a kind" in their local group, and that practice as a group might reduce this temptation. For these reasons, the Ethics Policy written at Greater Boston after Betrayal #2 required active participation in a local sangha teaching community.

What I've seen so far is that these local teacher communities mostly create or compound harm. The split of Greater Boston from Boundless Way (Betrayal #1) originated in dissension within the teaching group. Instead of being a place of support and collegial critique, it appeared to have turned into just another location where two teachers could assert their self-assigned superiority and exercise their manipulations. The Greater Boston teacher group seemed to me, during Betrayal #2, to become an echo chamber that reinforced teacher pride. I got the impression that they justified to each other their hard-heartedness toward the victim and animosity toward the board. Research confirms that professionals, including therapists and social workers, tend to not do much to address abuse committed by their peers. This might be because of personal friendship, a desire to not publicly embarrass their profession, fear of retaliation, or confusion about their responsibilities.[131]

After the departure, Greater Boston then drew on resources outside the larger sangha to create a new teacher community, as will be described in the next chapter. Our new teaching community seemed to get off to a good start. But it turned out that, within that group, we had very different attitudes toward teacher power and toward conflict.

## ATTITUDE TOWARDS CONFLICT

Zen teaches equanimity. Peace. Order. Silence. Respect. Inspiration. Our places of group practice can be places of refuge and calmness in a world on fire. We have our community, our sangha. Our sanghas often become spiritual homes for those cruelly excluded from or deeply disillusioned by their family of origin's faith community. Perhaps you have even been rejected by your family. Your group is led by a teacher who is warm and caring. People are empathetic. People are nice to each other. There's no conflict. We feel safe and loved. What more could you want? Because there are so few places in our contemporary world that make space for quiet, reflection, companionship, peace, and stability, it is tempting for sangha leaders to concentrate on supplying that.

But how about waking up? How about enlightenment? How about coming to know who we really are, and becoming intimate with the nirvana *and* samsara that are our lives? How about liberating all beings? How about hearing the cries of those harmed within our own community?

There's a reason that so many of those old Zen stories from China include hitting and shouting. While I wouldn't advise physical hitting, sometimes what we need is not comfort and solace but a good (metaphorical) kick in the pants. I remember hearing that "Jesus came to comfort the afflicted and afflict the comfortable." I think the same could be said about Shakyamuni Buddha. Zen equanimity is not about feeling only good things or becoming an emotionally flat-lined robot. Waking up requires setting aside a lot of old beliefs and habits that we had found comfortable. This is often very difficult and requires courage. Zen practice develops in us the inner ballast that allows us to ride the waves of nirvana and samsara as they come. We can experience our life fully without getting attached to joy and bliss or running away from conflict and pain. Facing directly into our lives, we can act as the hands of the bodhisattva of compassion in our raging world.

We do need places of refuge and peace—more at some times in our lives than others. However, if we always depend on conditions in the outer world to provide these for us, rather than learning to carry them *within* us in our hearts, we will be fragile. We'll continue to make our well-being dependent on circumstances. We will tend to turn away from suffering, controversy, conflict, confusion, or anything that disturbs us lest we be overwhelmed. But Zen that turns into a practice exclusively about *our* peace and *our* feelings of inadequacy and needs for support is not authentic.

I've heard it claimed that if we are truly compassionate, we will empathize with *all* beings and never engage in dispute or tolerate discord. I believe this is a grave distortion. As the earlier discussions of "unchosen empathy" and "blind compassion" pointed out, "niceness" can be a trap. Sometimes what is needed is a call for accountability. Zen isn't about avoiding the unpleasant.

Spiritual bypassing can affect whole communities, not just individuals. I've seen it in institutional form when sangha leaders take on an attitude of "don't scare the children" (i.e., the students) when conflict or misconduct arises in the inner circles. These are kept secret from the sangha at large in order to not disturb its—surface only!—peace and stability. Or the leaders may put top priority on protecting the reputation of their teachers or of Zen as a whole so as to avoid "disturbance." And just like what occurred in the Roman Catholic Church for decades, regarding priests and abuse of children, they ignore and silence the victims. Be wary of a sangha that advertises itself as providing stability and peace: Those may be maintained by actively suppressing dissent in a dictatorship or cult-like way.

If you want something warm and cuddly, getting a puppy might be a better idea than joining a Zen group. If you just want a place to chill out, and maybe learn some techniques for dealing with your emotions and life problems, there are also many other spaces to do that. A quick web search shows many centers and workshops that teach a variety of meditation or mindfulness *for something* practices. That "something" can include stress reduction, sobriety, better sports performance, or better management decisions. Those are all good things. They are often by-products of practicing Zen meditation. But they are fundamentally about self-improvement, not about awakening to who we really are.

The board at Greater Boston during Betrayal #2 was willing to risk conflict in order to try to bring about accountability. A number of people on that board and their supporters (including me) went on to form the Resilient Sangha Project. As its webpage explains: "Resilient Sangha is our expression for a sangha committed to turning the suffering of teacher misconduct into sangha wisdom for the benefit of all beings. In keeping with our Buddhist commitments, we believe wisdom can only be discovered by turning toward what's right here before us."[132]

On subsequent pages we explained, for the benefit of other sanghas as well as less-informed or future Greater Boston members, the many things we had learned. We followed up, in a second phase, with an online storytelling event and accepted invitations to present our experience to other groups. A group of survivors of teacher abuse, open to people from outside as well as inside the sangha, also met online for about a year. Through these sorts of actions, we hoped to support other victims, and help other sanghas prevent or respond appropriately to abuses while avoiding the hard bumps of our own learning process.

## FINAL THOUGHTS

I feel proud—and very lucky—to be in a sangha whose board demonstrated institutional courage instead of institutional betrayal. One of the Resilient Sangha Project web pages is a message from the survivor of sexual misconduct in our sangha, entitled "Why I Stayed." This sort of courage, I believe, leads to action that is ultimately not blaming and shaming, but rather is compassionate to all beings. Compassion should have a large component of empathy when extended towards those who have been harmed. Compassion must carry a substantial dose of accountability when directed towards those who *do* harm.

I can only hope that other communities will stop turning a blind eye to abuses of teacher power and punishing its victims. Only then can we become truly healthy communities of mutual support in awakening.

8

# BEYOND THE LOCAL SANGHA

If you are a new or middling-experienced student who believes you are in a healthy sangha—lucky you! You may not need this chapter, at least at this time. Your board is aware of its responsibility to the sangha even when that means disagreeing with the teacher(s). Your teacher keeps their ego in check, shares power, and uses the power given them by their students' trust only to care for their spiritual well-being. When they make a mistake, they admit it and seek to remedy any harm. You are finding trustworthy guidance in navigating the pitfalls along the path. Students in the teacher-idealization phase are gently but firmed moved on to a more mature realization of their own Buddha nature. Zen is a beautiful, transformative practice and you are feeling its effects!

This chapter is primarily addressed to those with more experience. I hope that—especially—teachers whose connections and influence extend beyond their local sangha will read this chapter. You have the power to use your writing, your relationships with peers, and your leadership roles to address the systemic sources of teacher misconduct. Less influential teachers should also find it informative. I believe that those practitioners who have unfortunately encountered abuses or allegations of abuse will find it helpful. What recourse and resources does, or should, the larger Zen community provide to aid your discernment and healing? How can we, teachers and dedicated non-teachers together, create a culture that holds abusers accountable for the harm they cause?

For a while I thought I was in a healthy, sustainable, resilient sangha. In early 2022 we adopted new bylaws, restructuring Greater Boston to create more clarity and a better balance of power between the board and the teachers. We had brought in two new senior teachers who expressed a sensitivity to abuses, a willingness to be gentle to the sangha in our healing process, and respect for the new structure. The Resilient Sangha Project (RSP) was endorsed by the incoming new 2022-23 board and the new teaching community. All sangha leaders signed onto our new Ethics Policy. At our summer 2022 annual meeting we publicly covenanted with each other to fulfill our duties. All the teachers completed the Healthy Boundaries course. We'd created resources for survivors while still welcoming newcomers. I found a new teacher and after a while received full Dharma transmission in the Taizan Maezumi lineage. What could go wrong?

But as a sangha we were still in many ways at the mercy of the culture of the larger Zen community. Within sixteen months of Greater Boston's adoption of the new bylaws both the board and teaching community fell apart. This chapter describes how a wider culture of secrecy, soft-pedaling, and concern for the preservation of status can foster betrayals of trust. I'm afraid that local sanghas will find it difficult to get or stay healthy until the larger Zen sangha wakes up to its frequent neglect of or complicity with teacher misconduct.

## "WE DON'T TALK ABOUT..."

I believe that there is a large-scale culture in Zen of avoiding talking about abuse, at least in any serious and helpful way. You may wonder why I've come to that conclusion.

### ABSENT STORIES

How many books and blogs have you read—whether introductory or about the precepts, history, or contemporary happenings in the Zen community—that deal seriously with dangers and abuses? By seriously, I mean giving it more than a passing mention, and not dismissing it as a problem only related to the occasional narcissistic psychopath. If you are aware of more than a few books, besides this one, please let me know! I have not been able to find them.

For example, even my favorite book about the precepts, *Waking Up to What You Do*, badly whiffs the topic. In her chapter on "Speaking of Others with Openness," Diane Eshin Rizzetto reports a student asking: "But say, for example, I'm with a group of people and someone makes a comment about how wonderful a person is, but I know this person has acted unethically. It could be someone we all know, even a spiritual teacher. If I keep silent, is this a statement of sorts?"[133]

In her reply, Rizzetto focuses only on the general issue of silence versus speech, using five sentences to say positive things about silence. One sentence mentions, in general terms, that sometimes there is value to speaking up. While I use this book often in teaching, I need to supplement it at this point. The student's question is too often *not* hypothetical. If the student (often with good reason) fears shunning or retribution for speaking up about teacher abuses, that is a reflection on our *social* karma. We also need to wake up to what *we* do, together, as a Zen community.

For another example, some years ago Juin suggested I contact Rick McDaniel who has written books and blogs based on interviews with North American Zen teachers. I believe Juin's idea was that I could inform Rick about the abuses that led to Betrayal #1. I sent Rick the blog posts I had written about those events and started to bring them up in my conversations with him. But his use of our conversations was limited to posting an upbeat profile of me on this website.[134] Meanwhile, his resulting book, *Zen Conversations*, featured interviews with Melissa and David, the teachers who were behind that Betrayal.[135] After Betrayal #2, I wrote in an email to Rick (on another matter) that "By now you probably know" about Juin's own misconduct. Rick replied that he didn't know and didn't need to know.[136] I find that to be an odd attitude for someone claiming to portray the breadth of contemporary Zen. In a blog post summarizing his book, he gives a two-sentence treatment, without naming names, to ethical violations of teachers. And he ends the post with a photo of himself with David, Melissa, and Dosho Port.[137]

I also pitched an article related to abuses to one of the leading Buddhist magazines. I never even received a response. When I've tried to engage with people on the topic of abuses, some have declined saying that their experience with misconduct has just left them too fatigued. In a few cases I can understand that. Some individuals have spent decades fighting abuse or are in (or fresh out of) of an intense experience with it. I suspect that others offer this simply as an easy excuse. Our human tendencies towards self-interest push us towards turning away from uncomfortable topics.

Perhaps some don't think abuse is a big issue because they haven't been personally harmed by it. I hope, in the interest of caring for the sangha of *all* of us, you might reconsider. Can we really "just get back to the Dharma" while many are being harmed in its name? Other times, avoidance looks like a *willful* ignorance, or even a deliberate cover-up. (As they say, "It's not paranoia if they really *are* out to get you.")

### ABSENT OVERSIGHT

Can a sangha, faced with teacher abuses of power, appeal to a higher level of authority? Catholics appealed to their diocesan authorities when priests sexually abused parishioners, especially children (for what it was worth). Mainline Protestant denominations also tend to have both national and regional groups that set standards, provide resources, and that may be appealed to in cases of misconduct.[138] Censure of a clergy member may include removal from the roster of those eligible for assignment to a parish—and often from any authority or income as a spiritual teacher. But Zen—much less Buddhism as a whole!—has no overarching supervisory or authorizing body.

Currently, the only Zen groups that I know of that function at the national or international level were created by teachers for teachers. Membership is voluntary, and historically their primary purpose has been to facilitate communications among teaching peers. Authorized Zen teachers who are also priests, for example, may become members of the Soto Zen Buddhist Association (SZBA), a formal organization with bylaws and a board. The American Zen Teachers Association (AZTA), which doesn't require that its members be ordained, describes itself as "a loosely structured peer group."[139] Teachers in the Taizan Maezumi lineage may apply to join the formally organized White Plum Asanga (WPA). These groups build community through regular conferences and communications. Such groups have the power to set standards of ethical behavior for membership if they so choose.

It seems these groups may be moving in that direction, though very slowly and in fits and starts.

The SZBA Ethics Statement that was in force when Betrayal #2 broke open in November 2020 said very little about teacher behavior towards students. It required that teachers follow the ethical guidelines of their own sanghas and to *self-report* to SZBA if they have violated those. The role of SZBA was seen only as providing sanghas with "a list of lay and ordained people trained as mediators" if asked. (Recall that mediation is not recommended in cases of abuse.) It did say it would consider suspending a member if misconduct were reported to them. The bulk of the policy dealt with teacher-to-teacher ethical issues, such as the poaching of someone else's student.[140]

The SZBA only very recently, in December 2022, adopted a broader and more detailed ethics policy. This set out more explicit responsibilities of its member teachers vis-à-vis students, including:

> The responsibility for maintaining appropriate and clear boundaries rests with the Zen priest.... Members [of SZBA] should not misuse status or authority to achieve privileges or other consideration or to inappropriately influence others.[141]

A detailed grievance policy adopted earlier the same year also notes that mediation is not appropriate in some cases.[142] These changes were long in coming. The drafting and adoption of these documents no doubt required considerable and protracted effort on the part of SZBA members who take abuses of power seriously. I feel much indebted to those individuals.

The WPA got there somewhat earlier. Their policy, adopted in 2014, reads, "Teachers should not violate trust or use power and/or position for personal gain or self-satisfaction. The ultimate responsibility for maintaining appropriate and clear boundaries between teacher and student always rests with the teacher."[143] The WPA also requires that the sanghas of its member teachers have ethics policies at least as strong as its own. The teachers of the Buddhist Healthy Boundaries course are primarily from the WPA.

The AZTA, while not as organized, has also had individual members and sub-groups who have tried to take action on abuse. For example, way back in 1992 members of the organization, at that time called the Second Generation American Zen Teachers, circulated a typewritten open letter concerning Genpo Merzel's early sexual misconduct with several women.[144] In 2021, after being informed about Greater Boston's Betrayal #2, I heard that the AZTA removed Juin from membership.

I have the greatest respect for those individuals who have fought long and hard to get these organizations to begin to face up to the issue of teacher abuse of power. The 1992 letter signers, for example, withstood typical DARVO flak and hostility. (Example: "it has become … a personal vendetta for some of you…trying to slander and undermine…. I question your integrity as spiritual leaders…"[145]). It is important to have a history of documentation and open letters concerning abuse. It is important to have ethical standards written out and agreed to. Those of us working at the sangha level need to have something to point to that says, "This conduct isn't permitted for Zen teachers!"

I am also aware that facing up to abuse is still a work-in-progress, as much for those organizations as for any of us. A distressing number of people who have signed open letters or are members of one of these organizations do not seem to me to be really "on board" with this project. Some of them, from my personal knowledge, have committed abuses themselves. Some punish those who speak up. Some have failed to speak up about abuse until it is *already* public, obvious, and egregious—that is, when it doesn't take any courage to do so. Being limited in resources and not of one mind, it's not surprising (though it's still disappointing) that these organizations—when they do decide to act—seem to take on only the most well-documented and easily provable cases of unethical behavior.

Combatting the serious cases that are *not* reported, as well as the more subtle cases of inappropriate comments, bullying, or misuse of sangha resources will, in my opinion, take more than a policy and spotty enforcement (however hard-won even these limited achievements have been). It will take a wholesale culture change. Of course, this is an uphill battle within a sexist and me-first larger culture. But that is no excuse to not clean up our own house. Teachers will continue to do damage, in the name of Buddha and Dharma, until that happens. I find that heartbreaking.

Yet, even if they had unlimited sources of energy, wisdom, compassion, and information, assuring adherence to ethical standards would still not be within the power of these teacher associations. They can exhort teachers to study their ethics policy, to inform themselves about the dynamics of power, and to keep a careful eye on their own behavior and that of others. They can publicly point out someone's misconduct through open letters, communications to their members, print and online publications, and social media.

The farthest they can go in actually sanctioning someone, however, is suspending or dismissing an offender from membership. Given that most Zen practice groups outside of Asia are led by more-or-less independent teachers, suspension or dismissal from a larger organization may hardly even crimp an abuser's style. Offenders often simply resign from the organization, at very little inconvenience to themselves, and continue to lead groups and abuse.

### SELF-POLICING SUCCESSES AND FAILURES

How often do teachers actually call out the abuses of other teachers? And is this ever successful in changing behavior or protecting students?

There is reason to be skeptical about self-policing. Self-policing of conduct hasn't worked for law enforcement: When situations of excessive force are adjudicated by commissions populated by other police officers, the offending officers usually get off. Excessive violence isn't stopped or prevented. It hasn't worked for the U.S. military: When victims of sexual harassment are required to report the problem up the same chain of command that engaged in the harassment in the first place, it's the victim who is usually punished. It hasn't worked for the Roman Catholic Church: Given a choice between protecting their peers and the reputation of their institution or protecting children from clergy sexual abuse, the leaders prioritized their peers and the institution. Only legal action forced any accountability. Self-policing didn't work within the Boundless Way council of teachers, nor did the group of transmitted teachers at Greater Boston prevent or even help to remedy Betrayal #2 there. Just because a particular in-group is "spiritual" doesn't mean it's immune from the issues endemic to in-groups.

Actions taken by national groups after Greater Boston's Betrayal #2 might be considered at least a limited success. The GBZC board sent a report of Juin's misconduct to AZTA and SZBA. The AZTA removed Juin from membership while the SZBA hired an investigator. After receiving the investigator's report the SZBA suspended him for two years with conditions for readmission. Soon after that our former spiritual director communicated to the Greater Boston leadership that he had disrobed and that he, at that time, had no intention of returning to Zen teaching.[146]

I am grateful for these actions by the AZTA and SZBA. Before these, those of us at Greater Boston who were speaking out about abuse were often dismissed as a bunch of vindictive whiners. After the national bodies acted, we gained at least a bit of credibility. Yet, if I understand correctly, the dismissal of our former spiritual director from AZTA and his suspension from SZBA was a first for each organization. And this was surely the low-hanging fruit! Juin *confessed* to having an inappropriate relationship, and the SZBA was able to start its investigation with a very detailed outline of the issues provided by our sangha's board.

The conditions that SZBA set for readmission were kept confidential and seem to have been weak. Greater Boston's report to the SZBA recounted not only the sexual abuse but also Juin's many subsequent attempts to discredit, deceive, and gaslight the student and members of the sangha's board. We've seen no attempts by him to be accountable or make restitution for those breaches of trust. Yet when the two-year suspension was up, the SZBA said that he had fulfilled their requirements and would be welcome if he chooses to return.[147] Because sincerely taking responsibility for *all* the harm one has done is a necessary prerequisite for successful rehabilitation,[148] this judgment seems to some of us to be vastly premature.

So any limited success must be seen in the light of a long line of failures, half-measures, tacit complicity, steps backwards or, at the very least, foot-dragging by these organizations. The 1992 open letter mentioned above asked Taizan Maezumi to withdraw Genpo Merzel's teaching authority. That didn't happen.[149] It wasn't until 2011, and decades more of sexual misconduct, that the WPA finally broke with Genpo.[150] While Genpo initially expressed remorse and said he would disrobe, this was only temporary. He soon reclaimed his former power. He still leads a sangha/business with a large following and his books still sell.

The cases of serial sexual abuse by Rinzai teachers Eido Shimano and Joshu Sasaki are other well-known failures. Shimano's abuse was apparent as early as 1964, and Sasaki's abuses began in the early 1970s. While the abuses happened in the United States, there was no U.S.-based teaching authority or institutional structure here that could sanction them, and their Japanese authorities apparently felt no need to. Some teachers tried their best to stop them.[151] Others willingly collaborated with them. It wasn't until 2010 that Shimano was forced out of the Zen Studies Society. (He then sued the ZSS.)[152] It wasn't until 2013 that Sasaki's title of Abbot was rescinded following "a tide of sexual abuse allegations."[153]

The recent SZBA investigation and censure of Dosho Port for ethical violations, which was also supported by clear documentation from the local sangha, resulted only in his resignation from SZBA. He continues to offer Zen training online (for a fee), blog prolifically, and write books. And as is typical, he has engaged in DARVO, attacking via his blog those who censured him.

I put my hope in two things. First, I hope that teachers wake up—as Zen practitioners should!—to our own power and the deep harm caused by our greed and delusion. Yet that hope, alas, is rather idealistic. Second, I hope we can support, use, and when necessary, build structures *outside* of our teacher groups that can bring about greater awareness and accountability.

### MINIMIZING AND MISINFORMATION

While missing from most writing about Zen, sometimes respected teachers *do* discuss abuse. And, unfortunately, they can write misleading and unhelpful things. I'm afraid my first Zen teacher, James Ford, seems to have been one of these. He is a former president of the SZBA and a prolific blogger and author. He is in a position of power where he could call attention to abuses. He rarely does. He argued, instead, in a 2012 blog post that the Zen world might be going overboard in its efforts to stop abuse.[154] In this post, he seems to excuse the behavior of his own teacher: "There have been various other scandals small and large around sex.... I think of...my own teacher John Tarrant, where I see not a predator, but rather someone who simply refuses to be bound by conventional and what I'd call Professional boundaries."[155]

As his evidence for the possibility of healthy teacher-subordinate sexual relations, he writes about "Unitarian Universalist clergy, where it was fairly common in the middle of the twentieth century for male clergy to have second marriages with subordinates...and where it seems many of these relationships would prove to be lifelong, causes me to be very reluctant to absolutely condemn when these things happen." He calls for equal attention to how (he apparently believes) *women's* sexual make-up "opens" them "to inappropriate sexual behaviors." Decrying the "tone" of public conversations about sexual misconduct, he seems to imply that those who oppose teacher-student sexual relationships are prudes: "[S]erious conversation probably can't happen unless we can start with a generous acceptance of the fact we are animals with natural sexual urges."

This respected teacher gives one sentence to the possibility of exploitation when he expresses a bit of remorse for not discussing the misconduct by Shimano, Sasaki, and Genpo in his earlier writing. And unfortunately, he refused attempts by RSP and me to engage with him about these matters.[156] So let's examine his arguments here.

- *The victims* don't care about whether the harm they suffered was caused by predation or more garden-variety boundary violation. The fact that someone might not fit the psychological profile of a habitual predator does not lessen the abuse. Nor should it affect the institutional response.[157]
- I wonder what the *first* wives and their children would think about the passage about Unitarian Universalist clergy. (Reread the passage above if you don't get my point.) We also might wonder what would have happened if, as many ethics policies now require, those clergymen's subordinates had been given a cooling-off period to consider their decisions more objectively.
- To ignore the cultural patterns of male sexual dominance of women (as contrasted to the reverse) seems to me to require wearing blinders.
- From what I've seen, it is not prudishness that motivates the fight against sexual exploitation. Most of us simply understand that abuse is a matter of power much more than of sexuality.

Neglect of power and boundaries can be contagious. I was still James' student at the time he wrote the above, and I don't recall having a reaction at the time. (Though, if I read it, I must have at least noticed his lack of awareness of the problem of patriarchy). The obvious problem is that when a respected Zen teacher implies that sex between teachers and students is, except for rare cases, possibly okay, many will follow along.

Another case of this occurred more recently. There is a new book out on the Zen Precepts that will, I'm sure, be used in the teaching of many precepts classes.[158] I think the author's chapter on the Three Treasures is especially insightful, and I assign it in the precepts discussions that I lead. Yet the student who was the target of sexual abuse at Greater Boston told me that she had found some passages in the book "disturbing." While the author clearly didn't intend the book to be "about" abuse (nor would I imagine the author would ever condone abuse), these passages seem to display a certain carelessness when addressing the topic of teacher power.

I'm afraid that the very value of the rest of the book could help spread some common misunderstandings.

One passage is: "What about sexual relations between teacher and student? Or between therapist and client? Or between two adulterers? Are these consensual? Here, perhaps what we need to look at—on both sides—is self-deception and motive, particularly unconscious motives."[159] A couple pages later we find the line, "It is very common that we arrange for ourselves to be seduced." Such statements are very problematic when applied within the context of teacher-student-sangha relations.

First, it is a mistake to mention sexual relations between a teacher and student in the same breath as "two adulterers." There may, in a few cases, be discernment needed concerning the size of the power differential between the two parties. But when there is an established and significant teacher/student or therapist/client relationship, sexual relations are non-consensual *by definition*. Such relations are unethical and can be grounds for civil suits and, in some states, criminal prosecution. So the question, "Are these consensual?" is already answered: no sangha needs to "look at" the question further.

Second, the "we" who are supposed to "look at—on both sides—... self-deception and motive," might be taken to include the readers of the book, and perhaps the sanghas to which the teacher and student belong, as well as the teacher and the student themselves. I heartily agree that the teacher should look into these factors within themself—preferably in an extended and supervised program of therapy and rehabilitation! The sangha should also be aware that unconscious motives might be behind the teacher's behavior.

But it really shouldn't matter to *anyone but the student* how naive *the student* has been. It doesn't even matter if their "unconscious motives" caused them to come on to their teacher sexually! Implying that the student may have "arranged to be seduced" in a relationship marked by significant differences in power smacks of blaming the victim. It's a teacher's job to see that the relationship functions always and only in the student's best interest. In contrast, the "self-deception and motive" of an abused student are their own private affair, preferably addressed in therapy. There, a student could privately examine the causes and conditions that made them a vulnerable "mark." Actions by the sangha to pry into the inner life of the student would only exacerbate the harm.

There are other worrisome passages. In the chapter on "Non-Lying," the author points to "a very important failure to tell the truth—namely, the failure to speak up. With all the talk recently about sexual and other forms of misconduct among dharma teachers, it's surprising how little attention is paid to students failing to speak up."[160] It is *not* a student's responsibility to speak up: It is the teacher's responsibility to not abuse their power. If we are talking about the student who was abused, how could it be compassionate to add to that trauma the labels of "failure" and a "precept-breaker"? If we are talking about students who witness abuse, they are also in a weak position vis a vis the teacher.

Why might a student victim or witness not speak up? This author only briefly and vaguely mentions that "fears around dominant-subordinate structures and our relation to power and authority" may play a part. In my opinion, this deserves more unpacking. The teacher may assert their power directly, for example, by threatening to reveal secrets confidentially shared in private meetings if the student talks to anyone. But such a direct show of power is usually unnecessary. Given the history of Buddhist sanghas in the Western world, the student probably already understands the likely consequences. The teacher would likely deny or at least minimize the abuse. The teacher is more likely to be believed than the student. The student victim or witness is more often than not labeled a liar, shamed, and ultimately driven from the sangha.[161] Or the teacher might just be a good manipulator, framing the situation in such a way that the student doesn't even realize they are being abused (until, perhaps, much later). The student victim is told they have a "special spirit," or the sex is called a "path to enlightenment." Or the teacher pleads that they would be heartbroken and have to leave Zen (or worse) if the student broke things off. Students in the teacher's inner circle may be praised or rewarded for ignoring complaints. Similar techniques may be used to hide emotional and financial breaches of trust.

Lastly, in the chapter on "Non-Misusing Intoxicants" this author writes, "We all know the substance category—drugs, alcohol, food, sugar, caffeine, nicotine. But there are other less obvious categories. Daydreaming.... So are blaming, analyzing, justifying, and storytelling. I need to tell my story; I need for you to know who I am.... Obsessing.... Tuning out.... Being a victim."[162]

Perhaps the issue here is more subtle than for the passages discussed above. It is true that it is possible for people to get overly attached to telling their personal story or identifying as a victim. But it is also true that those harmed by abuse of power by teachers are, indeed, victims! Sometimes the word "victim" is avoided in favor of euphemisms, or terms that only apply when a conflict is between people of equal power. Such reframing mischaracterizes the problem. One should of course hope that the person victimized will not attach permanently to victimhood and will get the help they need to move on to being a survivor. But simply *being* a victim is *not* a violation of the precepts.

Storytelling itself is also not a violation of the precepts. One of the most healing things one can do for a victim of abuse, in fact, is simply listen to their story. They have been silenced, their voices squashed and demeaned. Telling them to quit talking about themselves and "get back to the Dharma" would not be helpful.

One thing that *is* most definitely a violation of this precept is intoxication with power. The way people change when they hold power and may internalize it in a personalized, opportunistic way is a well-studied phenomenon in psychology—and it has negative consequences. But power, unfortunately, is not anywhere in the list of intoxicants that this author mentions. Nor is the issue of teacher power addressed anywhere else in her book.

Some readers will find the passages I criticized less disturbing, and for a valid reason. The author presents "failure" to keep a precept as a gateway to investigation and the Dharma, rather than as a moral judgment. So statements about "failing" to speak up, or about "what *we* need to look at" (emphasis added), or about "being a victim" could perhaps best be understood as pointing to something that an *individual* should take up privately, with their therapist or on the cushion, free of censure by others. But we live in a social world, and so whether our behavior is guided or not guided by the precepts is also a social concern. Mentioning something as in some sense "not approved" is therefore likely to invite some censoriousness. It would be wise, I believe, to take special care when we describe ethical issues that may arise within teacher/student/sangha relationships.

I'm afraid that these sorts of writings by esteemed Zen teachers may, through both their arguments and their omissions, encourage readers to pay too little attention to the dynamics of power in teacher-student relationships. If so, readers and their sanghas will be ill-prepared to prevent, recognize, or remediate abuses.

### DAMAGING ADVICE FROM TRAINERS AND CONSULTANTS

In the wake of Betrayal #1, many of us at Greater Boston had an understandable interest in learning more about ethics and abuses of power. In 2019, we hired a trainer to do a workshop. She was colleague of Juin's in the Soto Zen Buddhist Association and, at the time, the SZBA President. This trainer introduced us to the Right Use of Power™ (RUP) program. Later, as we struggled with Betrayal #2, Greater Boston asked for help from this trainer in finding a suitable consultant. We ended up (over the strong objection of two members of the board) hiring in early 2021 two consultants from the Right Use of Power™ Institute: Its founder and one of her colleagues.

The sales pitch for the RUP program looks good:

> Conscious Ethics. Power with Heart. Learning the embodied practice of Right Relationship - together. The Right Use of Power™ approach is a dynamic, inspiring, and relational approach to the ethical use of power to promote well-being and the common good.[163]

Spiritual groups, in particular, may be attracted to a program that promises these lovely things.

What we actually received, both in the training and from the consulting, many of us felt actually *damaged* Greater Boston's ability to deal with betrayal. According to the victim, it also compounded the harm she experienced. A blow-by-blow account of what happened would take a whole book on its own. But let me summarize what I see as the program's major failings.[164]

As I wrote about in the previous chapter, a strong ethics code will make a distinction between *interpersonal conflicts* between people of relatively equal power and *abuses* that exploit and harm those with far less power. An interpersonal conflict may be considered to be a simply a difficult relationship and, many agree, may be helped by intervention by a neutral mediator. Restoring right relationship, or at least a workable relationship, between (or among) the parties is the goal.

The case where a teacher uses their spiritual power to exploit and harm a very vulnerable and trusting person, however, requires a very different approach. It needs to start, not with neutrality, but with fact-finding and taking the side of the victim. It needs to result not in reconciliation between the abuser and victim, but in consequences for the offender and attempts at restitution. Think about it: Whether or not a good relationship between the victim and a person who raped them, stole from them, emotionally tortured them, or otherwise harmed them is ever restored is not the major concern! The goals, instead, should be accountability, justice, the restoration of the victim to wholeness, and prevention of repeat offenses.

The Right Use of Power™ paradigm, however, as presented to us during 2019-2021, minimized the power differential and collapsed everything into its "relational approach." The person with more power was said to be "150% responsible" for resolving the problem while the person with less power was said to be "100% responsible." The training we received included a list of 27 things the person with *lesser* power should do to restore the relationship. Many of these, it seems to me in hindsight, only accentuate an attitude of subservience. Included, for example, were "Offer authentic appreciations" and "Try not to put the superior on the spot."[165]

The idea that the student had 100% responsibility and could have made greater use of her "personal power" (another term used in the slides) encouraged our Greater Boston transmitted teachers to consider the student as something of a co-offender. This greatly complicated our attempts to make an appropriate institutional response.

Hiring Right Use of Power™ consultants after Betrayal #2 added to the harm. They urged the board and senior teachers to remain neutral, discouraged fact-finding, and implemented what they called "restorative processes." Very loosely based on the better-known "Restorative Justice" framework, their focus in practice seemed to be on restoring *the teacher who had offended* to the community.[166] After initial individual and group interviews, they facilitated a one-shot "Reparative Circle" including the teacher, the student, their support persons, and selected community members. This, they said, would be an effective process for achieving consensus on a set of "reparative agreements." As anyone who has dealt with serious abuse could have warned us, nothing of the sort resulted. The victim, in particular, did not feel at all "repaired." Throughout the process of working with these consultants, the many demands made by the offender seemed to be often granted, while the victim's (few) requests went unheard.

Judith L. Herman's research on trauma survivors notes that their vision of justice generally "is not centered on the question of the offender's fate...Survivor's visions of justice combine retributive and restorative elements in the service of healing a damaged relationship, not primarily between victims and offenders but rather between victims and the bystanders in their communities...the first duty of the moral community is to support and care for her. When the community embraces the survivor, justice is served."[167] The training and consulting services we received from Right Use of Power™ instead caused much of the community to turn a cold shoulder on the survivor, increasing the damage.

After the process at Greater Boston failed, some of us tried to engage with the consultants and trainer about what we felt was dangerous in the RUP program. I don't believe that the trainer or consultants are bad people, any more than I believe that the arrogant teachers I have encountered are "bad." It's clear we all share many common values. I've heard that the RUP trainer, in particular, was instrumental in SZBA dealing appropriately with a case of teacher misconduct in the Midwest. Yet our attempts to encourage changes in the program they use have so far been met with silence or defensiveness (or worse).

### TONE-POLICING

Betrayal #3 at Greater Boston is too recent and painful for me to recount in any detail. Yet it, and ongoing issues within the larger Zen community, have educated me about yet another way in which silence about abuses is enforced.

So let me start with a story—a koan, perhaps—from a recent article in the *New York Times*. The article explains why professional auditing services have failed to stop the practice of illegally employing migrant children in dangerous jobs. The parties involved include the professional auditing services companies, the auditors they employ, and the suppliers that are the companies' clients. The clients pay the auditing companies for their services.

> This spring, [an auditor] flagged labor issues involving… migrant workers at a warehouse that supplies Costco's potatoes. The plant's management complained that [the auditor] was demanding and argumentative, and his supervisor barred him from returning.... The supervisor said [the auditor] would have to complete a series of customer service trainings, and concluded with an inspirational quote that he attributed to the poet Maya Angelou. "People will forget what you said. They will forget what you did. But they will never forget how you made them feel," he wrote in an email. "Keep this in mind as you are interacting with our clients during your audits."[168]

The same auditor had also been put on a "remediation plan" after reporting abuses at a Walgreen's supplier.

There are two things going on in this story. First is the auditing company's prioritization of the interests of those in power over the interests of the vulnerable. The auditing company wants to keep its contract with its client and the client wants to get a clean bill of health. Criticizing and punishing the less powerful auditors, should they dare to report violations, thus serves to preserve and protect the power of the two entities as well as the collegial relationship between them. Exploited workers, on the other hand, get no relief from illegal and often inhumane labor practices. Second is the (mis-) use of language about feelings, sensitivity, interpersonal relationships, and communication. These are often associated with a softer, gentler, "feminine," and compassionate form of management. But the idea of attending to feelings and relationships has been twisted here in order to deflect attention from (an egregiously *not*-compassionate) situation of abuse of workers.

What the auditor in the story experienced is called "tone policing." This useful term was invented by those addressing racist oppression. Ijeoma Oluo in her book, *So You Want to Talk About Race*, defines it as "when someone (usually a privileged person) in a conversation about oppression shifts the conversation from the oppression being discussed to the way it is being discussed. Tone policing prioritizes the comfort of the privileged person in the situation over the oppression of the disadvantaged person."[169]

Those who carry out tone policing will insist that they are open to hearing about the oppression and abuse. They will insist that they are not trying to silence the speaker. They will "only" be adding the caveat that such communications must be done in such a way that no one (and especially no one in power) will ever complain.

Sometimes a kinder, more private and relationship-sustaining "calling in" conversation may be a more effective way of changing someone's mind or behavior than a more public "calling out."[170] Yet when there is continuing harm, urgent action to protect the vulnerable is required. And when personal engagement with someone in power has been refused or unsuccessful, another remedy must be found. A clear and public "calling out" is then both legitimate and necessary.[171]

Tone policing, however, will label *all* calls for accountability—no matter how expressed—as hostile and harsh, simply because the violator dislikes them.

Tone policing is thus another manifestation of the "reverse victim and offender" part of DARVO. The speaker of truths[172] will be labeled as abrasive, aggressive, condescending, insulting, and perhaps insufficiently attentive to the preservation of relationships simply because they spoke the truth.[173] As in the case of the auditor, a presumed deficiency in communications skills may be seen as the biggest problem. A program of re-education may be prescribed. Silence around the actual abuses is thereby preserved.

In my interactions within Zen communities both small and large, I have observed both the factors I pointed out in the *New York Times* story. I've observed excessive attention given to preserving harmony with and among teachers (and thus their status and power). I've observed the twisting of language about relationships and feelings in order to "kill the messenger" when the topic of abuses is raised. The auditing firm and its clients colluded. So, it seems, may Zen teachers. Instead of encouraging fair-minded investigation of allegations of abuse and the application of good judgment, current Zen structures may instead encourage piling abuse of whistle-blowers on top of the abuses the whistle-blowers are trying to report.

With this background, let me provide a rough sketch of what happened to those committed to building a resilient sangha at Greater Boston. The prioritization of the feelings of those in power over harms to the less powerful led to attacks on us from two sides. First, the 2022-23 board received a threatening letter from a senior Zen teacher who believed they were slandered by some text on the RSP webpages. Rather than investigating—and finding out that RSP had documentation to back up our supposedly false statements—members of that board instead became concerned about having offended the teacher. They regarded RSP with mounting distrust. Second, a similar reversal of their endorsement of RSP went on inside the Greater Boston teaching community. Attempts to engage in discussions about abuse or create a less teacher-centered form of sangha practice became increasingly condemned by the teachers other than myself as aggressive, offensive, and narrow-minded.[174]

By mid-2023, four out of the six board members had resigned their positions. Three of Greater Boston's four teachers had also resigned their positions and left the community. I also resigned from my Greater Boston teaching position, although I remain a member and active in RSP. Having an entirely vacant teaching community, I felt, would allow the sangha to better contemplate where it wanted to go next. There's only so much beating up by teachers that a sangha can stand.

Greater Boston went into its annual membership meeting in July 2023 with only two board members, a depleted general membership, and no teachers. But we were still a sangha. The newly elected 2023-24 board included a number of people strongly aligned with RSP.

Teacher abuse of power is truly "the gift that keeps on giving."

## RESTORING ACCOUNTABILITY

Much needs to be done. I have a few ideas, although I expect there are other good ideas out there, too.

### PUBLICATIONS AND MEDIA

If teachers' own opening experiences, teaching of the Buddhist ethical precepts, and courses offered by fellow teachers are not enough to stop us from abusing spiritual power, what other avenues can be tried?

The old-school way of bringing abuses to light involved the circulation of open letters written by teachers or other Zen leaders. These might be sent to individuals by mail or circulated in printed newsletters or other publications. In pre-internet days, these could enlighten (pun intended) at least fellow teachers or local communities about occurrences of misconduct.

Nowadays, open letters by teachers are also posted in blogs[175] or published in periodicals that have online versions.[176] And the internet also makes it possible for non-teachers, who have not (yet) developed similar networks of communication, to voice their concerns. In 2018,

I brought Betrayal #1 conflicts out of the proverbial "smoke-filled back room" with my blog post, "Letting in Some Air."[177] In 2020, a dozen or so former students, instructors, and staff of Dharma Ocean uploaded a pdf document to a Google Drive and circulated the link via social media and email.[178] Greater Boston put a notice about Betrayal #2 on our website.[179] While it was brief—only three sentences long—and placed deep in a subsidiary page out of a desire to not cause undue embarrassment to the offender's family, it was necessary. First of all, it validated the victim's experience by bringing it out of the sphere of the silenced and into public view. Secondly, the board believed that our Zen ethics require such a warning to potential future students or clients. Though this was of lesser concern, it was also advised to do so because the organization might be sued in the future if it *failed* to post such a warning.

But such information is still not necessarily easy to find. Perhaps someone with more resources and internet skills that I have could create something like a ratemyprofessors.com or Better Business Bureau for Buddhist teachers? (If the former, there would of course need to be some efforts to prevent multiple postings, to keep a single disgruntled student from trashing someone's reputation.)

While I have yet to hear of abusers changing their behavior because of such public revelations, these can at least potentially warn off people who might otherwise become their victims. But we could also do better. How about, when quoting inspiring and influential forebears, *not* glossing over or getting vague about misconduct they also committed? How about using our media resources to *prevent* abuses, by educating all Zen practitioners about spiritual power and its appropriate (and inappropriate) uses? How about including this information in every Buddhist magazine, and every book about Zen? How about resolutely refusing the dualistic understanding of teachers as "Zen masters" and students as their loyal and obedient disciples in our writings and posts?

And how about more internet-based workshops and seminars about abuses of power? On the two-year anniversary of the notice to Greater Boston about Betrayal #2, the Resilient Sangha Project held an on-line "Storytelling Panel of Harm, Healing & Hope." Though it was publicized almost exclusively by word-of-mouth and email, and selective about who was let in, it drew attendees from a variety of groups and locations. The Sogaku Institute has held an online class regarding sexual abuses, and the Buddhist Healthy Boundaries course is regularly offered.

## LEGAL RECOURSE

I am not qualified to give legal advice, but I can tell you what I've learned.

The law is a powerful but blunt instrument. Given that self-policing, boards, teacher education, and sanction by larger organizations don't seem to be as effective as one might hope, it's good that there is also a "big stick." Sometimes the threat of a stinging whack is the only thing that will get attention. (Ancient Zen teachers knew this.) Courts can *order* offenders to pay penalties or restitution, or to enter into rehabilitation, or even serve time in jail. Taking legal action makes the offense a matter of public record. The mainstream media will often pick up on stories about legal action which can be helpful even if the action is eventually unsuccessful in bringing the offender to justice.

The person who is charged or sued may be the teacher (or other leader) who committed the abuse. Cases of criminal sexual assault or financial fraud could probably be clear cases for legal action. Using spiritual authority to gain sexual favors may also be criminally prosecutable under some states' laws against clergy sexual relations with parishioners, or as coercion under federal laws concerning trafficking.[180] Criminal charges do not require action by the direct victim: People or organizations with knowledge of the crime can also initiate an arrest or investigation. Victims are treated as crucial witnesses.

Victims may also file civil lawsuits. In these, they formally ask for monetary compensation for damages they have suffered—although the moral victory of winning such a suit may be at least or more important to them. The boards of the organization that employs the offender, as well as the offender themself, may be the target of such a suit. The fact that the abuse occurred means that the board failed to properly perform its "duty of care."[181] The victim has more control over this process than over criminal proceedings but must also be both willing to come forward and be able to pay a lawyer (or at least find one willing to take them on for a contingency fee) to argue their case.

The law's bluntness is reason for caution. Bringing a lawyer into sangha problems carries with it its own risks. Suppose a victim sues the board of a sangha. The Faith Trust Institute *Handbook* warns that most lawyers would tend to understand their duty as protecting the sangha's (or its insurance company's) financial assets from the student. If, instead, the sangha wants to (as it should) do the right thing by the student, they will need to make sure their lawyer's actions align with the sangha's goals.[182] I've also heard of a case of a sangha being advised by a lawyer that they cannot make public statements about teacher misconduct because of the confidentiality of personnel records. This, I hear from other lawyers, is untrue, and likely arose from lawyerly over-caution about protecting the institution. It's also possible and even likely that a teacher or sangha, especially a rich and powerful one, will bring a countersuit. The law can serve as a vehicle for expensive and exhausting institutionalized DARVO.

On the whole, I feel like the Zen community would benefit by *more* legal action in response to abuses of power. It may be the only way to get abusers and those complicit in downplaying abuse to sit up and pay attention. This does, however, require considerable effort, time, and money as well as courage and focus. In the maelstrom of emotions, personalities, and true and false claims swirling in the wake of sexual or financial abuse, it can be hard to remember that the law might be appealed to, and to remember to preserve evidence. Starting a fund for legal fees for those survivors who are able to take this on would be an advance.

Unfortunately, as far as I can tell (remembering that I'm not a lawyer), there is less possibility of legal recourse for emotional abuse than for sexual or financial abuse. While bullying, berating, lying, psychological torture, trash-talking, and twisted forms of manipulation can be terribly destructive a of person's spirit, I don't know of legal cases about these. Tone-policing also seems to be entirely legal. Here Zen teachers, boards, students, and organizations seem to be on our own. My hope is that we can create a culture in which these harms can be recognized and addressed.

### NETWORK OF SURVIVORS

Other spiritual groups have developed support networks for survivors. The Survivors Network of those Abused by Priests (SNAP) started out serving only Catholics. It has since expanded to include other Christian and Jewish faiths and has chapters across the world.[183] Project Satya describes its purpose as "Investigating Institutional Sexual Abuse within Sivananda Yoga Vedanta Centres."[184] A Muslim group promoting reproductive justice and health aided survivors of abuse by a prominent imam.[185]

Buddhist Project Sunshine was an "independent healing initiative" that investigated sexual abuses at Shambala. But it existed only during 2017-2018.[186] Several people who have contacted our Resilient Sangha Project have been victims of sexual or emotional abuse at the hands of teachers. While a number of us RSP trustees have helped put such people in contact with each other for mutual support, we are a small, volunteer, overburdened, and pretty much unfunded group at this time. In 2021, a Tibetan Buddhist group started the Survivors Program: Connecting Survivors of Guru and Teacher Abuse.[187] Contributing energy and funds to survivor groups is a way to help move forward.

### NETWORK OF BOARDS

The fact that the Greater Boston board did its job during Betrayal #2 was shocking to many. The Greater Boston transmitted teachers seemed to expect the board to serve *them* rather than to carry out its legal duty to care for the sangha as a whole. It seems that the legal responsibilities of sangha boards are not well understood. The board had to start its research on clergy abuse of power and board responses from scratch, which was an exhausting process. Zen teachers have established networks to consult when they have a question about something; Zen boards do not. This exacerbates the power differential between teacher and student sangha members.

How about if we put together a network of Zen boards? We could compile resources, hold (and record) on-line informational seminars, establish a listserv or such for questions, and so on. Members of the network could get to know each other through online and in-person events. This idea was hatched in the Resilient Sangha Project some time ago but backburnered when no one had the time or energy to pursue it. More recently, a couple of us heard about a grant we could apply for that might allow us to run an on-line board training, and we looked into it. This was short circuited when Betrayal #3 developed, putting us back into crisis mode.

Or how about conferences or assemblies or communication channels that include not only board members but sangha members in general? My impression is that mainstream (and some non-mainstream) Protestant groups hold national meetings every year or two that include a substantial proportion of lay representatives. This could be done narrowly, locally or within lineages, or could encourage community-building among serious practitioners across lines of geography and tradition. I, along with a few others, have tried to create the beginnings of such a Zen-wide communication channel by creating the (ambitiously named) Zen Learners Association with a website and Google Group.

### THE SANGHA-LED SANGHA

Over the last few years, the phrase "a sangha-led sangha" has cropped up in many of our Greater Boston discussions. For many of us who remain at Greater Boston, this sounds like a good alternative to explore given the devastation we've experienced at the hands of teachers.

We can take inspiration from many sources. One is the pre-Chinese version of Buddhism. Shakyamuni Buddha did not establish lineage. The Buddha established *sangha*, the community of practitioners, whose rules for life together were laid out in the *vinaya*. We can take inspiration from Vietnamese Zen teacher Thich Nhat Hahn who said, "It is said that the next Buddha will be named 'Maitreya,' the Buddha of Love. I believe that Maitreya might not take the form of an individual, but as a community showing us the way of love and compassion."[188]

We can also take inspiration from Zen teacher Robert Aitken who, noting that the Japanese tradition in which he trained often led to high-handedness and distress, wrote "In my opinion modes of decision making by consensus, evolved from Quaker models in the movement for a New Society, offer the Western Zen movement the means to apply [the precept of not praising oneself while abusing others] in their sangha governance."[189] As to how "a sangha-led sangha" could best be implemented while still staying within the traditions of Soto Zen, that's something yet to be worked out.

Greater Boston now has the opportunity to experiment. The July 2023 membership meeting was well-attended, in spite of the exit of two teachers, my resignation from the Senior Teaching Community, and the collapse of the previous board. A new board was elected that included members of the Resilient Sangha Project. We have converted our programming (including sits and retreats) to be sangha-led. We've replaced Dharma Talks at our sits with Dharma Discussions that are led by member volunteers. The leaders start these off by offering some comments, a reading, and/or simply a question. I hope we can (safely) meet the needs of both long-time practitioners and newcomers, both those most harmed in the betrayals we've experienced and those with no knowledge of them.

I have been offering my services at Greater Boston as a (lineage-authorized) teacher to the sangha, for use when requested. I have been thinking of teaching as a *service* role, rather than a leadership one, and have suggested that my title be "adjunct teacher." I want us to think of Zen teachers as similar to math teachers. Math teachers are respected for their qualifications, but one wouldn't expect—or want—a math teacher to also be the principal and school board. I have offered private meetings and koan work to those who want it by zoom and at retreats and the occasional informative online talk. We have not revised our Ethics Policy yet, so I function under the rules we made for "visiting" teachers—that is, following all the ethical requirements laid out for senior teachers with the exception of participating in a Greater Boston teaching community. I am held accountable to these policies by the board. I also function as a teacher at Great Plains Zen Center, accountable to their ethics policies and board. All new initiatives at Greater Boston must be cleared with our board, and they don't just rubber stamp things. I've had various proposals denied or significantly modified.

The "sangha-led sangha" might not be possible in all communities, especially smaller and newer ones. To some, the notion may sound scary, like know-nothings are aiming to depose their revered teachers. But at Greater Boston we have a number of intelligent, wise, and committed people who have been practicing Soto Zen for many years or even decades. The responsibility for leadership of our sangha now rests mostly on the board and on the group of relatively senior students (including me) who serve as Practice Leaders for our various sitting groups. While progress is slow, I look forward to serving *with* them on task forces to make decisions about our programming and liturgy. We are starting to think about how to revise our ceremonies to emphasize community rather than lineage.

When the teacher is not in charge of running the sangha, what should we do about the tangible objects given in teacher transmission to signify authority? Earlier I suggested re-interpreting these as being about responsibility (power to care for) rather than opportunity (power to direct and control). Another possibility might be to do away with special clothing, sticks, and so on altogether. No less an authority than the (purported) Sixth Zen Ancestor Huineng seems to me to have suggested this. The sutra that is said to contain his teachings is, according to Zen scholarship, the first mention of the First Zen Ancestor's robe being passed down from teacher to successor.[190] Huineng's teacher is said to have referred to it as an "embodiment of trust" and distinguished it from the Dharma which "is transmitted from mind to mind and must be realized by people themselves."[191] When asked about to whom he would transmit this robe, Huineng said "The Dharma has already been given.... As for the robe, it isn't right to pass it on."[192] In some versions of the story Huineng explains: "Since receiving the robe, I have run into much trouble. There will certainly be more contention in later generations. The [transmission of the] robe will end and thus bring peace to the monastery."[193]

As Red Pine comments, "the Dharma doesn't come with any accessories."[194] After Huineng's death, however, the robe he had received was venerated,[195] and the passing on of newly sewn robes and other items became the tradition. Or consider that some ancient stories tell of teachers being praised for refusing to accept ceremonial robes and objects.[196] Do these outward symbols serve the Dharma, or mostly lead to pride and conflict? Perhaps this is a good time for the larger sangha to ask that question again.

Meanwhile, the future of Greater Boston remains unclear. While those in leadership all agree on what we *don't* want, figuring out what we *want* is much harder. Some like myself would prefer to include some teacher activities such as private meetings and occasional talks, as long as sangha leadership and decision-making is located elsewhere. A few, though, feel that a "sangha-led sangha" should be a group in which there is no teacher or perhaps even no teaching, even by peers. I understand that: In the name of teaching, we've suffered repeated lacerations to our spirits. I personally struggle with not allowing all my trust, vulnerability, and tenderness around teaching and being taught to be pushed into permanent retreat. Having done first aid on the wounds to the sangha, we now have to figure out how to collectively deal with the scar tissue. It doesn't help that our sangha leaders are a small group of busy people also in the process of searching for a less expensive place to rent. Yet, all things considered, I'd rather be a member of this local sangha than any other in any world!

## FINAL THOUGHTS

Teachers need to admit that we are not in control here, and that the problem of abuse by teachers cannot be solved entirely "in house" by teachers ourselves. Nor can it be solved at the level of the individual sangha. And then there are still the non-abuse sorts of dangers, such as dissociation and spiritual bypassing, which also present problems of great complexity. These may not all be solvable, but neither can we just irresponsibly shrug and say, "Well, harm is just inevitable—nothing can be done." There is a third option: Can we be humble enough to ask for help? Can we restructure our Zen culture, so it presents fewer dangers and more healing and awakening?

Can we learn more about the dangers of Zen so we can be better prepared? Can we learn from academics, lawyers, and/or therapists who particularly deal with clergy abuse? Can we be willing to learn from research, from other organizations, and—most importantly—from the students who have been harmed? Can we regularly incorporate knowledge gained from these sources into our training and criteria for ordination or transmission? Can teachers be humble enough to accept directives from their sangha boards as the boards act to maintain the mission of the organization? Can sanghas support victims rather than reputations when survivors of abuse appeal to the legal system for redress?

I hope so. I have reservations about remaining a Zen teacher if we cannot.

Conclusion

# WHY IT'S WORTH THE TROUBLE

ZEN PRACTICE, like any other thing we humans do, can be turned to the service of our own personal, self-centered ends. Do we fall into the common pitfalls of niceness, spiritual bypassing, or ego-inflation? Our traditions and institutions, like anything else created by humans, can become rigid and hollow. Do we get attached to the status we've gained within Zen communities? Do we find ourselves turning the *mythos* of spiritual practice into a *logos* justification of temporal power? Then our natural impulse will be to resist seeing these as delusions. We may not be able to see how our actions cause harm, much less accept accountability for it. Potential abusers of spiritual power are not just a few "bad apples" over there somewhere, and not our problem. "They" are "me." "They" is "us." If we persist in being silent about pitfalls and secretive about scandals, our inattention and complicity cause harm.

So why continue? If Zen practice, traditions, teachers, and sanghas are not "special" and somehow above normal human failings, what's the point? It might seem, given the hardships I have described, that the best course would just be to give up all the folderol and go take up golf instead.

## ONE BRIGHT JEWEL

A very old tale in the *Lotus Sutra* concerns a desperately poor person and their wealthy friend. The wealthy one secretly sews a precious jewel into the poor one's robe. The poor person doesn't realize it's there. I picture them covered in mud and dung from sleeping on the roadside. They probably stink, too. They certainly don't look like a jewel! Yet the jewel is still there, under all the muck. Eihei Dogen, commenting on the story, wrote about the jewel, "No one can take it away."[197]

No matter how much we humans screw it up, the jewel of the Dharma is still here. I've now talked with many people who have suffered harm in Zen communities and faced into it. Yet, for most of them, this experience has not shaken their confidence in Buddha Nature. They have lost their trust in Zen teachers and sanghas and may feel that all Zen institutions are disgustingly corrupt. And yet. They still often practice zazen on their own. They still usually find they want to live a Zen life. They still seem to deeply know that no matter how high the dung pile gets, there is a jewel underneath.

What is this jewel, and why is it worth the trouble of digging it out? I will attempt to speak from what I have experienced for myself. And then I'll explain why a very few secrets, silences, and scandals are necessary.

## SPEAKING FOR MYSELF

What's the jewel like? Here's a description in my own words. As I mentioned earlier, most of the time I walk around thinking that the stuff in my head is the central drama of my life—my thoughts, feelings, plans and regrets, sense of successes or failure, and my stories of progress and backsliding. Everything around me (including you, I'm afraid) are just the background, merely the set and props. Some planning and recalling are necessary to live in this world, but when not needed for those purposes, my mind runs in endless loops anyway, creating a backdrop of loud static. My everyday mind, being primarily wired for survival and self-protection, isn't particularly concerned with finding Truth. It especially tries to avoid facing the fact that I will die someday. It puts everything that comes in through my senses through a filter of "Is this good, bad, or neutral *for me*?" The answer to that question leads to attachment, aversion, or just letting something slide unnoticed. This self-centeredness doesn't necessarily look like greed: If I'm trying to protect my concept of myself as a "good person," I may do things that appear to be generous.

Yet the static and the filters keep me from being in touch with (and in) reality. Instead, I believe that what is in my head *is* reality.

Yet, at some moments, I can see through this delusion. When I'm awake, the foreground and background change places. I realize that everything—the chair I'm sitting in, the tree outside the window, you and me, people on the other side of the world, the stars, and even the process that creates my deluded thinking—are what is really happening. We may say "this is it" or call this "suchness." The *content* of what's going on in my head, however, is revealed as empty of reality. All those concepts, categories, and judgments, and all my self-centered defenses, justifications, and goals are just the secretions of my little brain. This includes the belief that I am a persistent, unchanging, autonomous self that is separate from the rest of the universe.

In the days before digital streaming, when people watched films in theaters, the projectors would sometimes jam. One moment you'd be sitting in the dark and absolutely engrossed in a thrilling action movie or romance. The next, the screen would show a frame of film bubbling and burning. You'd find yourself back in three dimensions in a theater with the house lights up, worn plush seats, and a sticky floor. Or maybe you'd have been terrified by a horror movie before the jam awakened you to the realization that you are actually safe and sound and holding the hand of your sweetie.

Awakening from our dream of self is a lot like that. We suddenly come back to earth, realizing that the projections our minds create are, like the light and shadow projected on the movie screen, just fictions our minds create. This may not be what you thought you wanted if you were dreaming of nirvana (and the perfect teacher, the perfect sangha). But it's what you need—and it's a huge relief if you were dreaming of hell.

And we realize that we are actually, as individuals, very small. I am not the central drama of the universe. I am not the protagonist I identify with on the movie screen. I'm just me, too often absorbed in a private looping film of my ambitions and regrets. Yet as my identification with my "small self" dramas disappears, what is left is not a void. Instead, I realize that I am one with the cosmos. I go from seeing my life as only the two dimensions on my screen to finding myself not separate from the three infinite directions (or four if you count time) of the universe. I don't stop at my skin. I am very large.

Where is the liberation in this? Believing that my looping mind track is reality creates suffering. I feel anxiety and endless disappointment as I keep trying to make my little life turn out the way I want it to. But if, after having even just once glimpsed or touched into reality, I can remember to not *believe in* my thoughts, then they aren't a problem. Instead of arguing with the universe at every turn, frustrated that it won't do things "my way," I can just try to harmonize and flow with it. Not being so concerned about myself enables me to actually engage with the reality I am in. This leads to (if I'm staying on the Way) responding with greater wisdom and compassion.

Awakening is usually talked about using visual metaphors such as "enlightenment." But being more touch-oriented than visually oriented myself, it often feels to me (as I mentioned earlier) like en-*lighten-up*-ment. It's a weight off my shoulders. I can take my beliefs, concepts, and self more lightly. I feel at home in my life. My life isn't something I have to earn, or force to turn out a certain way. I realize that I just need to play my bit part in the unfolding Dharma. This has profoundly affected the way I am in the world.

## THE (VERY FEW) NECESSARY SECRETS, SILENCES, AND SCANDALS

But you don't *see* that, *feel* that, or *taste* that until you do so *for yourself*. And how it comes about is itself a mystery. It doesn't come from your own efforts, nor is it given to you by a teacher. Waking up is therefore, in a sense, a "secret." No one other than yourself, including me, can really make you understand what it is. In a famous old Zen story, a monk named Huiming says, upon waking up, "I now understand, just as someone drinking water knows personally if it is hot or cold."

We are Buddha nature *and* we are limited human beings: both statements are always true. Sometimes we see the moon (a traditional symbol of the Dharma) and sometimes our view is blocked by clouds. Because no one in this world of change is ever permanently enlightened, we have to continue practicing, and continue waking up, for the rest of our lives. The silence that we keep while practicing zazen, and the quiet that tends to settle over our usually busy minds when we can really pay attention, are good kinds of quiet. I can't explain how or why this "works" to wake us up and free us. I can only point to the many practitioners over millennia who have found it worthwhile.

Students of Zen koans are encouraged to not talk about koan demonstrations. While apparently books describing the "correct" responses circulated in ancient Japan, such chatter is worthless. You see for yourself what you need to do, or you don't see it at all. The secrecy is meant to enhance koans' usefulness as tools for awakening.

Teachers of Zen often talk too much. Silence can be golden.

What sort of scandal could possibly be necessary? We need to scandalize our own egos! Our egos find it preposterous that we should entertain the idea that we are not permanent, or the idea that we are not a central figure in an important drama. We need to shock it and refuse to play by its rules and norms. It will protest. It will bite. That's to be expected, but we don't want to give in.

We also need to scandalize some who are lost in delusive idealization of teachers and sanghas. While I don't feel that I lack genuine respect for the Dharma and Zen and compassion for all who practice it, no doubt many will find my lack of *deference* and *reverence* for human teachers and human Zen institutions to be shocking and disgraceful. They will protest. They will bite. That's to be expected, but I don't intend to give in.[198]

## FINAL THOUGHTS

I'll let Keizan Jokin have the last words about secrets, silences, and scandals:

> Though you should not begrudge anyone the dharma,
> do not preach it unless you are asked. Even if someone

asks, keep silent three times; if the person still asks you from his or her heart, then teach him or her. Out of ten times you may desire to speak, remain silent for nine; as if mold were growing around your mouth. Be like a folded fan in December, or like a wind-bell hanging in the air, indifferent to the direction of the wind. This is how a person of the Way should be.

Do not use the dharma to profit at the expense of others. Do not use the way as a means to make yourself important. These are the most important points to keep in mind.[199]

# ACKNOWLEDGMENTS

This book could not have been written without the help of many people. Most important of these have been the authors and trustees of Greater Boston Zen Center's Resilient Sangha Project, especially Rebecca Behizadeh, Sarah Fleming, Jill Gaulding, Karen McCormack, Rebecca Moonspike, Cheryl Morrow, and James Peregrino. We've endured much together and come out spiritually alive. I'm eternally grateful.

A number of people contributed to the correction and refinement of the book by graciously responding to my requests for comments on drafts or portions thereof. These have included Susan Myoyu Andersen, Rebecca Behizadeh, Inger Bergom, Aaron Caruso, Paula England, Tae Hee Hong, John Genshin Knewitz (who read an entire draft with an eagle eye and commented on every chapter), Stuart Lachs, Jim Lopata, Genjo Marinello, Carol Merchasin, Rebecca Moonspike, Kameel Nasr, Lin Nulman, Janice Peterson, Juliana Rat, John Gendo Wolff, and Rick Archer's anonymous friend. All errors remain my own.

Many conversations and email exchanges also informed and/or encouraged me in my study of problems that arise in spiritual practice. I would like to thank Rick Archer, Willa Blythe Baker, Alex Bernstein and Sabaha Lee Round, Mitra Bishop, Caroline DeVane, Mary Gates, Ann Gleig, Shozan Jack Haubner, Amy Langenberg, Jac O'Keeffe, Douglas Phillips, Grace Schireson, Sozui Schubert, and Parnel Wickham. For extremely helpful advice about the Buddhist publishing world as well as discussions of problems within Zen, I would like to warmly thank both Scott Edelstein and Dave O'Neal. The emotional and personal support of my housemates at Arlington Friends House kept me going throughout the years of what we came to call my "sangha saga."

I also thank Paul Cohen, the publisher at Monkfish, for recognizing the importance of this topic, and Jon Sweeney, editor, whose work make the book better.

Lastly, I want to acknowledge the contributions of the many teachers other sangha friends from whom I am now estranged. First you taught me about the Dharma. For that I'm forever grateful. Then you taught me—alas, too often by demonstration—about the perils and pitfalls that can catch us along the way. I hope that in this book I have composted those later experiences into useful fertilizer for a revitalized practice. I sincerely wish for all of us that:

We may be happy.
We—and all our relationships—may be healthy.
We—and all who come to us for community and
guidance—may live in safety.
We may live in peace.

# NOTES

[1] Thanissaro Bhikkhu, trans., *Bodhi Sutta* (Britannica Online Encyclopedia and Project Gutenberg Consortia Center, 2001), Udana I.3, online.

[2] The Clinical and Affective Neuroscience Laboratory, *Meditation Safety Toolbox* (Brown University, 2019), online.

[3] Erik K. St. Louis and Ephraim Philip Lansky, "Meditation and Epilepsy: A Still Hung Jury," *Medical Hypotheses* 67, no. 2 (2006): 247-50.

[4] Debra A. Borys and Kenneth S. Pope, "Dual Relationships Between Therapist and Client: A National Study of Psychologists, Psychiatrists, and Social Workers," *Professional Psychology: Research and Practice,* 20, no. 5 (1989): 283-93.

[5] The Clinical and Affective Neuroscience Laboratory, 2019.

[6] Norman Waddell, trans., *Wild Ivy, The Spiritual Autobiography of Zen Master Hakuin* (Shambhala Publications, 2010), chapter 4.

[7] Ven. Lhundup Nyingje, "Retreat Lung: The Meditator's Disease," *Mandala* (Aug/Sept 2004): 10-11.

[8] Stephen Mitchell, *Dropping Ashes on the Buddha: The Teaching of Zen Master Seung Sahn* (Grove Press, 1976), 52.

[9] Keizan Jokin (1268-1325), "Zazen-Yojinki" ("Points to Keep in Mind When Practicing Zazen") Translation provided by Antaiji Monastery.

[10] Buddhist Text Translation Society, trans. The Surangama Sutra (2019), 47. Note that I have edited all quotes from this text to use gender neutral singular they/them/theirs pronouns.

[11] Most of the examples, texts, and terms I will use are from Japanese Zen, especially as it is evolving in the United States, since this is my milieu. Most of the concepts, however, are applicable across broader schools of Buddhism and meditation.

[12] Zenju Earthlyn Manuel, *The Shamanic Bones of Zen: Revealing the Ancestral Spirit and Mystical Heart of a Sacred Tradition* (Shambala, 2022).

[13] Steven Heine, *Dogen: Japan's Original Zen Teacher* (Shambala, 2021), xvi, xx.

[14] Bessel A. van der Kolk, "The Body Keeps the Score: Memory and the Evolving Psychobiology of Posttraumatic Stress" *Harvard Review of Psychiatry* 1 no. 5 (1994): 253-65.

[15] Margaret Thaler Singer, *Cults in Our Midst* (Jossey-Bass, 2003), xxiv.

[16] Amir Freimann, *Spiritual Transmission: Paradoxes and Dilemmas on the Spiritual Path* (Monkfish, 2018).

[17] Many of the interviews in Freimann's book describe this strong sense that the teacher was the source of the spiritual opening while—at least for those who left cultish groups—paradoxically being entirely one's own. In Ken Wilber's afterword to the book, he distinguishes the former as a phenomenon at the "functional" (or relative) level and the latter at the "ontological" (or absolute) level (196). As discussed later in this book, it may be inevitable that teachers become archetypes of spiritual realization in many students' psyches, at least until the students find their own paths. It's part of the teacher's role. But when the teacher believes that they really are a special variety of being—when they identify as something special—that's when cultishness starts

[18] A prime example of this is the tendency in a male-dominated culture to see women as the source of men's sexual conduct—for example, in the "But what was she wearing?" rape defense. An example from the Buddhist tradition can be found in the Surangama Sutra. The sutra says that a prostitute who was "wielding a spell that Kapila had obtained from a god of the Brahma Heavens" caused Ananda to end up in her bed. This would be hilarious if it wasn't also sad.

[19] Grace Schireson, "The Promise and Peril of Buddhist Meditation." *Psychoanalytic Inquiry* 40, no. 5 (2020): 349-58.

[20] This metaphor is thanks to Steve Hagen, *Buddhism Plain and Simple* (Tuttle, 2018), 141.

[21] Catherine Keller, *From a Broken Web: Separation, Sexism, and Self* (Beacon Press, 1986).

[22] I also used this paradigm in my previous career as an academic economist. "Economic man" is the discipline's central mythical "separative" character. In contrast, women have been regarded as "soluble" and have been all but invisible in the discipline. As I found many people mystified by this, I now think some ability to perceive the world spiritually and non-dualistically may be a

prerequisite. For more on non-dualism applied to economic life, see Julie A. Nelson, *Economics for Humans* (University of Chicago Press, 2018).

[23] Taizan Maezumi and Bernie Glassman, *The Hazy Moon of Enlightenment* (Wisdom Publications, 2007), 123. Note that misconduct by teachers, including Maezumi, will be discussed in chapter 5. Bernie Glassman is also a figure of controversy (see, for example, accounts in Lawrence Shainberg, *Ambivalent Zen* (Vintage Books, 1997). The question of what to take from (necessarily imperfect) teachers is discussed in chapter 4.

[24] Tina Fossella and John Welwood, "Human Nature, Buddha Nature: An interview with John Welwood." *Tricycle*, Spring 2011. Excerpt available at https://www.scienceandnonduality.com/article/on-spiritual-bypassing-and-relationship.

[25] Robert E. Buswell, *Tracing Back the Radiance: Chinul's Korean Way of Zen* (University of Hawai'i Press, 1991), 107.

[26] Masters, *Bringing Your Shadow Out of the Dark*, 130.

[27] Masters, *Spiritual Bypassing*, 22, 24, 26.

[28] However, it's possible that no matter how gently and compassionately one expresses one's discernment, one will still be accused of "blaming and shaming." This is an often-used technique for escaping accountability. (See "tone policing" in chapter 8).

[29] Masters, *Bringing Your Shadow Out of the Dark,* chapter 23.

[30] Masters, *Bringing Your Shadow Out of the Dark*, chapter 18.

[31] Thich Nhat Hanh, *Interbeing: Fourteen Guidelines for Engaged Buddhism* (Parallax Press, 1987).

[32] Zen Peacemakers, *Our Story, n.d.,* accessed May 19, 2023, https://zenpeacemakers.org/about/.

[33] Shunryu Suzuki, 1973, Zen *Mind, Beginner's Mind* (Weatherhill, 1973), prologue.

[34] Nyogen Senzaki and Paul Reps. n.d. "101 Zen Stories," *Zen Flesh, Zen Bones*, https://terebess.hu/zen/101ZenStones.pdf, accessed May 22, 2023.

[35] Joan Tollifson, *Death: The End of Self-Improvement* (New Sarum Press, 2019).

[36] You may well ask, is Julie Nelson one of these arrogant people who also likes to write (eloquently or not) about humility, while not having it? I don't *believe* so. But I could be deluded! And this is only about today and right now—there are no guarantees about tomorrow. I will have more to say about this in coming chapters, but I think this is where the absolute necessity of sangha comes in. If people close to me in my Zen community notice that I am too easily assuming

that I'm right—or that I am refusing to learn or expecting deference—I need them to call me on it. Delusion is delusion precisely because we don't recognize it in ourselves.

[37] Mariana Caplan, *Halfway Up the Mountain: The Error of Premature Claims to Enlightenment* (Hohm Press, 1999), ix.

[38] Sometimes, of course, the term "guru" is simply used to mean teacher or expert. I am using "guru model" to refer to situations in which the guru is furthermore revered and assumed to have no faults. For a discussion about this issue in Tibetan (Vajrayana) Buddhism, see the interview of Tenzin Peljor by Damchö Diana Finnegan. *Preventing Abuse in Tibetan Buddhism: Can Gurus be Infallible?*, January 28, 2024, https://www.youtube.com/watch?v=lhC0lVRl1kY.

[39] See Jeremy Hogeveen, Michael Inzlicht, and Sukhvinder S. Obhi, "Power changes how the brain responds to others," *Journal of Experimental Psychology: General*, 2014: 755-62 and essays in Joey T. Cheng and Gerben A. van Kleef eds., "Power, Status, and Hierarchy: Current Trends and Future Challenges," special themed issue of *Current Opinion in Psychology*, 2020, vol. 33.

[40] Masters, *Spiritual Bypassing*, 115-16, see also 92.

[41] Marilyn R. Peterson, *At Personal Risk: Boundary Violations in Professional-Client Relationships* (W.W. Norton, 1992), chapter 3.

[42] Masters, *Spiritual Bypassing*, 92, 94, 115.

[43] See Carlos J. Torelli and Sharon Shavitt, "Culture and Concepts of Power," Journal *of Personality and Social Psychology* 2010, 99 (4): 703-23 and essays in Cheng and van Kleef, eds., *Current Opinion in Psychology*, 2020, vol. 33.

[44] J.C. Cleary (trans.), *A Buddha from Korea: The Zen Teachings of T'aego* (Shambhala, 1988), 130.

[45] Reb Anderson, *Warm Smiles from Cold Mountains: Dharma Talks on Zen Meditation* (Rodmell Press, 1999), 18.

[46] Taizan Maezumi and Bernie Glassman, *The Hazy Moon of Enlightenment* (Wisdom Publications, 2007), 72.

[47] I did, in fact, become temporarily strongly attracted to one of my university students when I was going through a painful divorce. I'm human! I recognized, though, that this was a sign of my own long-suppressed emotions resurfacing rather than an indicator of "true love." I did not act on it in any way.

[48] Buddhists can sometimes learn from business commentators. See Rob Asghar, "Loyalty Isn't a Virtue, It's the Enemy of Workplace Ethics,"

*Forbes*, July 3, 2018, https://www.forbes.com/sites/robasghar/2018/07/03/loyalty-isnt-a-virtue-its-the-enemy-of-workplace-ethics.

[49] Red Pine (translator and commentator), *The Platform Sutra: The Zen Teaching of Hui-neng* (Counterpoint, 2006), sections 31 and 20.

[50] Adapted from *Wumen Guan*, Case 28 as recounted in Robert Aitken, trans., *The Gateless Gate* (North Point Press, 1991) and Kazuaki Tanahasi, trans., "Ungraspable Mind," *Treasury of the True Dharma Eye* (Shambhala, 2010).

[51] *Gateless Gate*, case 13.

[52] I'll return to the subject of patriarchy in later chapters.

[53] Dogen, "Receiving the Marrow by Bowing," in *Treasury of the True Dharma Eye.*

[54] Shohaku Okumura, *Living by Vow* (Wisdom Publications, 2011), 20, 35.

[55] When a patient is harmed by the actions of a medical provider, it's called iatrogenic harm. Iatros comes from the ancient Greek word for healer and genic means "caused by." A psychopomp is a spiritual guide (Greek: psyche = soul, pomp = guide).

[56] You haven't started this work yet? You might begin with Larry Yang's *Awakening Together: The Spiritual Practice of Inclusivity and Community* (Wisdom, 2017), Zenju Earthlyn Manuel's *The Way of Tenderness: Awakening through Race, Sexuality, and Gender* (Wisdom, 2015), or angel Kyodo Williams and Lama Rod Owens with Jasmine Syedullah's *Radical Dharma: Talking Race, Love, and Liberation* (North Atlantic Books, 2016).

[57] Board of the White Plum Asanga, "A Statement of the White Plum Asanga Regarding Allegations of Sexual Misconduct," November 17, 2017, accessed June 6, 2023, https://whiteplum.org/a-statement-of-the-white-plum-asanga-regarding-allegations-of-sexual-misconduct/.

[58] Mark Oppenheimer, *The Zen Predator of the Upper East Side* (Atlantic Books, 2013).

[59] Stuart Lachs, "For Whose Best Interest," *thezensite,* July 29, 2015, accessed June 6, 2023, https://www.thezensite.com/ZenEssays/CriticalZen/Sasaki_Lachs.html.

[60] Robert Aitken et al., "Diamond Sangha Teachers Open Letter to John Tarrant," *Sydney Zen Center Newsletter,* February-March 2000, 4, accessed June 6, 2023, http://www.ciolek.com/WWWVLPages/ZenPages/DOCS/szc-newsletter-feb-mar-2000.pdf. John Tarrant's license to practice psychology

in California was also surrendered in 2001 as the result of a "disciplinary action" by state's Board of Psychology (https://search.dca.ca.gov/details/6001/PSY/11288/4a7ada4e75660e81cd3479bcb5295730).

[61] Nelson Foster and Jack Shoemaker, "An Open Letter on Journalistic Integrity and the Shambhala Sun," *https://robertaitken.blogspot.com/,* February 17, 2011, accessed June 6, 2023, https://robertaitken.blogspot.com/2011/02/an-open-letter-on-journalistic.html.

[62] The custom in my sangha is to call teachers by their common (usually just first) names. However, when writing about Josh Bartok's misconduct I will refer to him in the text by one of his Dharma Names, Juin. It is important that his name be somewhat public in case he ever returns to working with students or clients without going through supervised rehabilitation first. (In fact, after saying he was leaving Zen teaching he reinvented himself as a "life coach.") However, his offense is in no way the worst among Zen teachers and I see no need to splash his name on every page as if he were the poster boy for teacher sexual misconduct. Sources: Soto Zen Buddhist Association, "Josh Bartok," October 15, 2021, accessed June 20, 2023, https://www.szba.org/josh-bartok; Greater Boston Zen Center, *Teachers & Other Leaders,* accessed June 20, 2023, https://bostonzen.org/teachers-practice-leaders-2/; Josh Bartok, "Josh Bartok (He/Him): Writer, Life and Writing Coach, Photographer," https://www.linkedin.com/in/joshbartok/, accessed February 4, 2024.

[63] Soto Zen Buddhist Association. *Dosho Port,* accessed June 20, 2023. https://www.szba.org/dosho-port, undated; and Nebraska Zen Center, *Board/Governance,* June-August 2021 minutes, accessed June 20, 2023, https://nebraskazencenter.org/board-governance/.

[64] Michael Downing, *Shoes Outside the Door: Desire, Devotion, and Excess at San Francisco Zen Center* (Counterpoint, 2001).

[65] Janet Jiryu Abels et al, "Open letter to Dennis Genpo Merzel signed by sixty-six Zen teachers" *Lion's Roar*, April 20, 2011, accessed June 6, 2023, https://www.lionsroar.com/open-letter-to-dennis-genpo-merzel-signed-by-sixty-six-zen-teachers/. While he initially disrobed, he later returned to teaching.

[66] Wendy Biddlecombe Agsar, "Lawsuit Against Ezra Bayda and Zen Center San Diego Ends with Settlement, *Tricycle*, June 28, 2022, accessed June 6, 2023, https://tricycle.org/article/ezra-bayda-lawsuit/

[67] Board of the White Plum Asanga, "Statement from the Board of the WPA Regarding

Michael Shikan Brunner," July 9, 2024, accessed July 31, 2024, https://whiteplum.org/statement-from-the-board-of-the-wpa-regarding-michael-shikan-brunner/.

[68] Timothy Miller, *The 60s Communes: Hippies and Beyond* (Syracuse University Press, 1999), 112.

[69] Mariana Caplan, *Halfway Up the Mountain: The Error of Premature Claims to Enlightenment* (Hohm Press, 1999).

[70] No Secrets in the Village group, "An Open Letter on Abuse in Dharma Ocean," May 15, 2020, accessed June 6, 2023.

[71] Andrea Michelle Winn, *Buddhist Project Sunshine*, 2018, accessed June 6, 2023, https://andreamwinn.com/offerings/bps-welcome-page/.

[72] Editors of the Bangkok Post, "Clergy reform long overdue," *Bangkok Post*, May 9, 2023, https://www.bangkokpost.com/opinion/opinion/2566030/clergy-reform-long-overdue.

[73] Spirit Rock's Ethics and Reconciliation Council, "Spirit Rock Meditation Center's Ethics and Reconciliation Council Statement Regarding Noah Levine," February 20, 2019, accessed June 6, 2023, https://www.spiritrock.org/file/Spirit-Rock-EAR-Council-Statement-regarding-Noah-Levine.pdf. Also archived at https://tricycle.org/wp-content/uploads/2019/02/Spirit-Rock-EAR-Council-Statement-regarding-Noah-Levine.pdf, accessed April 13, 2024. See also Madison Marriage, "The Retreat" podcast series, *Financial Times*, https://www.ft.com/untold, January-June 2024.

[74] Project Satya, *Investigating Institutional Sexual Abuse within Sivananda Yoga Vedanta Centres*, 2020, accessed June 6, 2023, http://www.projectsatya.org/.

[75] While I'm appalled that students don't get to know about these, I'm constrained by the lack of documentation or firsthand experience from mentioning them in this book. I want to be careful not to spread rumors in case any are unfounded or exaggerated.

[76] Robert Aitken, *The Mind of Clover: Essays in Zen Buddhist Ethics* (North Point Press, 1984).

[77] Marilyn R. Peterson, *At Personal Risk: Boundary Violations in Professional-Client Relationships* (W.W. Norton, 1992), 3.

[78] Rev. Patricia L. Liberty, "Why It's Not an Affair," *AdvocateWeb*, 2000, accessed December 6, 2020, https://www.advocateweb.org/publications/articles-2/clergy/affair/.

[79] Research with MRIs has found that such behaviors are associated with a form

of neurodivergence in which the usual connections involving the part of the brain associated with emotions such as empathy are lacking. However, having such a brain structure need not necessarily lead to highly antisocial behavior. For example, neurobiologist James H. Fallon, who discovered late in life that he has this trait, describes the mitigating effects of a healthy environment and his choice to deliberately train himself to treat people better. (See *The Psychopath Inside*, 2013, Portfolio and videos with the same title.) See also Patric Gagne, *Sociopath: A Memoir* (Simon & Schuster, 2024).

[80] Dan Rockwell, https://leadershipfreak.blog/, March 22, 2023, accessed June 19, 2023, https://leadershipfreak.blog/2023/03/22/7-ways-to-meet-the-need-to-feel-seen-heard-and-understood/.

[81] Evan Asano, "6 Easy Steps to Get People to Trust You Quickly," Forbes.com, August 28, 2015, accessed June 19, 2023, https://www.forbes.com/sites/quora/2015/08/28/6-easy-steps-to-get-people-to-trust-you-quickly/?sh=78b-8973f344c.

[82] Peterson, *At Personal Risk,* 159-60.

[83] Of course this was explained as "spreading the Dharma." Unfortunately for our sangha finances, the move was followed closely by the Covid lockdowns, the spiritual director's misconduct, and subsequent dwindling membership.

[84] Soto Zen Buddhist Association, "Ethics Statement for the SZBA," 2011, accessed September 6, 2021. https://terebess.hu/zen/szoto/SZBA_Ethics_Statement_2011.pdf.

[85] Jennifer J. Freyd, n.d. *Research*, accessed September 19, 2023. https://www.jjfreyd.com/about-research#:~:text=Betrayal%20blindness%2C%20a%20key%20concept,systems%20upon%20which%20they%20depend.

[86] Center for Relational Recovery. undated. "Betrayal Blindness." Accessed November 30, 2023. https://www.relationalrecovery.com/betrayal-blindness/. While this website was written specifically for blindness involving intimate partners, I've made what I think are reasonable word changes to adapt it to the issue at hand.

[87] Scott Edelstein, *Sex and the Spiritual Teacher* (Wisdom Publications, 2011).

[88] Jennifer J. Freyd, "What is a Betrayal Trauma? What is Betrayal Trauma Theory?" September 16, 2022, accessed July 2, 2023, https://dynamic.uoregon.edu/jjf/defineBT.html.

[89] For a discussion of the difference between accountability and blame see,

for example, Sigall K. Bell et al., "Accountability for Medical Error: Moving Beyond Blame to Advocacy," *CHEST,* 2011, 140 (2): 519-26.

[90] Andrea Celenza and Glen O. Gabbard, "Analysts Who Commit Sexual Boundary Violations: A Lost Cause?" *Journal of the American Psychoanalytic Association*, 2003, 51 (2): 617-36.

[91] An accounting of the ceremonial apology and Juin's later thoughts can be found at https://rbmcdaniel.ca/2023/06/07/josh-bartok. Later developments are discussed in chapter 8.

[92] Celenza and Gabbard, "Analysts Who Commit Sexual Boundary Violations: A Lost Cause?"

[93] Faith Trust Institute, "Responding to Spiritual Leader Misconduct: A Handbook," 2022, https://drive.google.com/file/d/1R00_BIx-0ysCIm8bTHlv5AkBt0Ia-Awt/view?usp=sharing; Celenza and Gabbard, "Analysts Who Commit Sexual Boundary Violations: A Lost Cause?" 633.

[94] Gendo, "A Statement of the White Plum Asanga Regarding Allegations of Sexual Misconduct," November 3, 2017, accessed July 28, 2023, https://whiteplum.org/a-statement-of-the-white-plum-asanga-regarding-allegations-of-sexual-misconduct/.

[95] Many Zen stories about interactions between teachers and their Dharma heirs (and especially those in Keizan Jokin's *The Record of Transmitting the Light Zen Master Keisan's Denkoroku,* ed. Francis Doun Cook (Wisdom Publications, 2003)) end, after all, with "On hearing this, the [Dharma successor] was greatly awakened."

[96] O'Brien, *Circle of the Way,* 139.

[97] Keizan, *The Record of Transmitting the Light.*

[98] John R. McRae, *Seeing Through Zen: Encounter, Transformation, and Genealogy in Chinese Chan Buddhism* (University of California Press, 2004).

[99] Willam M. Bodiford, *Sōtō Zen in Medieval Japan* (University of Hawaii Press, 1993).

[100] Karen Armstrong, *The Battle for God* (Alfred A. Knopf, 2000), xii-xv.

[101] A fad in the 1970s, mood rings contain a substance that changes color based on finger temperature. Different colors are said to indicate different emotional states.

[102] Fortunately, it couldn't be used as a device for measuring personal achievement: The more we tried to *achieve* enlightenment for ourselves the more yellow the ring would be. Only by letting go into the Dharma would the color

start to turn. In a way, one can think of spiritual friends as being something like such rings: We all (including teachers!) too easily take yellow for blue when looking at our *own* thoughts and actions.

[103] "Continuous Practice" in *ShoboGenzo*, ed. Tanahashi, 332.

[104] "Confirmation" in *ShoboGenzo*, 387-88, 392-93.

[105] Keizan Jokin, *The Record of Transmitting the Light*, 225.

[106] I recently discovered, to my horror, that our Greater Boston website still contained the text, "... if you follow the Zen path long enough to become a lineage holder yourself..." As if that were where everyone's path leads!

[107] See the interviews in Amir Freimann's *Spiritual Transmission* (discussed in chapter 2).

[108] Victor Sogen Hori, *Zen Sand* (University of Hawai'i Press, 2003), 44.

[109] What if a teacher claims to have some magical sort of spiritual power? The old stories are rife with ancestors walking on water, seeing into other worlds, hearing things from miles away, and similar miraculous events. I've heard a few reasonably credible contemporary accounts of people who, at least for a time, felt they had such a power, as well. But as with *makyo* (chapter 1), remember that, even if such accounts are true, they are not the point of Zen. There is nothing in these demonstrations themselves that mark a person as a qualified—much less trustworthy—spiritual advisor.

[110] Bodiford, *Sōtō Zen in Medieval Japan.*

[111] O'Brien, *The Circle of the Way*, 122 (citing work by Taigen Dan Leighton).

[112] Ross Bolleter, *Dongshan's Five Ranks: Keys to Enlightenment* (Wisdom Publications, 2014), 183.

[113] Stuart Lachs provides a devastating view of the ways in which Zen culture reinforces hierarchical power, from the perspective of the Sociology of Religion, in "Means of Authorization: Establishing Hierarchy in Ch'an/Zen Buddhism in America," 1999, accessed January 16, 2023, https://www.thezensite.com/ZenEssays/CriticalZen/Means_of_Authorization.htm.

[114] Jack Zimmerman and Virginia Coyle, *The Way of Council* (Bramble Books, 1996).

[115] Jennifer J. Freyd, "Institutional Betrayal and Institutional Courage, Feb. 7, 2023, accessed July 21, 2023, https://dynamic.uoregon.edu/jjf/institutionalbetrayal/.

[116] Barry Magid, *Nothing Is Hidden: The Psychology of Zen Koans* (Wisdom Publications, 2013), 183.

[117] Laura Niemi and Liane Young, "When and Why We See Victims As Responsible: The Impact of Ideology on Attitudes Toward Victims," *Personality and Social Psychology Bulletin* 49 (2), 2016: 1227-42.

[118] Diane Fitzgerald, *Greater Boston Zen Center Podcast Series,* December 2020, accessed August 31, 2023, https://bostonzen.libsyn.com/not-finding-fault and January 2021, accessed August 31, 2023, https://bostonzen.libsyn.com/right-here-is-where-the-what-is.

[119] Being heard is a very important step in healing!

[120] Faith Trust Institute, "Responding to Spiritual Leader Misconduct: A Handbook," 90-91.

[121] Freyd, "Institutional Betrayal and Institutional Courage."

[122] Nancy Mujo Baker, *Opening to Oneness: A Practical & Philosophical Guide to the Zen Precepts* (Shambhala, 2022), 14-16.

[123] Bays, Jan Chozen Bays et al., n.d. *Buddhist Healthy Boundaries: Boundless Hearts, Safe Hands.* Accessed January 19, 2024. https://www.buddhisthealthy-boundaries.org/.

[124] James Ford, "Zen Becoming Western: A Reflection on Boundless Way Zen on the Occasion of Dr James Cordova's Dharma Transmission," *Monkey Mind...Easily Distracted.* December 4, 2016, accessed August 25, 2023. https://www.patheos.com/blogs/monkeymind/2016/12/late-afternoon-thoughts-zen-america-least-small-corner-project.html.

[125] Aitken, *The Mind of Clover*, 44.

[126] Zenju Earthlyn Manuel, *The Shamanic Bones of Zen: Revealing the Ancestral Spirit and Mystical Heart of a Sacred Tradition* (Shambhala, 2022).

[127] Bodiford, *Sōtō Zen in Medieval Japan,* 92.

[128] Manuel, *The Shamanic Bones of Zen,* 10, 42.

[129] Manuel, *The Shamanic Bones of Zen,* 8, emphasis added.

[130] Manuel, *The Shamanic Bones of Zen,* 75.

[131] Andrea Celenza, *Sexual Boundary Violations: Therapeutic, Academic, and Supervisory Contexts* (Jason Aronson, 2007), chapter 8.

[132] Rebecca Behizadeh, et al., "The Resilient Sangha Project," June 2022, accessed August 25, 2023. https://bostonzen.org/resilientsangha/.

[133] Diane Eshin Rizzetto, *Waking Up to What You Do: A Zen Practice for Meeting Every Situation with Intelligence and Compassion* (Shambhala, 2005), 78.

[134] Richard Bryan McDaniel, "Julie Nelson," May 13, 2021, accessed September 26, 2023, https://rbmcdaniel.ca/2021/05/13/julie-nelson/.

[135] Richard Bryan McDaniel, 2021, *Zen Conversations: 42 Zen Teachers Talk About the Scope of Zen Teaching and Practice in North America* (Sumeru, 2021).
[136] Personal email correspondence, May 20, 2021.
[137] Richard Bryan McDaniel, 2021. "AZTA Conference – July 8, 2021." July 14, 2021, accessed August 4, 2023, https://rbmcdaniel.ca/2021/07/14/azta-conference-july-8-2021/. The sanctioning of Dosho by the SZBA was mentioned earlier in the present book, in chapter 5.
[138] See, for example, The Church Council of the Evangelical Lutheran Church in America, "Definitions and Guidelines for Discipline: Rostered Ministers, Congregations, and Members of Congregations," November 2021, accessed August 4, 2023, https://download.elca.org/ELCA%20Resource%20Repository/Definitions_and_Guidelines_for_Discipline_2021.pdf.
[139] American Zen Teachers Association. undated, accessed August 24, 2023. https://zenteachers.org/.
[140] That document seems to no longer be available on the SZBA website. However, the version I downloaded at the time seems to be the same as the "Proposed Ethics Statement for the SZBA" available at https://terebess.hu/zen/szoto/SZBA_Ethics_Statement_2011.pdf.
[141] SZBA, "SZBA Code of Ethics," December 2022, accessed 1 25, 2023, https://www.szba.org/s/SZBA-Code-of-Ethics-Adopted-Dec-2022.pdf, 7.
[142] SZBA, "Grievance Process." March/April 2022, accessed 1 25, 2023, https://www.szba.org/s/SZBA-Grievance-Process-Adopted-April-2022.pdf, 10.
[143] The White Plum Asanga, "WPA Ethics Policy," October 29, 2014, accessed August 24, 2023, https://whiteplum.org/wpa-ethics-policy/.
[144] Second Generation American Zen Teachers. 1992. "Genpo-Letter-August-1992.pdf." *SweepingZen.* June 19, accessed August 6, 2023. https://web.archive.org/web/20120302121828/http://sweepingzen.com/wp-content/uploads/2011/02/Genpo-Letter-August-1992.pdf.
[145] SweepingZen, *Open Letters to Kanzeon Zen Center,* February 15, 2011, accessed August 6, 2023, https://web.archive.org/web/20120929022304/http://sweepingzen.com/open-letters-to-kanzeon-zen-center.
[146] Josh Bartok, Letter to the GBZC Leadership, November 2021.
[147] SZBA, "Letter to the Greater Boston Zen Center Board of Directors." January 18, 2024.
[148] Faith Trust Institute, 31.

[149] I am unclear about whether withdrawing teaching authority is actually possible with Zen lineage traditions.
[150] Board of The White Plum Asanga, "The White Plum Asanga issues statement regarding Dennis Genpo Merzel," *Lionsroar.com.* June 29, 2011, accessed August 6, 2023, https://www.lionsroar.com/the-white-plum-asanga-issues-statement-regarding-dennis-genpo-merzel/.
[151] For Shimano, see Kobutsu Malone, archivist, "The Shimano Archive," last revised May 23, 2016, accessed February 2024, https://shimanoarchive.com/. My thanks to Nelson Foster for pointing out that Robert Aitken had no authority over Shimano at the time the abuse began (Aitken was not even authorized as a teacher for another decade) and made efforts to stop it.
[152] Mark Oppenheimer, "The Zen Predator of the Upper East Side," *The Atlantic*, December 18, 2014, https://www.theatlantic.com/national/archive/2014/12/the-zen-predator-of-the-upper-east-side/383831.
[153] Paul Vitello, "Joshu Sasaki, 107, Tainted Zen Master." *The New York Times*, August 4, 2014, https://www.nytimes.com/2014/08/05/us/joshu-sasaki-a-zen-master-tarnished-by-abuse-claims-dies-at-107.html.
[154] James Ford, "A Few Random Thoughts in the Midst of Zen's Various Sex Scandals," November 28, 2012, accessed August 7, 2023, https://www.patheos.com/blogs/monkeymind/2012/11/a-few-random-thoughts-in-the-midst-of-zens-various-sex-scandals.html.
[155] Ford, "A Few Random Thoughts in the Midst of Zen's Various Sex Scandals."
[156] He was also given the opportunity to review this section of the book before publication, but declined to comment.
[157] Faith Trust Institute, *Responding to Spiritual Leader Misconduct: A Handbook*, 2022, 33.
[158] The book is Nancy Mujo Baker's 2022 publication, *Opening to Oneness: A Practical & Philosophical Guide to the Zen Precepts*, which I cited earlier. Because I understand that Baker's ability to respond to my critique of these passages is impaired by severely ill health, I will not mention her name in the text.
[159] Baker, *Opening to Oneness,* 53. I have chosen not to draw attention in the text to the last paragraph on page 53 because I'm sure that it must be an error that slipped past both the author and editor: "When it comes to children.... Failing to speak up...whether we or others are the victims, is a serious breach of the third precept." I can't imagine the author actually intending to imply that silenced child victims of sex abuse have seriously mis-used sex.

[160] Baker, *Opening to Oneness*, 62.

[161] While this author correctly states that "It is also important to realize that telling the truth can be done without blame" (Baker, *Opening to Oneness*, 62), I think this tends to overlook the possibility of such negative consequences. I can tell you from personal experience that those who do not want to hear the truth will *hear it* as "blame," no matter how much compassion the truth-tellers express towards the person who committed the misconduct. The victim or vocal witnesses *will* be accused of blaming, finger-pointing, vindictiveness, mental imbalance, not "being Zen," and so on.

[162] Baker, *Opening to Oneness*, 70-71.

[163] Right Use of Power Institute. n.d, accessed September 12, 2023. https://rightuseofpower.org/.

[164] A critique informed by the entire Resilient Sangha Project group can be found at https://bostonzen.org/resilient-sangha/our-concerns-with-right-use-of-power/.

[165] Powerpoint slides from Right Use of Power™ workshop given on May 18, 2019. Pdfs were shared with all attendees by email on May 28, 2019.

[166] The Restorative Justice framework generally requires that the victim be protected from further harm and that the person who did harm is ready to take full responsibility for it. See Judith L. Herman, *Truth and Repair: How Trauma Survivors Envision Justice* (Basic Books, 2023), chapter 6. Another commentary on Restorative Justice notes that while it should be "offender-sensitive" it must be "victim-centric." See Elizabeth Beck and Andrea Wood, "Four Restorative Justice Practices," in *Social Work and Restorative Justice: Skills for Dialogue, Peacemaking, and Reconciliation*, ed. Elizabeth Beck (Oxford Academic, 2010), 65. The process offered by Right Use of Power™ diverged from these very basic points.

[167] Herman, *Truth and Repair*, 131, emphasis added.

[168] Hannah Dreier, "They're Paid Billions to Root Out Child Labor in the U.S. Why Do They Fail?" *New York Times*, December 28, 2023, https://www.nytimes.com/2023/12/28/us/migrant-child-labor-audits.html.

[169] Ijeoma Oluo, *So You Want to Talk About Race*, New York: Seal Press, 2018, 205-6. See also Barbara Applebaum, "False Equivalences, Discomfort, and Crossing the Line of Civility: Who is Afraid of Incivility?" *Philosophy of Education* 75, 2019: 278-91 and Alison Bailey. "On Anger, Silence, and Epistemic Injustice." *Royal Institute of Philosophy Supplement* 84, 2018: 93-115.

[170] Jessica Bennett, "What if Instead of Calling People Out, We Called Them In?" *New York Times*, February 24, 2021 (updated), https://www.nytimes.com/2020/11/19/style/loretta-ross-smith-college-cancel-culture.html.

[171] See, in Bennet (2021), "Not that Professor Ross is conflict averse. 'I have no problem calling out politicians who aren't living up to the oaths that they swore to,' she said.... 'The thing I am sharply critical of is punching down, calling out people who have less power than you simply because you can get away with it. But there is a very strategic use of punching up.'"

[172] I do not mean, by referring to some statements as "true," to imply that there is some universal standard of Truth and much less to imply that I always speak from such a standard. But some claims are verifiable by a preponderance of the evidence when evaluated by a neutral party. Others are not. That is the point of doing an investigation.

[173] Tone policing can also adopt and twist the language of "focusing on impact versus intent." This term was invented by disadvantaged people repeatedly harmed by clueless racist and sexist statements and actions. They were tired of the actual fact of systemic harm (e.g., an "impact" such as being excluded from a group) being neglected in favor of a focus on the speaker's inner thoughts and "intent" (e.g., "I didn't mean to...!"). What is needed by the disadvantaged is, instead, an acknowledgement by the person with advantages that, however unintended, harm *was* caused. This language is co-opted and twisted when authority figures engaged in misconduct portray themselves as being negatively "impacted" emotionally by insufficiently polite truth-telling. And they can even put on a show of being compassionate and non-judgmental by saying that they are sure that the truth-speaker "didn't *mean* to be abrasive"!

[174] While some of these charges were in relation to other RSP trustees, some focused on me personally. Since his exit, one of the (now former) Greater Boston senior teachers has continued to voice these accusations, engaging in a (discouragingly successful, from my point of view) campaign to discredit me in the eyes of other teachers and exclude me from one of the organized teaching communities.

[175] See, for example, James Ford, compiler, "Letters from Zen Teachers to the Zen Studies Society," December 31, 2010, accessed August 22, 2023, https://www.patheos.com/blogs/monkeymind/2010/12/letters-from-zen-teachers-to-the-zen-studies-society.html.

[176] See, for example, Grace Schireson, "Zen teachers issue open letter confronting abuse," *Lion's Roar*, January 13, 2015, Accessed November 30, 2023, https://www.lionsroar.com/openletteronabuse/.

[177] Julie Nelson, "Letting in Some Air," August 26, 2018, https://julieanelson.com/2018/08/26/letting-in-some-air/. The comments and "postscript" give more details, and examples of both support and challenging of my points.

[178] No Secrets in the Village, "An Open Letter on Abuse in Dharma Ocean."

[179] Greater Boston Zen Center, undated. "Teachers & Other Leaders," accessed June 20, 2023, https://bostonzen.org/teachers-practice-leaders-2/.

[180] Prosecuting sexual abuse by spiritual leaders under trafficking laws is being explored by lawyer Carol Merchasin. She explained at a recent conference that the law applies "[w]hen someone entices or recruits someone to perform sex in return for something of value (like enlightenment) done with fraud or coercion." The charges also have to include "a dash of interstate commerce," a qualification she believes can usually be easily satisfied. (Carol Merchasin, Jens Augspurger, and Angela Gollat, "Investigating Alternative Spiritual Movements: What Experience and the Law Tell Us About Sexual Abuse in Alternative Spiritual Communities," presentation at "Uses and Abuses of Power in Alternative Spiritualities," Cambridge, Harvard Divinity School, 2023.)

[181] The individual board members usually do not need to fear losing their personal assets in a lawsuit, however. Most incorporated organizations purchase "directors and officers insurance" and lawsuits against individual officers are rare.

[182] Faith Trust Institute, "Responding to Spiritual Leader Misconduct: A Handbook."

[183] Survivors Network of those Abused by Priests, undated, "Survivor Support," accessed August 23, 2023. https://www.snapnetwork.org/snap_locations.

[184] Project Satya, "Investigating Institutional Sexual Abuse within Sivananda Yoga Vedanta Centres," 2020, accessed June 6, 2023, http://www.projectsatya.org/.

[185] HEART and MAWPF, "Removing Roadblocks: Examining barriers to Justice & Healing to Build more Victim-Centric Services for Muslim Survivors of Sexual Assault," May 2017, 6, accessed August 23, 2023, https://hearttogrow.org/wp-content/uploads/2020/05/Removing-Roadblocks-May-2017-MAWPF.pdf.

[186] Andrea Michelle Winn, "Buddhist Project Sunshine," 2018, accessed June 6, 2023. https://andreamwinn.com/offerings/bps-welcome-page/.

[187] Heartwood Center for Body Mind Spirit, "Survivors Program." October 2021, accessed November 1, 2023, https://www.heartwoodcenter.com/meditation/survivors-program/.

[188] Thich Nhat Hanh, "Dharma Talk: Sangha." The Mindfulness Bell. September 1997, accessed August 24, 2023, https://www.parallax.org/mindfulnessbell/article/dharma-talk-sangha/#:~:text=We%20have%20to%20learn%20to%20practice%20meditation%20collectively%E2%80%94as%20a,Love%2C%20Mr.

[189] Aitken, *The Mind of Clover*, 77.

[190] O'Brien, *The Circle of the Way*, 78.

[191] Red Pine (translator and commentator), *The Platform Sutra* (Counterpoint, 2008), section 9.

[192] Red Pine, *The Platform Sutra*, section 49.

[193] Keizan, ed. Cook, *The Record of Transmitting the Light*, 175.

[194] Red Pine, *The Platform Sutra*, commentary on section 11.

[195] Eihei Dogen, "The Power of the Robe," in *Treasury of the True Dharma Eye*, 112.

[196] Thomas Yuho Kirchner, *Entangling Vines: A Classic Collection of Zen Koans* (Wisdom Publications, 2013), 93.

[197] Dogen, "One Bright Pearl" in *Treasury of the True Dharma Eye*.

[198] For another personal account of how speaking out about abuses by a Zen teacher meets with resistance, see Natalie Goldberg's *The Great Failure: A Bartender, A Monk, and My Unlikely Path to Truth* (Harper One, 2004), especially 123-24, 133, 141.

[199] Keizan, "Points to keep in mind when practicing zazen (Zazen-Yōjinki)."

# INDEX

# ABOUT THE AUTHOR

Julie Seido Nelson is a transmitted teacher (Sensei) in the Maezumi Roshi Zen lineage. Her home spiritual community has been the Greater Boston Zen Center in Massachusetts. She is also a teacher at the Great Plains Zen Center in Monroe, Wisconsin. She has written for popular Buddhist audiences in *Tricycle* magazine and on her blog. She is now a professor emeritus after a career in research and teaching. Nelson is the author of *Economics for Humans* as well as many academic publications, some of which draw on Buddhist philosophy and practice. Having begun Zen practice in about 2004, she has found it to be of immense value. She is deeply saddened when people, either in addition to or instead of realizing the benefits, suffer great harm.

www.ingramcontent.com/pod-product-compliance
Lightning Source LLC
Jackson TN
JSHW021856150425
82159JS00001B/1
* 9 7 8 1 9 5 8 9 7 2 7 8 6 *